**Thirteen
Days
That
Shook
The
Kremlin**

Thirteen Days That Shook The Kremlin

by Tibor Meray

translated by Howard L. Katzander

FREDERICK A. PRAEGER, *Publishers*

New York

BOOKS THAT MATTER

Published in the United States of America in 1959
by Frederick A. Praeger, Inc., Publishers
15 West 47th Street, New York 36, N. Y.

© 1959 in the United States of America
by Frederick A. Praeger, Inc.

Library of Congress catalog card number 59-7884
Printed in the United States of America

This book is Number 77 in the series
of *Praeger Publications in Russian History and World Communism*

Preface

Imre Nagy was still alive when I began this book during the summer of 1957. At that time, I wrote in the preface: "I want to tell what I know about him. If there were still any hope that he would one day be free and could tell this story himself, I would seek another subject for my efforts. But there is no longer much hope. I do not know what the future holds for him any more than I know what my own future will bring. But in these days it is better to put onto paper what one carries in one's head. Paper is a less perishable repository than is a human head."

Since then, they have killed him. Today, it has become even more imperative for those who were close to him to set down in the utmost detail what they remember about him. Yesterday's timely stories, now a sheaf of memories, have been transformed by his destiny into history.

I have not sought to present the colorful or the picturesque in this book. I have sought to present only the truth. I knew Imre Nagy well. I witnessed the events that climaxed and ended his career. I spoke with him frequently, during the Revolution as well as in the months before. Whenever I have been unable to set down the results of my own observations, I have tried to report either the known facts or the evidence of reliable witnesses. Only in extreme instances, and then with great reluctance, have I made use of logic or of my insight into the psychology of the personalities involved in order to illuminate events. In these instances I have tried to exercise the greatest prudence.

It is obvious that my work, like all attempts to trace the history of the period, has been handicapped by the fact that many essential documents remain inaccessible—the precise details of conversations between Moscow and Budapest and of the secret sessions of the Politburo. All such details have been pieced together from what Nagy reported to me and to others of his friends. But the cooperation of Khrushchev, Rakosi, Kadar, and many others would be required if the picture were to be made complete. Perhaps the day will come when all such material will become available as the collective treasure of a free and happy world, serving simultaneously as an object lesson—and as an object of horror. In the meantime, those who, like myself, attempt to write of events so recently past run the risk of being contradicted by later revelations.

This is a risk I gladly assume.

I want to analyze with the utmost care the attitude of Nagy and of the Hungarian people during the Hungarian Revolution. Those thirteen days out of all of Hungary's thousand years of history had great impact abroad and produced considerable confusion and contradiction in the free world. This is particularly true insofar as the role of Nagy is concerned. As for the years that led up to the Revolution and to the general situation in the country, I will give only as much background as is necessary to make the events of the Revolution comprehensible—in particular, the reasons why Nagy, though a Communist, commanded the devotion and loyalty of the Hungarian people, and why, despite their loyalty, he had so many difficulties keeping the Revolution under control. In another book, *The Revolt of the Mind,* in collaboration with Tamas Aczel, I have discussed in detail the situation of the Hungarian intellectual movement and its vital role in the rebellion —matters that are only briefly touched upon in this volume. In many ways, that book and this book are complementary.

—T. M.

Paris
August 15, 1958

CONTENTS

BOOK I

**Before
The
Deluge**

I

In June, 1953, a few days after the East Berlin uprising of June 17, the Soviet Politburo summoned a Hungarian delegation to Moscow with the utmost urgency. This delegation was composed of Matyas Rakosi, Secretary-General of the Hungarian Workers' Party and President of the Council of Ministers; Istvan Dobi, President of the Hungarian Presidium; Erno Gero, Vice-Premier and economic chief; Mihaly Farkas, a member of the Party Secretariat and Minister of National Defense; and Imre Nagy, Vice-President of the Council of Ministers. In addition, the delegation included a young man named Bela Szalai, who was also a member of the Party Secretariat.

The recipients of this summons were given no hint as to its purpose. The composition of the delegation, specified by the Kremlin, was a surprise. Dobi, a relic of the Smallholders Party, was not, even as a matter of form, a Communist. Neither Szalai nor Nagy were among the Party's dominant leadership. Jozsef Revai, who with Rakosi, Gero, and Farkas was one of the infamous quartet that for a decade had led the nation and the Party, was not among those invited.

At the Kremlin another surprise awaited the delegates. In an anteroom they encountered Lavrenti P. Beria, then Soviet Vice-Premier, who was also to attend the meeting. Beria, approaching

Rakosi, said in an almost brutal tone of voice: "Well, now, are you still around? Are you still head of the Hungarian Government?"

The Hungarians could hardly believe their ears. For many years Rakosi had been the unchallenged leader of Hungary's Communists. He had spent sixteen years in prison under the Horthy regime, then had gone to Moscow in exchange for some Hungarian regimental standards which had been captured by the Russians in 1848. He had returned with the Red Army in World War II as "Stalin's best Hungarian disciple." Since then, he had been regarded as the Kremlin's confidant. His photograph was posted in every factory, in every office, and in most shop windows. The press never mentioned his name without accompanying it by such obligatory epithets as "wise father of the Hungarian people," "our Party's master thinker," "great son of Hungary," or "first of the Hungarians"—and frequently all these were used simultaneously. Thus the tone adopted by Beria in speaking to Rakosi seemed more than mere insolence, and it presaged nothing good.

The meeting with the Politburo justified the Hungarian delegates' worst fears. They were made to feel as though they were standing before a tribunal rather than being gathered at a friendly meeting held between the leaders of brother parties on a basis of equality.

The Soviet leaders had before them a minutely detailed report on the political and economic situation in Hungary. Its content and tone differed radically from that of the idyllic editorials in *Pravda* and in the Hungarian Communist paper, *Szabad Nep,* as well as from the confidential reports regularly submitted to Moscow by Rakosi. The document had been prepared, under the direction of E. D. Kisselev, the Soviet Ambassador in Budapest, by Soviet specialists who had been sent to Hungary—as well as to other satellite countries—for that purpose shortly after Stalin's death. Their aim was to give the new Soviet leaders an accurate picture of conditions in the Soviet empire. Prepared with the utmost secrecy, the report painted a somber picture of conditions in Hungary.

The Rakosi regime, the Russians said, had brought the Hungarian economy to the point of collapse. It had given no consideration to the country's basic possibilities and, over a period of several years, had imposed upon it a pace of industrialization and, particularly, a pace of growth in heavy industry that nothing could justify. Mikoyan said: "There are certain haphazard characteristics evident in the economic planning. This is notable in the excessive expansion of steel-making facilities. Hungary has neither iron ore nor coking coal. It must import them. No one has tried to calculate the cost to Hungary of a ton of pig iron or of steel. Immense steel mills have been erected before anyone has made arrangements for the delivery of raw materials to Hungary. In 1952, for example, Hungary had a shortage of 700,000 tons of coke."

Hungary's once-famous agriculture, the Soviet leader said, had been at a standstill for ten years. The herds of livestock had shrunk instead of increased in number. Collectivization of the rural economy had been carried to extremes: a recalcitrant peasantry had been forced into *kolkhozy,* and, throughout the countryside, class warfare had taken on inadmissible characteristics. Under the pretext of eradicating the rich peasants, the regime had introduced a series of clumsy measures that had caused thousands upon thousands of farmers to leave the land. The total of such abandoned farmland, called "reserves" by Rakosi's reports, amounted to ten per cent of Hungary's arable terrain.

At the same time, continued the Soviet denunciation, the Hungarian leaders had committed crimes against socialist law. Arbitrary acts had been committed against the people, particularly in the countryside, while the courts had handed down sentences of a severity that nothing could justify. The prisons were crowded with the innocent.

All of these faults, for which Rakosi as head of the Party was primarily responsible, had resulted, said the Russians, from the fact that the Party was led, not by elected bodies, but by a clique. Thus, there had grown up a cult of personality and a mania for authoritarianism. Above all, the Russians said, it had been a grave error to allow the country to be led by four men, all of whom were Jews. In a country like Hungary, where anti-Semitism has strong roots, this was intolerable and had been a great mistake. In short, the failures and crimes of the Rakosi quartet had brought the situation to such a point that, unless there were a radical change, the people might at any moment rise up against their leaders.

"They will chase you with pitchforks," said Nikita Sergeievitch Khrushchev, Secretary of the Central Committee.

The Hungarian leaders were nonplussed. The report on which the Russians had based their charges was too well documented for them to be able to deny the slightest detail. But this was secondary. The big question was: What could have provoked this about-face by their Soviet comrades? Both the accused and the accusers knew very well that neither the cult of personality, nor the excessive industrialization, the rapid pace of collectivization, nor the other arbitrary policies were Hungarian inventions. These measures had been ordered and approved by the Kremlin, and, if the Rakosi quartet had shown excessive zeal, it had been only out of a desire to please their masters. To raise these points, however, would be not only useless, but dangerous. After all, who would dare say to Mikoyan or Malenkov: "Weren't you the ones who pushed the Stalin cult of personality to its climax?" Who would reproach Beria with having committed illegal executions? Or Kaganovich with the fact that the standard of living of the Soviet worker was so low? Or Khrushchev with the frantic collectivization of farms? Could Rakosi and Gero defend themselves by pointing out that their Five-Year Plans had been inspired by their Soviet advisors?

It was evident that the reversal in the attitude on the part of the Soviet leaders was to be explained by the recent events in East Berlin. Here, at the summit of Communism, it was clear that the East Berlin riots were no isolated incident. Apart from East Berlin, there had already been trouble in Czechoslovakia, at Prague and at Pilsen; in Hungary, there had been trouble in the industrial complex of Csepel, in Budapest, and at Ozd, while, at Diosgyor, there had been an attempt at wildcat strikes; and there had also been demonstrations by the peasants of the pusta, the great Hungarian plain, and, particularly, in the southeast corner of the country in the region called the "storm center," which was the birthplace of rebellions. Obviously, the Soviet leaders could not believe the official explanation that these events were set in motion by "provocateurs in the pay of the imperialists." They must have been fully aware of the fact that the discontent of the masses, now hardly contained, was the result of their own policies or, more precisely, of the policies of the Stalinist era.

In the case of Berlin, the Soviet leaders had realized that it was not enough simply to crush the revolt with their tanks. They had also quickly agreed to a number of economic and political concessions aimed at improving conditions. Now, the net import of their criticisms of the Hungarians indicated that a radical change was forthcoming in the whole socialist camp. The Hungarian Five-Year Plan had provided for expansion of military forces. But now the Hungarian leaders were being sharply reprimanded for having allocated too much of the national resources to the armed forces. This was the period of the armistice in Korea, and the Soviet leaders were apparently anticipating a long period of peace. If the signs were to be believed, they were ready to pay an even higher price for a more durable peace than for a cease-fire in the Far East. At one point in the heat of the discussion, Molotov angrily turned on Rakosi, saying: "Will you finally understand that you cannot eternally govern with the support of Soviet bayonets?"

The violence of the tones used in the discussion could, of course, be explained by other complex reasons. There is no doubt that some of the leaders nurtured a sharp antipathy for Rakosi, for an acrid cloud of anti-Semitism hung over the Politburo. This antipathy showed itself with particular force when Rakosi provoked the anger of his critics with his quibbling.

"Listen to me, Rakosi," said Beria, turning toward that "beloved leader of the Hungarian people." "We know that there have been in Hungary, apart from its own rulers, Turkish sultans, Austrian emperors, Tartar khans, and Polish princes. But, as far as we know, Hungary has never had a Jewish king. Apparently, this is what you have become. Well, you can be sure that we won't allow it."

Rakosi was as white as a sheet. Yesterday, he had been cock of the walk. Today, they were speaking to him as though he were a valet whom they were about to dismiss. In a hesitant and uncertain voice he tried to defend himself. There was no doubt, he said, that the criticisms of his Soviet comrades contained certain truths, but he was afraid that they also contained some exaggerations. He was not permitted to go very far with this argument. The Soviet leaders listened only grudgingly, paying little attention to his words. Their constant interruptions and indications of impatience finally silenced him. It was obvious that their decision had already been made.

They were not long in making this decision known. The Soviet Politburo ordered a radical revision of Hungary's economic plans: measures would have to be taken to restore a rule of law and to instill a new spirit into the "fraternal Party." Then the Russians launched into the question of personalities. Two members of the Rakosi quartet would have to give up their posts. The first of these was Mihaly Farkas, Minister of National Defense; the second was Jozsef Revai, Minister of People's Culture, whose banishment Rakosi vigorously applauded—probably partly from jealousy, since Revai was perhaps the best-endowed of the four. Gero could remain a member of the Party leadership, but he would have to relinquish his control over the economy. As for Rakosi, he would retain his post as Secretary-General of the Party, using the title of First Secretary. He would thus have an opportunity to repair his faults and to correct his mistakes. But he would have to renounce his post as Premier.

The question of Rakosi's successor then came up. Malenkov said that several weeks earlier, in May, he had discussed with Rakosi the question of terminating this duality of Rakosi's function. But Rakosi had been unable to propose anyone to succeed him. He had had something to say against everyone whose name was mentioned. He had voiced suspicions against everyone except himself. "This astonished us," Malenkov said.

Rakosi now protested. He had not wanted to remain Premier, he said.

"Perhaps," said Molotov, brusquely. "But you wanted a Premier who would have no authority and who would be incapable of arriving at a decision."

Khrushchev said: "We do not want the direction of the Party and the State to remain concentrated in the hands of one man or in a small group. This is not desirable."

Who, then, was going to be named Premier?

From all that the Soviet leaders had said, it became clear that what they wanted was a man deserving of their confidence, a man possessing sufficient authority to be able to make decisions, and a man who was not Jewish.

The Hungarian delegates remained silent. The choice in the end would be made by the Russians. Some might find it strange that the Premier of Hungary should be named in Moscow, but to those participating in this conference such an action seemed quite natural.

The Soviet leaders—Molotov, Malenkov, and Khrushchev—then put forth the name of Imre Nagy. They proposed his candidacy, they said, if only because he had, since 1948, been predicting that the policy of forced collectivization would end in disaster. The Party had refused to listen to him at that time; it had, indeed, castigated him as an opportunist and, for several years, had even excluded him from the Politburo. But time had shown that Imre Nagy was right.

Unanimously, the members of the Hungarian delegation gave their approval.

That was how this thick-set little man, with a flowing moustache and owl-like spectacles and a calm manner of speech, became Hungary's Premier.

II

Who was this man in whom the leaders of the Kremlin had more confidence than did the Hungarian leaders themselves?

No doubt his dossier in the files of the defunct Cominform contained more details on his youth, as well as on his adult life, than were known even to the members of his entourage in Hungary. But anyone seeking the details of the Nagy's first forty years would have to go to many other sources—and the crumbs that he would accumulate might barely satisfy his curiosity.

An old friend of his, the miner Janos Zgyerka, told the story of how both Nagy and he had once (about 1925) been arrested because of Communist agitation and of how they had spent some time together in the ill-famed Budapest prison known as the *Gyujtofoghaz*. Imre Nagy quietly managed to keep up his spirits throughout the entire period of the imprisonment. He had a bowler hat which he used as a pillow in his cell, and on it he slept very well—as befitted a man of good conscience.

This small episode was highly characteristic of Nagy's personality. He was a convinced Communist who, in the service of the cause, took every risk without hesitation. Born in the town of Kaposvar, in Transdanubia, he had left his home and gone to Budapest when he was still hardly more than a child. His family* had been a Protestant one in a predominantly Catholic district where the Church had huge estates, and it is possible that this "minority start" was the cause of his rebellious turn of mind. At any rate, he had joined the Workers' Movement shortly before World War I, at a time when the movement was growing rapidly in Hungary. Soon he was working in one of the biggest iron foundries of Hungary (the MAVAG), and it was here that he first learned something of Marxism, including the famous slogan: "Iron-worker, do not give in!"

But it was not until he arrived in Russia that he became a Communist. As a soldier in the Army of the Austro-Hungarian monarchy —like Josip Broz Tito—he was taken prisoner, again like Tito, by the Tsarist forces. This was a decisive event in his life. For, although it was the Tsarist army that had captured him, it was the Bolsheviks, triumphant over the Tsar, who held him a captive to the day he died.

As a volunteer in an international brigade composed of liberated prisoners, Nagy fought some bloody battles during the Civil War that followed the overthrow of the Tsars. But, while these battles were, for most of his comrades, only a passing episode or an adventure of youth—as were the Party membership books in their pockets —they became for Nagy a reason for living, a love that endured to his death. He became a professional revolutionary, a convinced and, eventually, a learned Communist, and a propagandist who had faith in Lenin.

Hurled by life into many situations and localities—into the

---

* Nagy was born in 1896. No positive information regarding his parentage is available. There is a belief that his father was a small peasant landowner. There is another belief that the father was a rural artisan.

illegal skirmishes of the Hungarian Party in Budapest, into work among the peasants of the Transdanubian villages, and also into work among the Communist exiles from Hungary in Vienna and Moscow—he was a man who could always be relied upon. When it was necessary, he went to prison for his convictions, or, during the war against Hitler, he worked as a propagandist at the Hungarian section of Radio Moscow, or he lectured on agronomy at Soviet universities. Nagy's companions in Moscow called him "the Kulak" because he had a country accent and was built like a farmer and wore a peasant's moustache. This bothered him not at all: the others were urban Communists; he was from the country and he was passionately devoted to the land.

When the emigres returned to Hungary in the vanguard of the Red Army, Nagy was with them. In December, 1944, a Provisional Government was constituted at Debrecen, and in it Nagy was given the portfolio of Minister of Agriculture. Within the Party he was regarded as a specialist in agrarian matters. Then, too, the Party wanted a man in that post who would make a good impression on the peasants and on the leaders of other parties. At that time, the Communists were not yet so ambitious as to hope to crush the other parties; they hoped only to win the collaboration of such parties. In such a framework, "the Kulak" was well cast.

Even though his appointment as Minister of Agriculture was, in some respects, made for tactical reasons, Nagy himself saw it as the realization of his fondest dreams—not simply because he had reached the eminence of a cabinet post, but because of the nature of the task assigned to him. This man who had left his native soil seventeen years earlier, dedicating his life to "uplifting the poor and humiliated peasants of the Hungarian villages and to endowing them with land," as he later said,[1] now saw himself as the artisan and instrument of that endowment.

For dozens of years, the most intelligent Hungarian opinion had held that the first task in revitalizing the country lay in dividing the estates of the great landed proprietors among the poor peasants. The principal objective of the land division program was the division of the great estates of some three hundred owners, consisting of 5,000,000 acres. The Catholic Church owned 1,136,000 acres;

the Esterhazy family, 315,000; Count Gyorgy Festetics, 97,000; and Count Pallavicini, 72,000. By contrast, 1,600,000 peasant landowners had 11,600,000 acres.

This task now fell to Nagy, and he worked feverishly, but with the cool-headed approach of the man of science. It was he who prepared the decree reforming the agricultural system,[2] submitting it to the Council of Ministers, and, on March 29, 1945, he drove the first stake into the soil at the foot of the statue of Prince Arpad at Pusztaszer, symbolizing the beginning of the division of the land. Addressing the assembled peasants, he said:

"I have come here to witness this glorious moment when the people of the Hungarian countryside begin the final and definitive liquidation of feudal Hungary. . . . I am happy that it was my party, the Communist Party, that has brought this about and that I have been able to contribute to this great task."

Nagy's reference, first to the Party, then to himself, was revealing. In his mind, this was the natural order; for him, it was the essential order, regardless of the task assigned to him by the Party.

On November 15, six months after the beginning of the land division, he was removed[3] from the Ministry of Agriculture and named Minister of the Interior. But he was not the man to last long in what was essentially a police post. On March 23, 1946, he was removed, the Party leadership having found him "too tolerant" and lacking in the requisite "mailed-fist" approach. This post, it was decided, required a stronger, more decisive man. His successor was Laszlo Rajk, Hungary's "strong man" from 1945 until 1949.

Nagy's new assignment indicated that the Party wanted to make use of his prepossessing personality, of his good manners, and of his way of speech—a way of speech which derived its flavor from the soil. He was shunted into a siding as President of the National Assembly. He presided over the Assembly's sessions, made speeches on anniversaries, congratulated new members of the Kossuth Academy, and even led a delegation on a tour of Western Europe. He performed the least of his tasks conscientiously. There was not a speech that he did not prepare with care, writing it himself. Through this period he spent his nights at his desk, sending his staff home to dine with their families. He had a villa, an automobile, a high position. He had only to wear a pleasant smile in all circumstances, to watch his words, to close his eyes to what was going on about him, and to keep a tight rein on his curiosity.

But this he was unable to do. Twenty years ago he had gone to prison for his Party. He had gone in a bowler hat, and there was some spite in that behavior—some spite against those in power, but, at the same time, this behavior also differentiated him even from the others imprisoned with him. Professional revolutionaries at that time wore no hat at all or a cap with visor. A Communist with bowler hat! He must be a different kind of Communist.

In 1930, he had had a serious conflict with the Party. During a discussion with his comrades, he had committed the most embarrassing sacrilege: he had said that he would not stand at attention during the playing of the *Internationale*. The others had created a scandal about this and had forced him to admit his error. Now, two decades later, he again found himself in conflict with the Party.

Even in 1945, as Minister of Agriculture, he had not always behaved as one would have expected a convinced Bolshevik to behave. At that time the country had been crowded with Soviet troops, and not only had these troops expelled the German and Hungarian fascists (for which they truly merited the nation's gratitude) but they had also conducted themselves in a manner which boded no good either to the Hungarian people or to future Hungarian-Soviet friendship. They had raped women, stolen watches and jewelry, looted shops and houses, and ruined lands and forests.

A fanatic Communist was forced to close his eyes before such "details," being allowed at most to say that such incidents were a part of warfare and that, after all, Hungarian soldiers were behaving no better in the Ukraine. But Imre Nagy had not been satisfied with such explanations. As Minister of Agriculture, he had to protect the peasants' land crops. He had sent one protest after the other to Marshal Voroshilov, the president of the Allied Control Commission, demanding that the discipline of the Soviet army be enforced. One of his official notes had said: "The orchards on the outskirts of the town of Kecskemet have suffered huge losses from the honored soldiers of the liberating army who are spending their leaves there, as well as by transient troops. The soldiers have chosen the quickest way of picking fruit from the trees; they have cut down branches and even entire trees. Up to now, several thousand trees have been thus destroyed. I ask Your Excellency to take the necessary steps. Signed: Nagy, Hungary's Minister of Agriculture."

Marshal Voroshilov had received many such notes at that time from peasant politicians, from bishops, and from the representatives of the Social Democratic Party—all of whom raised their voices more than once against the abuses. But for a Communist to write such a note! And, furthermore, a Communist minister who had once been exiled to Moscow!

It is true that the note was not an ultimatum. It was only a warning, and in the somewhat liberal and chaotic atmosphere of 1945, even such notes were permissible. And thus it was not these protests but something else that had created the trouble—three years later, in 1948. By this latter date the atmosphere had already become much more "lofty" and the Party discipline much more severe. Rakosi and his followers had nationalized the factories and the banks and had absorbed the Social Democratic Party into the Communist Party, throttling all opposition. Up to that point, everything had come about as though by the wave of a wand: one success had followed another, and it truly seemed as though nothing was impossible for the Party. Then, in 1948, the Hungarian Communists had taken upon themselves a task exceeding all previous ones. They had planned, in the course of a few years, to take the entire farming population of the country into cooperatives, following the example of the Soviet Union.

When Nagy learned of this plan, he was appalled. The Hungarian peasants had waited for centuries to become the possessors of their own land. Hardly three years had passed since the large estates had been divided. It would be tragic for them to be obliged to give up their patches of ground and to be integrated so precipitously into *kolkhozy*. Nagy himself favored, without reservation, a rural economy based on cooperatives—but to be achieved by stages, with proper pauses between each, and not with what he regarded as criminal haste.

Listening only to his conscience and his convictions, Nagy expressed his views in a discussion with Rakosi. At that period, the cult of personality was at its peak, at a point where Khrushchev could be commanded by Stalin to do a Ukrainian dance for his amusement. But in Hungary there was still one man, Nagy, who dared to say: "This is the wrong way to build socialism."[4]

Nagy stood alone. This was the era of iron-fisted government in Hungary, when even Laszlo Rajk, "strong man" of the Ministry of Interior could be arrested as a Titoist spy; when the war of the classes was daily being intensified; and when "vigilance for the Party" was the order of the day. It was no longer possible to discuss such matters. Imre Nagy was forced to make a confession of error, a confession that was humiliating. Did he obey because he feared arrest?[5] Partly perhaps, but another reason was his devotion to the concept of majority rule within the Party: since he was in a minority, there was nothing for him to do but to give way.

For nearly two years Nagy found himself in the discard. He was named Vice-Chancellor of the Agrarian University of Godollo, near Budapest, where he taught young agricultural engineers the principles of cooperative farming, the production methods used on the Soviet *kolkhozy,* and the Leninist principles of agriculture. He was completely divorced from politics and he was in disgrace; but he was happy, not only because he was back in his preferred field and because he liked his students and the time he had for scientific work, but, above all, because he was prevented by his disgrace from participating in a series of tragic events that would have been more painful for him than was his confession of error.

Thus Nagy had no part in the execution of Rajk and of a long list of faithful Communists, nor in the liquidation of a major portion of the top military staff, nor in the imprisonments, the internments, the deportations, and the many other terrorist acts. Because of this fact, he remained the only Communist leader whose hands were not stained with blood. In making Nagy the victim of his anger, Rakosi had unwittingly rendered him a great service.

Still, the events of that period did not pass unnoticed by Nagy, and, when he was readmitted to the Party leadership, it was with the lesson clear in his mind that, if he wanted to keep his head, he would have to learn to hold his tongue. He was determined to execute all orders of the Party without flinching. He was put in charge of the forced collections of agricultural products from the peasants (a job in which, nonetheless, he tried to lighten the peasants' burdens). He made speeches on such occasions as a Party reunion in the Budapest Opera House, in which he vaunted the superiority of the Soviet system and denounced the West's intervention in Korea and delivered menacing prophecies of the early demise of the capitalist system.

It is reasonable to suppose that, during this time, Nagy, like so many other Communist functionaries to whom the excesses of its leaders were distasteful, was a victim of the kind of self-hypnosis that enabled him to ignore the tortures, the personal tragedies, the executions, and all the injustices that were a corollary to the building of socialism—on the ground that, in spite of everything, the ultimate aim was the good of all the people and a better life in the future. As a matter of fact, it was Nagy who, on the morning after Stalin's death, delivered the eulogy before the Hungarian Parliament, evoking with great emotion the memory of the "great leader of all humanity." Less than a month before the trip to Moscow, during which the Soviet Politburo elevated him to the Premiership, Nagy, in his speech on entering the Hungarian Academy of Sciences, discussed in detail Stalin's last book on Marxist theory.

It was precisely this kind of a man whom the Soviet leaders, now embarking on a new course, needed. He was a Communist who was deeply devoted to the Party's ideals, but he was also a Communist who had long been aware of the Party's misguided policies. He was a Communist who had long been a member of the leadership, but who had been guilty of no personal offenses. He had submitted to an order to make a confession of error even when he had been in the right, and yet he still clung to his convictions. He had suffered too much from the old leadership to be under any obligation to it, but he had worked too long with its members to be in a hurry to liquidate them. In short, from the Kremlin's viewpoint, he was ideal. In their search for a man who would serve as the instrument of their new policies, the Soviet leaders would have found it difficult to have hit upon one more deserving of their confidence at that moment than was Imre Nagy.

III

Nagy took over the post of Premier on July 4, 1953, secure in the knowledge that he enjoyed the full confidence of the Soviet Politburo, and, particularly, the confidence of Georgi Malenkov, who had given him strong personal assurances of his support. He began his work with complete self-assurance, with patience, and with the dignity that was his way. On the day that his twenty months' incumbency began, he presented his program to Parliament*, which unanimously endorsed him in the post. He announced modifications in the country's economic programs, a higher standard of living, a more tolerant attitude toward questions of religion, a new level of esteem for the intellectuals, more humane treatment for the workers, and new liberties for the peasants. His Government authorized those peasants who so wished, to leave the cooperative. He closed the internment camps, proclaimed a broad political amnesty, ended deportations, suppressed blacklists of so-called kulaks,† and dissolved the police tribunals.

Hungary's history has perhaps known more audacious, more dramatic, and more eloquent parliamentary debuts by a new premier, but it has never known one whose implications were as broad. And the elements of Nagy's program were not the only indication of the author's courage, for the circumstances in which he announced his plans gave even greater indication of his character. For at least five years, there had been no room in Hungary for criticism, only for adulatory praise. The workers had been told: "The factories belong to you"; and then they had been exploited worse than they would have been exploited under capitalism. The peasants had been told: "The land is rightfully yours"; but they

---

* This program was first presented to the Central Committee for approval in June, and, therefore, it became known in Party circles as the "policy of June."

† Peasants who were comfortably enough fixed to own a little land.

had lacked the bread to keep body and soul together, and, after the harvest, they had often been left without grain for the next sowing. The intellectuals had been told of the joys of freedom of thought; but their every original idea had been denounced as heresy. The citizens had been urged to enjoy their new freedom from fear; but, in reality, they had trembled in constant fear of internment, of being denounced by their neighbors or by petty police spies, not daring to receive mail from abroad (even from members of their immediate families), and in terror at the sound of an automobile stopping near their doors at night.

Under such circumstances, the program which Nagy presented, despite its relative moderation, was more revolutionary than would be the rise in a Western country of a torch-waving incendiary calling on the people to overthrow their government.

The program was received on almost all levels of society with profound relief and with almost incredulous joy. There were many who refused to admit that such a drastic change was possible; they were so completely resigned to their fate that they had lost all hope of anything better. But the first reaction of disbelief and surprise gave way quickly to a burst of enthusiasm. Emotions long held in check were now liberated. The impression of servitude diminished in the people, and within a few weeks the whole country hummed with activity. The country people recalled suddenly that the new Premier was the same man who had presided over the division of the land. Now, once again, he had taken a stand in their favor. Obviously, Nagy was on their side. In the factories, the back-breaking speed-up was relaxed, while pay envelopes grew fatter. The people could once more feel free, speak out, live, seek some diversion. Thousands of little artisans were again able to obtain licenses to work. Blacksmiths and barbers reopened their shops. It was once again possible to have a pair of shoes soled, or a radio fixed, without waiting for months. In Budapest, tailors, beauty parlors, jewelers, and photographers opened their places of business. It was possible to buy books by Western authors without being accused of anti-Soviet leanings. The young people listened openly to jazz; Budapest's pretty women resumed their use of rouge and eye-shadow without risking the displeasure of Party functionaries. It was not that the Nagy regime of 1953 was completely free, or that it brought a general prosperity, but that, nevertheless, life had become more calm, more attractive, more joyous.

Nagy worked with all his strength. His ambition was great: he wanted to establish the country's economic life on a scientific basis. He was motivated by an idea that was almost an obsession. It was that Marxism-Leninism is a science which would, if applied with discernment to the economic and social situation in a given country, produce astonishing results. He regarded himself less as a man of politics than as a man of science, and he was convinced that, with the help of specialists and technicians, he could erase all the mistakes of his predecessors.

He called together the best agricultural technicians, freed them for a month from all other responsibility, and installed them in a hotel in Budapest. He directed them to draft an ideal agricultural program for Hungary. As a beginning, he enumerated in minute detail the principles that were to guide them. In professorial (and somewhat dull) fashion, he expressed his views on the cultivation of various grains, on fodder for animals, on crops useful in industry, on potatoes, fruits, grapes, insecticides, and fertilizers—plus his views on farm mechanization, the breeding of livestock, and the veterinary arts. He was firmly convinced that his methods were right. Everything must be sacrificed to work. It was neither political intrigue nor personal rivalry that would help the country; only the labor of its people could achieve his ideal.

Yet, neither the political intrigues nor the rivalries around him stopped. If his program was hailed by almost the entire country, there remained a hard core of irreconcilables who opposed him. These were the Party functionaries, the members of the Party apparatus. In less than ten years this group had grown to number many thousands of persons, and these constituted a privileged elite. Their political origins were varied. Among them were old militants of the years when the Party was illegal, and young fanatics, and careerists, and seekers after power. These occupied all key positions. Some were permanent members of the Party staffs; others were functionaries in the ministries or in the police force, or they were members of the security organizations, or officers in the army. They were the secretaries of the trade unions, the directors of the press, of the arts, and of sports. In short, they controlled through the

Party and the Government the country's entire life. Each carried in his pocket his little red Party book, and most of them had little comprehension of the abilities their assigned tasks required of them. It was through the Party that they achieved their success, gained their daily bread, held their social position, their apartments, and their power. Not that they were so well paid, but, in any case, they received more than they deserved for their lack of competence and for the amount of work they did. Their rise was due to the fact that they submitted without hesitancy to the orders of their superiors, to the fact that they were enthusiastic in carrying out commands, and to the fact that they were possessed of an enormous capacity for flattery. Their careers and their privileges were indissolubly linked to the Party and its leaders. In this country of slaves, where the principal slogan was "Liberty," it was these functionaries who were the least free. The people themselves were subjugated, but the functionaries were the valets. It was of small importance that many of the functionaries were men of conviction who worked day and night with indefatigable zeal for the Party.

It was on this apparatus that Matyas Rakosi relied (and with good reason) when he began his campaign against Nagy's new order—against what came to be known as the "policy of June." Rakosi was not a man to give up easily; he had experienced too much in his adventurous and tormented existence. While he was hypocrite enough to have been capable of going along with Nagy, he was possessed of too strong a passion for power to allow him to give in. Once, during his exile in Moscow, Rakosi had taken a walk with Gero and Nagy. Suddenly, he had turned to Nagy and whispered: "Just look at Gero. He is always half a step ahead of me!" It is difficult to suppose that this man, who had been for ten years the unquestioned leader of a country, would now stand aside quietly while another man took his place.

From the beginning of the Nagy Government, Rakosi remained under the impression that the agreement among the masters of the Kremlin was less unanimous than it had appeared to be at the meeting where he was shorn of his power. Then, only five days after the Nagy Government was proclaimed, Beria, the Number Two man in the Kremlin and the head of the political police, was arrested. It was Beria who had attacked Rakosi most vociferously

for wanting to be a "Jewish king." Now Beria was accused of
having been for many years an agent of the imperialists. Rakosi had
prepared too many similar inquisitions against possible rivals and
enemies to put any credence in these charges, but he was no less
inclined than ever to believe that Beria had played a dominant
role in his disgrace and in the formation of the new Hungarian
policy.[6]

Eight days after Nagy presented his program, Rakosi, in an
address to the Party apparatus, reassured the functionaries, by quot-
ing the old Hungarian proverb: "Gruel is never eaten hot off the
fire." He lost no time. He began immediately to gather information, to
compile statistics, to seize upon various Nagy slogans and proposals
with which to attack the new policy. To say that the new policy did
not conform to Rakosi's character, or to his ambitions or his perverse
leanings, is not sufficient explanation for his opposition. He was
opposed to the "policy of June" not only by nature or by custom,
but also because of fear. The fact is that Rakosi was afraid. His
hands were soiled with blood. Moscow was just at this time demanding the rehabilitation of many falsely-accused Communists,
and particularly those who had been accused of Titoism. This was
part of the Kremlin policy of rapprochement toward Yugoslavia
and of liquidation of the Stalinist terror of which Beria had been
the principal instrument. In Hungary, the Stalinist era had been
the Rakosi era. Stalin was dead, but Rakosi was alive. And he had
every intention of remaining alive.

Nonetheless, every time the Hungarian leaders went to Moscow,
whether to seek the Kremlin's arbitration in a disagreement or to present a new phase of the Nagy program, the Soviet leaders supported
Nagy against Rakosi. Once, Rakosi tried to go to Moscow without
Nagy, but he was informed that, if he did so, he would not be
received. On one occasion he was upbraided by Malenkov for not
having "taken the lead in the movement to right the wrongs of the
past." Another time Khrushchev said to him, insultingly, in connection with the rehabilitation of fallen Communists: "You were
responsible for the arrest of these men. You do not want to free
them because you know you were guilty and because their presence
would eventually compromise you. You must proceed with the
rehabilitations in a way that will not destroy your authority. But

keep this in mind: We will defend your authority only as long as it is not to the detriment of the Party to do so."

These trips to Moscow were like a rest cure for Nagy, who returned from them relaxed and refreshed, full of new enthusiasm and energy for his work. In his place any other politician, Communist or not, would have rid himself of an adversary who continued to intrigue against him. It is hard to say whether Nagy's indulgence of Rakosi was a reflection of political weakness or of his usual good nature, but he was not one to take action against his fellows. The situation in Hungary was improving; the atmosphere was lightening. He could devote himself to his creative work, and Moscow was giving him full support.

But, after each setback, Rakosi began again. He spent his days by his telephone, rallying his partisans to his support. On Sundays he attended Party meetings—frequently meetings of lower echelons—in an effort to hold on to the loyalty of the functionaries.

Nagy had no interest in such political pyrotechnics. He had no desire to seek easy applause. He went his way, step by step, solving each problem, probing each question. He had plenty of time, he thought. There was no one to pressure him. His position was strong and assured. He spent his weekends at his villa, staying away from Party conclaves and completely absorbed in building a charming arbor at the bottom of his garden.

IV

On January 7, 1955, the Russians once again summoned the Hungarian leaders to Moscow. The composition of the delegation was approximately the same as it had been in June, 1953: Nagy, Rakosi, Gero, Bela Szalai, and Mihaly Farkas. Farkas, following his removal from the quadrumvirate directing the Party, had been accepted back into the Party leadership by Nagy on the insistent recommendation of Kisselev, the Soviet Ambassador to Budapest, who assured Nagy that Farkas had mended his ways. On the Soviet side were Malenkov, Khrushchev, Mikoyan, Molotov, Kaganovitch, and Bulganin. There were reports spread out in front of the Soviet leaders' eyes, and their faces were stern.

The only difference between the two meetings lay in the fact that this time the Russians' barbs were directed entirely against Nagy. What had happened to bring about this change?

The answer to that question lay in the fact that Rakosi had finally succeeded in gaining the ear of the Soviet leaders. And, because of a new shift in the Kremlin, these leaders were once again disposed to listen to him. This is what had happened:

During the summer of 1954, Gero and Rakosi had prepared a new economic plan with a view to torpedoing the "policy of June" by reducing the standard of living of the workers and by increasing the taxes on the peasants; and a wave of so-called "rationalization" had already been instigated in the various official departments with the result that thousands of employees and intellectuals had lost their jobs. "The country's standard of living is too high," said Gero and Rakosi, "and rigorous economies must be imposed."

The Hungarian Central Committee had debated the Rakosi-Gero program. Nagy had vigorously attacked it. "Whose standard of living is too high?" he asked. "The workers'? The peasants'? The intellectuals'? Neither their incomes, their diet, their clothes, nor their lodgings indicate this to be so. . . . How can we support a socialism that does not assure the workers bread? What enthusiasm can we expect for a socialism that is not capable of providing meat, milk, and butter for the workers? The old economic policy gave no consideration either to the people or to society, and through it the concept of socialism became a narrow one conceived only in the idea of maximum industrialization. This is not socialism!"

The entire Central Committee had been swept along by his words. For the first time, it looked as though the majority of the Party cadres were about to break with Rakosi's extremism, which it now described as the Party's principal danger, and were about to range themselves behind Nagy. For most of the functionaries, this was a matter of opportunism, but it must be assumed that, for at least some of the Party's high priests, memories of their youthful idealism had been revived, together with recollections of the days when they had been ready to assume any risk to advance the cause of what they had then believed promised to uplift the people.

This was in October, 1954. Nagy's star was at its apogee. An article on his policies, which he wrote for *Szabad Nep,* had enormous repercussions across the country. Tibor Dery, the country's best-known Communist writer, interpreted the entire country's feelings in an open letter addressed to Nagy in *Irodalmi Ujsag* of October 23, 1954: "Dear Comrade Imre Nagy," Dery wrote, "I have just finished reading your article in *Szabad Nep,* and I want to write to you immediately to tell you of the great pleasure it gave me. . . . I am writing in haste, for it will shortly be nine o'clock in the morning and the deadline [of *Irodalmi Ujsag*] is only a few hours away. But I do not want my letter to wait until next week. I hope you won't mind that I want to inform you of my joy and confidence—and, I think, at the same time of the joy and confidence of our entire people—quickly and without any formality."

And, at the end of October, when Nagy spoke before the Congress of the Patriotic Popular Front in Budapest's largest theater, asking those in the hall (in a provincial accent which recalled the voices of Protestant pastors in small villages)—this question: "Do the honorable delegates of the Patriotic Popular Front grant to the Government the help and confidence needed for the realization of the 'policy of June' and for the realization of the governmental program in order to overcome our difficulties?" —the assemblage of workers, peasants, writers, scientists, and Party functionaries rose and shouted: "We grant it!"

After this rebuff, Rakosi had left the country. He spent two months at a health resort in the Soviet Union. Gero had withdrawn into a hospital reserved for Party leaders in order to undergo treatment for his stomach ulcers, which had considerably worsened, and for his eyes, which were threatened with blindness. Thus, it had seemed there was only one leader in the country—Imre Nagy.

But the fact is that Rakosi had shown himself extremely agile for a convalescent, going from one Soviet leader to another with stories critical of the situation under Nagy in Hungary. This was not his first effort in that direction, but it was the first time he had struck a sympathetic response.

The reason for the sudden willingness of the Soviet leaders to listen to him was that a turning point had come about in the basic policies of the entire socialist camp. October, 1954, was a month when a meeting took place about which even today little is known, though it put its mark on every succeeding event between the iron curtain and the bamboo curtain. That was the month when Khrushchev, Bulganin, and Mikoyan went to Peiping. During this trip, according to most reliable Communist sources, the three Soviet leaders—the Ukrainian, the Great Russian, and the Armenian—reached an agreement among themselves and possibly also with Mao Tse-tung, looking toward the elimination of Malenkov. The levers to be applied against him would be the restoration to primacy of the dogma of heavy industry and new measures to improve the agricultural system. The liquidation of Malenkov was most important to Khrushchev. To achieve this, he was even ready to align himself with such hard-core Stalinists as Molotov and Kaganovich.

It was to Kaganovich that Rakosi now made his detailed reports. And the information that he brought from Hungary—whether true or not—fitted in well with Khrushchev's plans for undermining Malenkov, who had been Nagy's leading sponsor. The example of Hungary would be used to show where Malenkov's policies were leading the Soviet Union.

As was usual at such sessions, the Soviet leaders presented a solid front of agreement. Hungary, Nagy's accusers said, was nearing collapse under a crushing burden of foreign debt. Industrial production was falling off. While it was true that the standard of living had risen slightly, there was nothing, really, to justify the rise. Part of the system of peasant cooperatives had collapsed, and the country was threatened with political chaos. Foes of the Party were speaking their minds openly. Demagoguery was showing itself in the Party leadership. The country's military potential had been reduced and, as a whole, the Government had gone much too far along the route of liberalization. The one person responsible for all this was, of course, Imre Nagy.

The most vociferous in his criticism of Nagy was his former protector, Georgi Malenkov—perhaps because that one suspected his own danger, or perhaps because of the old Bolshevik tradition under which the one nearest the victim delivers the coup de grace. Whatever the reason, the fact remains that Malenkov frequently read the dossier before him, which included translations of excerpts from Nagy's latest speeches and from his article in *Szabad Nep*.

Malenkov emphasized every weak ideological point:

1. Imre Nagy had previously written in *Szabad Nep*: "The old economic policy gave an absolutely incorrect interpretation to socialism, taking into account neither the man nor the society. . . ." ("This," thundered Malenkov, "is unacceptable. This is slander against the Party. It is possible that there have been some mistakes, but we have never forgotten to take men themselves into account.")

2. Imre Nagy had stated in *Szabad Nep*: "The Party members should have an important role not only in carrying out the tasks ordered by the leadership, but also in the formation of the policy of the Party." ("How do you imagine this could be achieved, Comrade Nagy? We do not want to transform the Party into a club for discussions. These opinions of yours are in contradiction with the Leninist principle of centralism.")

3. Imre Nagy had said at the Congress of the Patriotic Popular Front: "The Patriotic Popular Front should be the living conscience of the country." ("As an old Communist, Comrade Nagy, you should know that the country's conscience is the Party. You are underestimating the Party's governing role, and you want to subordinate it to the Popular Front.")

4. Imre Nagy had mentioned in his speech at the same Congress that "the hearts of nine and one-half million Hungarians are set on the same goal." ("This statement," said Malenkov now, "is proof of a bourgeois nationalism. What does it mean, nine and one-half million Hungarians? Among these Hungarians there are workers and capitalists, peasants and kulaks. To mention them together is to deny the class struggle. It is opportunism.")

5. Imre Nagy, in the same speech, had quoted Hungary's greatest poet, Sandor Petofi, as saying: "The poet's idea is fulfilled: if the Earth is God's hat, our beloved fatherland has, through the work of our magnificent people's hands, become the most beautiful bouquet on this hat." ("This comparison befitted a poet of the nineteenth century, but it does not befit the Premier of a Communist country. It is chauvinism. It is demagogy. It strains for its effect. . . .")

Nothing was overlooked, ranging from the country's economic difficulties and the decline in the quality of its exported goods to an anti-Soviet demonstration the previous summer during a water polo match in Budapest. Malenkov cited fact after fact, adding accusingly after each: "This is not what we told you to do. It is not that we are imagining these things."

Nor could Nagy imagine these things. He was unable to imagine that these men, who, he thought, had confidence in him, would be capable of changing their opinion so suddenly for no apparent reason. Just as, a year and a half earlier, they had refused to let Rakosi speak, they now reduced Nagy to silence. In vain did he try to explain that if there were still economic problems in Hungary, these were the inevitable heritage of his predecessors' policies; that if the people were voicing criticism—sometimes too violently, perhaps—it was a sign of renewed public life rather than of chaos. But each time he was interrupted before he could make his point. The lesson learned from this experience made him ask himself a question that he should have asked at the time he had been named Premier by these same men: How could they speak of fraternity and of socialist equality when they treated the Premier of a so-called independent country like a servant by refusing to listen to him, and when they decided the future of his country as their private concern, as if it were simply an ordinary vassal state?

His bitterness, his anger, and his resentment reached a peak when he was told by the Soviet leaders that he had not kept before his eyes "the magnificent example of the Soviet *kolkhozy*." He burst out:

"You made not a few mistakes of your own when you formed your *kolkhozy*."

Now it was the turn of the Soviet leaders to be startled. These men had never known a Communist from another country to dare to criticize the Soviet Union. It is possible that this remark did Nagy more harm than all the intrigues of Rakosi.

The decisions taken by the Politburo were just as categorical as were those that attended Nagy's accession to power. The mistakes of Imre Nagy would have to be corrected with the utmost haste. The expansion of heavy industry and the emphasis on military production would have to be resumed. All critics who might be prejudicial to the Party leadership must be pitilessly suppressed.

But the Soviet leaders added that they had no thought of dismissing Nagy. He would have to recognize his past errors and be the first to correct them.

After the delegation's return to Budapest, Nagy resumed his work and ran the country's affairs as though nothing had happened. But he could not keep up this front for very long. At the end of January, overwork and, above all, the shock he had received in Moscow struck him down. For some time he had been suffering palpitations. Now he had a mild heart attack.

In the press, a brief communique announced that "because of the state of his health, Comrade Imre Nagy will not be able for some time to fulfill his functions as Premier."

V

Rakosi never took seriously the Kremlin's instructions that the errors committed in Hungary would have to be corrected "by Imre Nagy"; and the fall of Malenkov early in February served to free him of all further restraint. Officially, the Soviet Premier was forced to resign because of having underestimated the importance of heavy industry and because of a mishandling of the agricultural policy. It was on these two points that he made his confession of error. But the leaders of the satellite parties were informed that the charges against him were far more grave. His biggest mistake was that he "had not broken with Beria early enough." They were told that, after the East Berlin riots in June, 1953, Beria had presented to his colleagues a plan for a general settlement of conflicts with the West—a plan which included the reunification of Germany, based on dissolution of the East German People's Republic. For a while, Malenkov had supported this conception.

The fact that the removal of the Soviet Premier was linked to the case of Beria—who had been Rakosi's most violent critic—gave further encouragement to the Hungarian First Secretary. Events in the Soviet Union were retroactively justifying Rakosi's course. It was with considerable pleasure that Rakosi took note of Molotov's speech before the session of the Supreme Soviet which ratified the fall of Malenkov—a speech which by its intransigence and its threats constituted a clear return to Stalinism. For Rakosi, who pinned all his hopes on an accentuation of international tensions, this speech was like balm. He decided to settle his accounts with Nagy once and for all.

Nagy still held his title of Premier, but in name only. During his illness, no member of his Cabinet visited him, although visits were not forbidden by his doctors. The insecurity of his situation did nothing to help his condition. He wrote to Rakosi, but he got no reply.

On February 25, he addressed a letter to the Central Committee, protesting against the fact that a meeting was to be held in his absence. He wrote: "There are those who wish to silence me, to influence the members of the Central Committee with only one side of the story. I regard this as an arbitrary attitude, contrary to the spirit of the Party and inadmissible."

Nevertheless, the session was held without him, from March 2 to March 4, and it confirmed Rakosi's triumph. The same assemblage that five months earlier had seen Rakosi's leftist deviations as the Party's principal danger, now, with the same unanimity, saw the danger as deviationism of the right. And for those who did not clearly understand the inference, the resolution said: "It has been possible for rightist conceptions to become so dangerous in our Party because Comrade Imre Nagy has supported anti-Marxist conceptions in his writings and speeches and has even been the first to proclaim them!"

After twenty months of intrigue and of gnawing away at Nagy's support, Rakosi was determined to exploit his victory to the end. Although the Central Committee resolutions which criticized his own policies in June, 1953, had not been published, those of March, 1955, condemning Nagy's policies, were in the hands of all Party organizations within two hours of their adoption. As for their publication in the press, this was held up until March 9, as a birthday present for Rakosi, who was once again the "wise leader and father of the Hungarian people."

The publication of the March resolutions was followed by thousands of speeches by Party functionaries at meetings around the country. At these meetings the terrorized people, again resigned to their fate, hailed with enthusiastic unanimity the leadership's newest decisions.

But the Central Committee had failed to decide one question—Nagy's future. To the people of Hungary, accustomed as they were to associate the idea of political disgrace with charges of treason and with staged trials, it was astonishing that Nagy continued to hold his titles. No doubt Rakosi and his followers were obeying the counsel of the Soviet leaders who, aware of Nagy's popularity, seemed to prefer a bastardized solution to frank liquidation. Besides, Hungary was soon to celebrate the tenth anniversary of its liberation by the Red Army, and so it was obviously preferable to avoid troubling the air with a governmental crisis at this time. The Central Committee, too, preferred to delay action until Rakosi's position was again firmly established and until such time as he could be provided with the right opportunity to express his views before the Party's highest councils.

For Rakosi, who had proposed this course himself, it was, however, only a matter of choosing his own time. As soon as the liberation festival was over, and after several hundreds of thousands of workers of Budapest had marched past Rakosi (a little bald man with radiant visage standing dwarfed at the feet of Stalin's statue), the First Secretary called a new meeting of the Central Committee for April, 1955. The only item on its agenda was the destruction of what reputation remained to Nagy. As a preamble, Rakosi read a long and exhaustive report and listened to the denunciations that followed. Since the entire Party was seeded with his corrupt followers, it was easy for him to arrive at his goal.

These were the charges against Nagy:

1. Fractional activity. The principal proof was a conversation between Nagy and Istvan Dobi, in the course of which Nagy was reported to have said: "You know, Istvan, all that is needed in this country is eight or ten honest men who know how to be firm. Then everything would be all right." This statement was interpreted as an attempt at anti-Party agitation aimed at organizing a group in opposition to the Central Committee. One aggravating circumstance in connection with this charge lay in the fact that Nagy had

made the statement in the presence of his wife, who was not a Party member.

2. Personal ambition. During the negotiations that preceded the Congress of the Patriotic People's Front, Nagy was said to have suggested that he be elected president of that organization. The Politburo did not accept this proposal, but this was no less a proof that Nagy saw himself exercising broader functions than those of Premier. No one thought it useful to point out that, before the advent of Nagy, Rakosi had been Premier, President of the Patriotic People's Front, and also Party Secretary-General, all at the same time.

3. Nepotism. Nagy had named his own son-in-law, Ferenc Janosi, as Secretary-General of the Patriotic People's Front. This was true, but it was also true that, under Rakosi's administration, Janosi had already been a Vice-Minister. His influence in this role was what had made it possible for him to be elected to the post.

4. Clerical leanings. Minister of War Istvan Bata, who was a witness against Nagy, declared that there were times when he was unable to obtain an audience with the Premier, but that "it was quite otherwise when it came to bishops, for whom Nagy always found time." There was also the charge that Nagy had consented in 1945 to the marriage of his daughter in a religious ceremony and that he had even attended the ceremony. This was true. Nagy's son-in-law, the same Ferenc Janosi, a man with a baby-like face and a tendency toward obesity, had been a Protestant pastor and had been serving as an army chaplain when, during the war, he had been taken prisoner by the Russians. It was in Russia that he had made his acquaintance with Marxist doctrine and also with Nagy's daughter, Zsoka, an attractive redhead. After Janosi's return to Hungary, he had remained, by order of the Party, chaplain in the new Hungarian army in order "to help extend democratic influence." Obviously, it would have been difficult for a chaplain with the rank of colonel to be married outside the church, and there was nothing in Party regulations that forbade a father to attend his daughter's marriage. Yet these facts did not prevent the inclusion of this ten-year-old incident on the list of Nagy's "crimes."

The Central Committee session ended by deciding to "exclude

Comrade Nagy from the Politburo and the Central Committee and to deprive him of all functions stemming from the Party's confidence in him."[7]

Rakosi led his adversary to his execution with a ruffle of drums. The issue of *Szabad Nep* which announced the removal of Nagy as a Party leader contained commentaries accusing him of "anti-Party, anti-people policies," the gravest accusations which could be made in a Communist country. A few hours after the paper appeared, Parliament met. At the start of the session, Istvan Dobi submitted a resolution stating: "The Parliament discharges Comrade Nagy from his functions as President of the Council of Ministers for not having properly fulfilled his duties, and it designates for this post Comrade Andras Hegedus."*

The resolution was greeted with prolonged applause. The same deputies who in June, 1953, had appointed Nagy with an ovation now rejected him with a similar ovation.

Shortly afterwards Nagy, still ailing, was visited by a delegation of minor Party functionaries who informed him that, although he would not be forced to give up his home, he would be deprived of the right to make purchases at commissaries reserved for high dignitaries of the Party, and that he would be deprived of his automobile and of the right to receive treatment at the Party hospital. He would also have to resign from all political and social positions, including that of Vice-President of the Patriotic People's Front, from his mandate as a deputy, from his positions as a municipal councillor and as a member of the bureau of the Hungarian Peace Council, and from his chair at the University and his seat in the Academy of Sciences. As a disciplined member of the Party, Nagy accepted its decisions, protesting only his removal from the Academy of Sciences on the ground that this honor had come to him, not from his Party activities, but as a result of his years of

---

* Andras Hegedus, then less than forty years of age, had up to a short time beforehand been the personal secretary of Gero. Having no other talent than an unlimited penchant for opportunism (and being outwardly unprepossessing, with his head always withdrawn between his shoulders), he nevertheless found himself elevated inside of one day to the post of Premier of Hungary.

work in the agricultural sciences. His protests were, however, in vain. He was given the choice of resigning from the Academy or of facing the loss of his pension of 2,000 *forints* a month (approximately one hundred and fifty dollars on the official rate of exchange, but with a purchasing power of about half that amount).

Stricken by his illness and now by these events, Nagy remained confined to his bed on the first floor of his villa on Orso Street. Whenever he opened a newspaper, it was to see his name followed by maledictions; whenever he turned the radio dial, it was to hear himself denounced. The huge portraits that the people had carried in his honor as recently as April 4 were burned; his books were removed from book stores and from library shelves. Of all his past activities, only his "errors" were mentioned publicly. Each time the doorbell of his villa rang, he expected it to be the police. He could be arrested at any moment.

VI

Why did Nagy not recant his views and confess his errors? Often, in the past, he had been forced to renounce his ideas. Often he had been humiliated, and he had grown accustomed to submitting to the will of the majority. Why, now, did he refuse to give way to the pressure that was applied both with naked force and with glowing promises?

Nothing would swerve him on this point. Before his disgrace had become total, but during the period when he was being avoided by his colleagues, he had been visited at his villa one day by a distinguished Communist personality, M. A. Suslov, a member of the Soviet Politburo who was in charge of supervising relations with the Hungarian Party. Suslov was about to take part in that Central Committee meeting whose outcome has already been described.

At the start of the conversation, Suslov told Nagy that he had come to persuade him to make his confession of error. It was apparent that the Soviet leadership was looking for a "Malenkov solution" in Hungary as well. In order to present an outward appearance of Party unity, the Russians were willing to keep Nagy in the Government, if not as Premier, at least as Vice-Premier and as a member of the Politburo.

The Soviet dialectician argued long and forcefully. He raised the questions of the Party's best interests, of the discipline to which Party members were obliged to submit, and of the dangers that Nagy's headstrong attitude could provoke. But his arguments were in vain. Nagy refused to play the role of a Malenkov. He insisted on the right to explain his theories before the Central Committee, after which its members could decide his case. If he were to be defeated after an open debate of his policies, he would then accept the Committee's decision. But it was just such a debate that the Party leaders wanted to avoid. Suslov was forced to admit his failure, and Rakosi was thenceforth given a free hand.

What gave Nagy the strength and the determination to resist when, always before in his conflicts with the Party, he had submitted? First, he was convinced of the correctness of his position. The measures taken by his Government, even though they were open to some criticism, had nonetheless ameliorated the situation of most of the people and had served the cause of socialism. The standard of living of the workers had risen by fifteen per cent, and more than 1,500,000 acres of land that had been lying fallow had now been sown with seed. If he were now to renounce his views, he would lose a precious asset—the confidence of the people.

On the other hand, if he were to make a confession of error, he would have to bow before men like Rakosi—men who had already pushed the country to the brink of a precipice and whose hands were soiled with the blood of their own comrades. He would rather be reduced to a nonentity than recoup his fortunes by aligning himself behind Rakosi.

Apart from political considerations and from his profound moral indignation, there was yet another factor: this time Nagy felt that he was not standing alone. During his previous conflicts with the Party, in 1930 and in 1948-1949, he had been a man isolated. This time not only was he a member of the Party leadership, but the conflict was now in the open before the entire country. If the people were ignorant of the details, they at least understood the broad lines that distinguished the policies of Rakosi and those

of Nagy. Banished by the Party and the target of the most per-
fidious attacks, he was still able to write these lines with complete
serenity: "There have been formulated against me false accusations
that I am an anti-Party man. My calumniators should consult the
people if they wish to know who is their enemy. The people would
reply, and it would not be I who would be confounded by their
answer."

During his period of isolation, Nagy drafted a defense of his
position and an analysis of Communist policy in Hungary. In a
chapter entitled "Ethics and Morals in Hungarian Life," he painted
this picture of the decay and the decomposition in the leadership
of the Party:

"The degeneration of power is seriously endangering the fate
of socialism and the democratic basis of our social system. Power
is increasingly being torn away from the people and turned sharply
against them. The People's Democracy, as a type of dictatorship
of the proletariat, in which the power is exercised by the working
class and in which power depends on the partnership of the two
large working groups—the workers and the peasants—is obviously
being replaced by a Party dictatorship. This Party dictatorship does
not rely on Party membership. Instead, it relies on a personal
dictatorship and attempts to make the Party apparatus, and through
it the Party membership, a mere tool of the dictatorship. Its power
is not permeated by the spirit of socialism or democracy but by a
Bonapartist spirit of minority dictatorship. Its aims are not determined by Marxism or by the teachings of scientific socialism, but
by autocratic views that are maintained at any cost and by any
means. . . . Political guidance, that is, the persuasion of the masses,
is being increasingly replaced by the use of force and by the devices
of power, all of which raise the AVH above society and the Party,
making the AVH the principal organ of power. . . . An all-powerful
material dependence, an anxiety for bread, is killing the noblest
human virtues—virtues that should be most specially developed in
a socialist society: courage, resolution, sincerity and frankness, consistency of principle, and strength. In place of these, the leaders
have made virtues of self-abasement, of cowardice, of hypocrisy,
of lack of principle, and of lies. . . . An atmosphere of suspicion
and revenge is banishing the fundamental feature of socialist moral-

ity, of humanism; in its stead, cold inhumanity is appearing in public life. It is a shocking picture which the moral situation of our social life reveals."

This was written in December, 1955, before the Twentieth Party Congress had denounced the cult of personality and the policies of the Stalinists.

Although the support Nagy enjoyed among the people did not penetrate his room in Orso Street, there were some supporters who did. These consisted of a small group of men, none of them lacking in political importance, who saw in him a worthy political guide. They were men who had decided to link their fortunes with his own; they were members of the Party, but they were Party men who, in Nagy's words, had "chosen to fight for their honor." They were men in whom he could have confidence.

During these weeks and months there was a movement evolving in Hungary which was to prove of historic importance to that country. A number of members of the Party, among them many who were part of the leadership, left the apparatus. This was a phenomenon which classic Marxist theory had previously observed throughout history in other ruling classes. There always arrives a moment when the reign of a ruling class becomes an anachronism because it has become too sullied with blood and filth, because it has run the country into the ground, politically, economically, and morally; and because, in the end, the most conscientious and clear-sighted leaders—those with the most integrity and who are the least compromised—find they can no longer be accomplices. Though these have lost their illusions and have come to hate those who have abused their ideals, they still retain hope of salvaging something from the ruin. These were the men who now aligned themselves with Nagy. Chiefly, they were writers, journalists, artists, young scientists, students, and other intellectuals. All had been members of the Party, and many had passed decades in the movement.

The reasons why these men now rallied to Nagy were many and varied. First, there was disillusionment with the role played by the Soviet Union—a role which they had now come to understand was far less disinterested than the speeches of Soviet leaders and the editorials of the Soviet press sought to imply. Those who still retained their national pride could no longer endure the humiliation of what they had now come to recognize as Hungary's colonial status—a status little different from that of the colonies in Africa, whose liberation they had so often demanded. There was resentment of the economic policies which slavishly followed the Soviet pattern, and there was resentment of the Soviet exploitation of their resources, which had brought Hungary, once the bread-basket of Central Europe, to the brink of ruin. There was the realization that the people, to whose attitudes the Party had long been blind and deaf, were totally out of sympathy with their leaders. There was the fact that many of these men had recently been freed from prison or had been brought back from the obscurity into which they had been exiled by the Stalinists during years of suffering and privation. Among these in Nagy's camp were Geza Losonczy, Sandor Haraszti, Ferenc Donath, and Szilard Ujhelyi, all old militants who had passed long years in prison suffering tortures and humiliations. There were Jozsef Szilagyi, exiled for many years for having voiced doubts of Rajk's culpability, and Miklos Vasarhelyi, who had lived for years under the threat of arrest for being an intimate friend of Losonczy. There was also Julia Rajk, she whose own husband had been hanged as a Titoist and who had seen her son taken from her and who had spent five years in prison completely cut off from contact with the world.

Those who had not suffered in the Stalinist purges, who had not lived under fear of arrest, who had even believed that the victims of Stalinism were, in one way or another, guilty of the crimes charged to them—these, to whatever extent they still had consciences, underwent a profound emotional crisis when the innocence of such men was admitted by the Party and when the extent of their sufferings was made known. They were consumed with a sense of guilt, even though they had not participated directly in the persecutions. "It is my crime to have believed in yours," wrote a Hungarian poet to a victim of a prefabricated trial.

There were a number of other factors, one of which was the degree of culture of those concerned. The dissidents who supported Nagy came mainly from the leading ranks of the intellectuals— among them, for example, Miklos Gimes, who was undoubtedly one of the most learned men in the country. There was also the quality of moral courage. It was no accident that most of Nagy's supporters had served time in jails or in the extermination camps of the Nazis or had taken up arms, at least clandestinely, against Hitler and his Hungarian accomplices.

It must also be remembered that there were differences—and sometimes even serious ones—in the views of those supporting Nagy. The majority of his supporters did not want to change the existing system. They wanted only to improve it—to reform it. Yet they all condemned one thing in the system: its inhumanity. Imre Nagy's dream was of a humanist socialism—a socialism which would respect individual freedom as well as national independence.

Six months after the fall of Imre Nagy these Communist intellectuals thought that the time had come for action. Events in the Kremlin had taken an unexpected course after the resignation of Malenkov. If the ruling trio, Khrushchev and Bulganin and Mikoyan, had begun by tightening the bonds between the Soviets and the satellites by means of the Warsaw Pact, they had also made spectacular attempts to lessen international tension. The Soviet leaders had gone to Belgrade to seek the forgiveness of Tito and to acknowledge that there were many roads to socialism and that each country must choose the road best suited to its circumstances. Then they had gone to Geneva for the conference at the summit and, while no substantial accord had been reached, the atmosphere was relaxed and the cold war attenuated.

In Hungary, however, this new international entente was in no way apparent. Though Khrushchev had rehabilitated Tito, Rakosi still refused to whiten the name of Rajk, who had been executed as a Titoist. And, while the Polish press opened its columns to a certain amount of free criticism, in Hungary conformism and sectarianism still held sway. The Party leaders forbade certain stage dramas; they forbade the publication of certain books already set in type; and they seized the organ of the Writers' Association, *Irodalmi Ujsag.*

It was precisely this absence of synchronization with the Soviet Union that was pushing the intellectuals to some action. Why should Hungary remain behind in matters of liberalization when it had always, under Stalinism, been in the vanguard of repression? Some intellectuals dreamed of launching a broad protest movement, in which the best writers, artists, and scientists, would participate by presenting a manifesto to the Soviet Union. Many even dreamed of an appeal to the United Nations.

Nagy was categorically opposed to these projects. He was convinced that the battle had to be fought within the Party and within the country itself, not beyond its frontiers. Finally, it was decided that the Communist intellectuals would address a memorandum to the Central Committee. In the memorandum they would protest against the "administrative methods" employed in opposition to the intellectuals and against the abuses of policy perpetrated by the bureaucrats.

Fifty-nine writers, composers, scenario writers, actors, and journalists, among whom were many holders of the Kossuth and the Stalin literary prizes, signed this memorandum which, in spite of its moderate tone, constituted for the Party leadership a snub such as Rakosi had never before received. The signatories made it known that they had had enough of the situation, that they demanded a change in intellectual life and also, though they did not say so in precise terms, a change in the country's leadership. Though it did not mention the name of Imre Nagy, the document was a profession of faith in Nagy's policies and in his new course.

Rakosi's reply was not long in coming. The scandal was too broad; the entire country was aware of the revolt of the intellectuals. It was impossible to arrest Nagy and to make him the victim of a second Rajk purge trial. The Soviet leaders would not stand for such a jarring note in the euphoric state of international relations. But Rakosi held in his hands a document that made it possible for him to denounce its signers as "contrary to the spirit of the Party." At his bidding, the Party passed a resolution denouncing the intellectuals' movement as "anti-Party and anti-people." Disciplinary measures were taken against the leaders.

Nagy's name did not figure in the document, and no charge could be brought against him. But Rakosi could have had no doubt that his adversary was fully aware of the action—that he was perhaps, even the initiator. And lack of proof had never restrained Rakosi.

In November, 1955, the Central Control Commission, the Party's highest authority in disciplinary matters, summoned Imre Nagy to appear before it. Its president, Karoly Kiss, a former shoemaker who was always morose and who was the victim of a pro-

nounced myopia, enumerated the charges against him: 1.) his
refusal to make his confession of error; and 2.) his having gathered
around himself an anti-Party group which had become the "rallying
point of the enemies of socialism."

Nagy replied with indignation. It was not he, but Rakosi, he
said, who was providing grist for the mill of socialism's enemies.
Then he read a long resume of the dissertation he was preparing
for the Central Committee. In it, he denounced the crimes of the
leadership, analyzed the steps which had driven the country to the
brink of catastrophe, and enumerated the efforts that had been
made to discredit him. The members of the Commission remained
deaf. Obviously, they were not free men. Kiss had in his pocket
instructions from Rakosi as to the disposition of the Nagy case.

Nagy was asked to leave the room while the Commission members deliberated, after which he was informed of their decision.
He was expelled from the Party for "rightist deviationism," for an
"attitude incompatible with the spirit of the Party," and for "divi-
sive actions."

Stunned, Nagy listened to this condemnation as it was read
in a gloomy voice. He had dedicated his entire life to the Party.
Within recent weeks he had restrained the hotheads among the
intellectuals who had drafted the memorandum, imploring them
to do nothing that could be considered as "anti-Party." Arrest
would have distressed him less than did expulsion.

Strangely enough, several members of the Commission had
been his supporters during his brief term of power. Karoly Kiss
himself had drawn the wrath of Rakosi by instituting an inquiry
which showed that Rakosi, Gero, and Farkas had spent 28,000,000
forints of Party funds to build sumptuous villas for themselves.
Rakosi, thirsting for vengeance, had tried to have Kiss expelled,
but Nagy had defended him successfully. Now Nagy addressed Kiss:

"You are in an excellent position to know what crimes and
abuses of power have been committed in the Party, and you know
very well that I am not the one who has committed them. Was it
not I who protected you against the vengeance of the man whose
orders you are carrying out here today?"

Then he addressed himself to Ferenc Nezval, a former worker
who had become a high Party functionary. As a member of the Commission of Rehabilitations, Nezval had been in charge of revising

verdicts in the purge trials, and he had often been stunned by the enormities that had been committed. To Nezval, Nagy said:

"You know very well how many innocent persons have been assassinated or imprisoned, and you also know who is guilty of these crimes. And yet it is not he who is expelled from the Party. It is I who opened the prison doors.

"And you also know," he thundered, "that you are committing an unspeakable injustice and that the day will come when you will be ashamed."

At this point he took his Party book from his pocket and placed it on the desk before Karoly Kiss. Then he turned on his heels and left.

He barely found the strength to return to his home. In his battle with Rakosi, he had known he would have to take as well as deliver blows. But nothing else could have brought him such sadness. Another man might have been content to leave this organization of evil-doers that the Hungarian Workers' Party had become. But this was Imre Nagy and he had been a Communist for forty years.

In the afternoon, a young writer named Tamas Aczel, one of the most courageous leaders among the intellectuals, visited him. At the door, Aczel encountered Professor Haynal, one of Europe's best heart specialists, and his assistant. Aczel went in.

"I'm only staying a moment," he said, when he saw the state Nagy was in.

"Come in, come in," Nagy said, in his low voice.

There was a long silence, which was finally broken by the old man in a voice tinged with bitterness.

"Look what they've done to me. . . . After so many years as a Party militant. . . . These absolute nonentities. . . . But I told them the truth. . . . I told them the truth."

He could say no more. He subsided with a sob.

VII

There ensued two months of complete uncertainty for Nagy. Obviously, Rakosi did not yet feel himself strong enough to give the order for the arrest of his foe. He was cautious in the extreme about the publication of the news of Nagy's disgrace, withholding it from the general public by publishing it only in *Partelet,* the bulletin issued for Party functionaries, rather than in *Szabad Nep,* the Party newspaper. Nonetheless, expulsions, exilings, and other disciplinary measures against Nagy's supporters followed one after the other. The movement of the intellectuals, having been denounced by the Party, was forced into retreat.

It was otherwise a period of outward calm, explained in part by the fact that the Communist Party was preparing for the fateful Twentieth Party Congress in the Soviet Union. The entire Communist world was busy preparing for this event, though none of its leaders outside the Kremlin, and perhaps none except Khrushchev within its walls, knew what the meeting was to bring.

During this period Nagy remained close to home. He continued work on the political dissertation that was intended to be his defense before the Party of his "new course." He still hoped that the Central Committee's debate on the document would clarify Party policy and also his own relations with the Party.

Undoubtedly, the most important section of this dissertation is the chapter entitled "The Five Basic Principles of International Relations and the Question of Our Foreign Policy." The five principles set forth by Nagy were: national independence, national sovereignty, national equality, territorial inviolability, and the precept of non-interference in internal affairs. During this period, these five principles formed the leitmotiv of Soviet and of Chinese Communist policy. They had already been adopted by such active neutralists as Nehru and Tito. The Bandung Conference of Afro-Asian powers also embraced the formula. The conclusions Nagy drew from these principles were as simple as they were revolutionary: "The five basic principles cannot be limited to the capitalist system or to the battle between the two systems, but must extend to relations between the countries within the democratic and socialist camps. . . . National independence, sovereignty, and equality, and territorial inviolability and non-interference in internal affairs have the same importance in all countries, whether they are capitalist, socialist, people's democracies, or any other type of regime."

What Nagy was saying is quite clear. In his insistence on a respect for national independence and for the principle of non-interference in internal affairs—and even in relations between socialist countries—it was clear that he believed that the Western powers were not the only ones which should free the colonial or semi-colonial peoples: the Soviet Union itself must respect the sovereignty of the people's democracies, including Hungary.

There was nothing brilliant in his style. His studies were full of quotations from the Marxist-Leninist "classics"; and, knowing his past, there is nothing surprising in that. The surprising fact was that, after having spent forty years in the Party, he still had not lost his liveliness of spirit. If there were anybody in those years who could add something to the rigid theories of Marxism-Leninism or who could discover original ideas within this worn and limited ideology, that person was Imre Nagy. And if there were anybody who fulfilled the demand of official Communist propaganda that he be "a patriot and an internationalist simultaneously," that person, too, was Imre Nagy. In advancing the idea of his political idol, the great Hungarian patriot of the nineteenth century Lajos Kossuth, about a Danubian confederation, Nagy was not only voicing the basic interests of the Hungarian people but, at the same time, the interests of all small nations in the valley of the Danube. This confederation, based on the neutrality of its participants and on the policy of active coexistence, could be the best guarantee against every chauvinist tendency and against any policy of anti-Sovietism.[8]

In the ideological desert of the slavish conformity which rules all publications of the Soviet press and all Soviet political institutions, Imre Nagy's opinions seemed—even in their moderation and restraint—an oasis.

Many of Nagy's friends, on reading his opinions, were fearful that Rakosi or the Russians might learn of these ideas. It was not that they were in disagreement with Nagy—for, frequently, their views went beyond his; but the phrases that Nagy employed, while they might seem timorous and circumspect to a Western reader today, resounded like a revolutionary proclamation in the context of the times. Nagy, however, was so firmly convinced of the rightness of his theories, and that the route he was following was that of "authentic Marxism-Leninism," that he saw no reason to be cautious. He had his dissertation copied and he sent ten of these copies to the Central Committee with a request that they be circulated among the Committee's members. As a courtesy, he also sent a copy to the Soviet Embassy in Budapest.

In mid-February, shortly after the circulation of Nagy's polemic, the AVH arrested a young journalist who was widely known to have contact with Nagy's circle. Some of Nagy's followers, frightened by this move, burned their copies of his dissertation. Nagy was indignant. "My dissertations are not to be burned, but to be defended," he told them.

But the Twentieth Party Congress, held in Moscow from February 14 to 26, 1956, seemed to justify Nagy's views in all particulars. When Khrushchev explained to the Soviet Party that all countries should choose their own route to socialism, he was expressing the same idea that Nagy had inscribed on paper during the period of his disgrace. The Soviet Party's First Secretary, in speaking of "coexistence of the socialist and capitalist camps," and in underlining the necessity of "cooperation between the Communists and the Social Democrats," was repeating, in a manner of speaking, the views of a Hungarian Communist who had been expelled from the Party and who was living under constant threat of arrest. The revelations contained in Khrushchev's "secret report" on the crimes of the Stalinist era could well have served as added evidence for Nagy's dissertation on the moral and ethical crisis of the Party.

It would be difficult to say how many in Hungary believed in the sincerity of Khrushchev and his supporters, or in the theses adopted by the Twentieth Congress. But if there was one man who believed in them (even though he did not agree with every point), it was Imre Nagy. In re-editing his dissertation, he serenely wrote in its preface: "Having reread this work after the Twentieth Congress, I find myself confirmed in my belief in the justice of my previous conceptions; I believe that my point of view on the fundamental questions discussed is sound."

How was it possible that once more he had confidence in the Soviet leaders? Not long ago he had fully relied on them, only to be abandoned by them from one day to the next. They had sacrificed him brutally during their internal quarrels.

It was natural that his confidence was more cautious this time. Yet, how could a convinced Communist like himself abandon the

hope that there would appear one day some ray of light in the
"beacon of the Revolution"? True, he had been offended and
by-passed by them. But all this could prove to be a detour on the
great road, a step backward—to vary Lenin's formula—to make
two steps forward. It was a fact that the Russians had not allowed
him to be arrested. And his expulsion from the Party's leadership
had been more the action of Rakosi than of Khrushchev. Now,
after the beautiful declarations of the Twentieth Congress, Khrushchev and his supporters could be still considered "liberals" by comparison with the Hungarian dictator. After all, they had now
declared war against dogmatism, against Stalinism, and against
criminals inside the Party.

Thus, Nagy was again encouraged to hope for relief. His
energies returned and his optimism revived. The state of his health
improved to the point where his doctors permitted him to take long
walks. From the end of March, through April and into May, he
would walk daily down Orso Street to Pasareti Avenue, the route
of the Number Five blue omnibus, which would already be jammed
when he boarded it at Viragarok or Aran Gabor Street. He would
ride to the end of the line, to Vorosmarty Place in the heart of the
city, and many of his fellow passengers would recognize him so that,
as a result, someone would always get up and offer him a seat.
He told his friends, not without pride, that, when the bus drivers
saw him between two stops, they would frequently pull up to allow
him to board.

Then he would stroll along the Corso from Vaci Avenue to
Lajos Kossuth Street. Sometimes he would encounter an attractive
woman who would smile in recognition. At this, his eyes would
light up and he would discreetly tip his little round hat. Often he
would venture as far as the bookshops on Museum Boulevard and,
along the boulevards, to the Emke Cafe. Passersby would smile
affectionately and greet him. The more courageous would ask after
his health, then whisper in a low voice, "When will you come back
to us, Mister Prime Minister?"

Some days he would take with him two little children, the
daughter and the son of his daughter Zsoka. He would seat them
on the terrace of Gerbeaud's confectionery, on Vorosmarty Place,
and order a cream puff or ice cream for them. There was nothing

remarkable about any of this. He behaved like any other man, like any other grandfather. What is remarkable is that a similar attitude and behavior would have been unimaginable in another Communist leader—a Rakosi, say, or a Gero, neither of whom ever mingled with the people or gave themselves the luxury of being human beings like everyone else.

It was a period of relaxation in which tongues again began to loosen and in which it was becoming apparent that Rakosi had done a great service to Nagy by persecuting him, without arresting him, during this long year. The moral support and popularity Nagy had won by refusing to make a confession of error now became evident. Had he followed the example of Malenkov, he would be able, without doubt, to tour the city in a luxurious Ziss limousine like the other Party leaders, but in such an event he would not have inspired such sympathy as he was now receiving from the people. By being the only Communist leader who had dared to say "No," he had become the first and only one to whom the people said, "Yes."

Sometimes, in the evening, he would go to the theater. Tamas Major, director of the National Theater, or Aladar Toth, director of the National Opera, could hardly contain their joy at seeing him in the audience. His public quickly recognized him, and all heads would turn in his direction. On leaving the stage, actors would bow in his direction, and it frequently came to pass that the audience would rise to applaud, not the actors but Nagy.

It was during this period that the National Academy of Music gave the premiere performance of a new work by Hungary's greatest living composer, Zoltan Kodaly, a friend and ally of Bela Bartok. It was a choral work, the text for which was taken from the poems of a seventeenth-century writer named Miklos Zrinyi. The leader of an army, as well as a writer, this man of genius had wanted to fight at one and the same time the German menace in the west and the Turkish menace in the east and south. To the music of Kodaly, the chorus once again raised Zrinyi's warning cry: "HANDS OFF THE HUNGARIANS!" The audience was astonished. There were tears in the eyes of many. At the final chord, they rose as one man and turned toward the white-bearded composer, beside whom was sitting Imre Nagy. Then, in a frantic ovation, they cheered the two patriots, both of whom were working toward the same end: freedom for Hungary.

During the same period a sculptor named Zsigmond Strobl Kisfaludy, who was highly regarded by the regime, returned from Moscow, where he had shown his work. During his stay in the Soviet capital he had made a bust of the Soviet President, Marshal Voroshilov. One day the sculptor and his model, both lovers of vodka, had indulged themselves generously in their favorite drink. Suddenly the Marshal turned toward the sculptor and said: "Things do not go well in your country. . . . Rakosi? A vulgar blackguard. . . . And Gero is just as worthless. As for the others, better not speak of them. . . . There is only one honest man in the whole Party leadership. He is Imre Nagy."

Early in June this "honest man" reached his sixtieth birthday. That day, toward five o'clock, Orso Street, normally a quiet byway, was the scene of unaccustomed animation. People were arriving in a steady stream. They did not come by official cars, but by autobus, by streetcar, and even on foot; and they all headed toward Imre Nagy's villa. At the door, many would stop and face into the street, standing motionless for a second. They did this because they knew the villa was under surveillance from the house across the street and that visitors to the fallen leader were photographed by the police. So they did their best to make the photographs clear. They wanted to be sure that the authorities knew that they had paid a visit to Nagy. Having accomplished this feat, they then opened the gate and crossed the little garden to the door, where they were received by a tall, thin woman, Nagy's wife. Behind her stood Nagy himself, his color good, his manner alert and youthful.

"Thank you for coming," he said to his guests, visibly pleased at the attention he was receiving.

Each of the visitors brought a little gift—a bottle of old wine, some flowers, a piece of porcelain, or a tiny flask of apricot brandy from Kecskemet. Nagy protested to each: "Now, now, why do you put yourself to expense for me?" But his eyes were gleaming with inner emotion; he was visibly touched by the affection that surrounded him.

The furnishings of the villa showed excellent taste. From the entrance hall, doors opened on the left into a winter garden and on the right into a gallery. On the walls hung paintings chosen with discernment. In these rooms were gathered the intellectual elite of the country. Near the door stood Zolton Kodaly. In the winter garden Peter Veres, who had begun life as a peasant and who was now President of the Writers' Association, was telling an interminable story. Around the tables, talking with each other, sat scientists, writers, actors, professors, opera singers. Taking advantage of the occasion, young instructors, who a few years earlier had been Nagy's students, drew him aside to ask his advice about their work.

Nagy found time for each of these guests. It was his habit to find time for everyone and for everything. He loved to pass the time talking to his friends, never motivated by a desire to draw attention to himself or to shine in any way, but by his innate interest and human curiosity.

Rakosi's sixtieth birthday had also been an event, but of a different order. It was observed by a gala night at the opera, by a Rakosi exhibition, and by the writing of books in honor of "the wise father of the Hungarian people." On that occasion, there was an enormous banquet, at which were served the finest delicacies to be found in the people's democracies, from smoked salmon to caviar. But in the villa on Orso Street there were only ham and cheese sandwiches and a few dry cakes made by Nagy's wife and daughter, who also carried the platters to the guests. The few bottles of wine which were opened and which were not among those brought as gifts, were of mediocre quality. Nagy apologized to his guests for the poor fare; he could do no better. There were no toasts. He wanted no speeches. His guests were content to sip their wine and look upon the source of their hopes for a better future.

The next day the report circulated within the Party that Nagy's villa had been the scene of a forbidden political meeting, of an "attempt to organize in opposition to the State" under the pretext of celebrating Nagy's birthday. Making one call after another, Matyas Rakosi telephoned those visitors whose names had been brought to him by the secret police. He began with a member of the Government, Sandor Zottner, the Minister of Mines and Power, and this one was forced to make a confession of error at the next meeting of the Council of Ministers. From the others, however, Rakosi got little satisfaction. "We were invited," they replied, "and we went. We are Hungarians, you know, and Hungarians are accustomed to respond to a polite invitation by accepting."

VIII

During the weeks and months that followed the Twentieth Congress, the contrast between the trends developing in Russia and those developing in Hungary became more and more noticeable. In Russia, the Congress had concentrated its fire against "extremism of the left," against "sectarianism," and against the "heritage of Stalinist dogmatism"; but in Hungary, it was the danger of rightist tendencies that was still considered the primary enemy, and one of Stalin's most fervent disciples, Rakosi, remained the country's leader.

Yet, the resolutions adopted by the Twentieth Congress and the resultant relaxations of international tensions (and among these, above all, one could cite the improvement in relations between Yugoslavia and the Soviet Union, as well as the visit of Khrushchev and Bulganin to London) had forced Rakosi to make some concessions in deeds as well as in words. After the visit of the Soviet leaders to London, where the British Labour Party had submitted to Khrushchev a list of the names of Social Democrats imprisoned in the people's democracies, Rakosi was forced to free the Hungarian Socialists on that list.

A month after the Twentieth Congress, Rakosi went to Eger, in northern Hungary, and, speaking before that region's Party militants, wound up his speech by "doing justice" to a man who had been executed in 1949, Laszlo Rajk. Here Rakosi said: "Once Beria, the agent of the imperialists, and the band of Gabor Peter were unmasked, the record of Rajk's trial was revised as a result of the initiative of our Party's leadership. It was established that his trial had been based on a provocation. That is why the Supreme Court, acting on the basis of the Central Committee resolution adopted last June, rehabilitated Comrade Laszlo Rajk as well as others."

To the Hungarian people, this statement was like oil poured on a fire. They boiled with indignation at the cynicism of a man who boasted that he personally had unmasked "the traitorous Rajk band" and who now spoke of his victims as "comrades." None believed that the responsibility for these crimes could be laid at the feet of Beria and Gabor Peter, and none believed that all the credit for having uncovered the injustice rested with Rakosi and the Party leadership. At the general assembly of the Writers' Association's Party cell, a young critic openly compared Rakosi with Judas.

The pressure of public opinion was such that, in less than two months, Rakosi was forced to make a confession of error. The trembling voice and the beaten look which were evident on Rakosi's face when he thus took upon himself the responsibilities for his misdeeds indicated that he was aware that he was going too far in his self-criticism. Yet, for the masses of the people, even his admission proved too little to satisfy them.[9] Being of the opinion that the power of the tyrant was reaching its end, the majority of the Party members and of the public in general were no longer satisfied to see the man responsible for so many murders escape by simply reversing his opinions.

On the other hand, it seemed clear that the Soviet leadership still had no desire to effect a change in the Hungarian situation, despite the resolutions of the Twentieth Congress. Although the Russian leaders knew perfectly well that in the old Hungarian Party leadership there was only one man—Nagy—who was innocent of all the crimes committed, they continued to give evidence of their confidence in Rakosi. In fact, rather than seeking to replace him, they appeared to be doing everything to shore up his tottering position. On the anniversary of the liberation of Hungary on April 4, Khrushchev and Bulganin sent a personal telegram to the Hungarian Party's First Secretary. Early in June they sent Suslov to Budapest with instructions to inform the Hungarian leaders that the Kremlin did not want a change. And when, early that summer, Tito visited Moscow, the Kremlin leaders sought to persuade him that the best solution was to keep Rakosi in power in Hungary. Tito himself reported this in a speech published in *Borba* on November 16, 1956. He said:

"When we were in Moscow, we also discussed the events in Poland, in Hungary, and in other countries. We declared that Rakosi's regime—and that Rakosi himself—had no qualifications whatsoever to lead the Hungarian state or to bring about national unity, but that, on the contrary, only very grave consequences could result from such a course. Unfortunately, the Soviet comrades did not believe us. They said that Rakosi was an old revolutionary, that he was honest. . . . The Soviet comrades said he was a clever man, that he would succeed, and that they did not know anyone else upon whom they could rely in that country."

Such a situation could not long continue. It was difficult to grant more freedom of expression and more democracy within the Party and at the same time to retain as the country's leader a man against whom there had accumulated so much hatred. The struggle undertaken by the Communist writers to overthrow Rakosi had won wide mass support and had found an effective instrument in a youth organization controlled by the Party itself. This organization was known as the Petofi Circle. From mid-March on, the Petofi Circle organized discussions of economists, of historians, of philosophers, of agronomists, of Party militants who had won their chevrons in the days of illegality, and of young intellectuals who had graduated from the "people's colleges"—young intellectuals whom the Party had once taken into its nurseries but who now had become nonconformists. The number who took part in these meetings grew from week to week. The tone of the discussions became more and more impassioned; the picture of the country's situation became more and more dramatic; and the need for action became more ineluctable. It is important to note that, of the twenty members of the Petofi Circle Committee, seventeen were Party members, and that all of these either led or took part in the debates. It became obvious that the division in the Party was even more profound than had been suspected, that the number of those opposed to the Party leadership was growing steadily, and that those Communists who were still men of honor and goodwill had openly to declare themselves partisans of Nagy.

It was on June 27, 1956, exactly three years after the inauguration of the "June policy" which was still synonymous with the name of Nagy, that the debates of the Petofi Circle reached their climax. The subject of that evening's discussions seemed on the surface to be a purely theoretical one. It was: "The Problems of Information and of the Press." But the thousands of persons, who, from early afternoon, thronged the streets leading to the building of the Army Officers' Club, where the meeting was to be held, knew that behind that cold and formal title smoldered a fire that could burst into flame at any moment.

The debate began at 6:30 p.m. and continued until 4 a.m. Several of the best writers, journalists, and scientists of Hungary took part in the discussion. In its course, the truth of the crimes committed by the Stalinist system headed by Rakosi was unfolded before an audience of 6,000 persons (which meant, ultimately, all Hungarian opinion). Three members of the Central Committee, taking part in the discussion, were able to make only the most embarrassed defense.

The last speaker was Geza Losonczy, a Party member, a brilliant publicist, and a man of politics who had passed years in prison for crimes he had never committed. This man with thick black hair, wearing glasses and speaking in a soft voice, told with the utmost clarity the whole story of what he called the "Nagy affair." He said it was impossible to speak of democracy within the Party or to invoke freedom of speech or to mumble criticisms and self-criticisms and still refuse Imre Nagy the right to defend himself against his accusers.

At the mention of Nagy's name, the entire audience rose and began chanting for his return to the Party.

Within forty-eight hours, Rakosi convoked the Central Committee. The monolithic regime could not tolerate such a dualism between the leaders and the members of the Party. It could not tolerate two assemblies—the Petofi Circle and the Parliament— nor two leaders—Matyas Rakosi and Imre Nagy. The Central Committee members—who were shortly thereafter further frightened by the fact that, a few hours after this angry meeting, the workers of Poland revolted at Poznan—adopted a resolution condemning the Petofi Circle's activities as "anti-Party and anti-people," holding responsible the "rightist elements grouped around Imre Nagy."

Rakosi, however, was not satisfied. He had drawn up a list of four hundred persons who, according to him, would have to be arrested immediately if order and calm were to be restored. The first name on the list was that of Imre Nagy.

In actuality, this move on the part of Rakosi was the final straw. As a result, the Russians themselves lost their patience. The negotiations with Tito were still under way, and they were anxious to "restore friendship between the two countries." They were now ready to throw on the scales the head of the Hungarian leader who was so detested by Tito. Khrushchev dispatched Mikoyan in haste to Budapest to give the order for the removal of Rakosi.

Exactly three weeks after the feverish debate before the Petofi Circle and hardly a fortnight after the unanimous denunciation of the Petofi Circle and Nagy, the same Central Committee relieved Rakosi of his functions with the same unanimity and named Erno Gero as Party First Secretary. Rakosi was forced to leave the country without delay and take refuge in the Soviet Union. To reinforce the position of Gero—a fanatic afflicted with a serious stomach disorder who was no more popular than his predecessor—the Party placed at his side as a secretary a recently rehabilitated Communist, a man who a short while earlier had been freed from prison, Janos Kadar.

In spite of everything, the Party tried to present this change as a demonstration of its strength, for the Party was anxious to avoid losing face or appearing to make concessions to the "right"—and to its leader, Imre Nagy. Premier Andras Hegedus, after having delivered an eulogy on Rakosi who, "at his own request," had been relieved of his duties, found it useful to state: "We must prepare ourselves, for the enemy would like to make use of the departure of Comrade Rakosi as an excuse for creating trouble. It could be that the rightist elements grouped around Imre Nagy will attempt action. We must be alert to repulse categorically every subversive move."

Erno Gero used a softer tone in the speech in which he set forth his program for the country, but he also denounced the activities of the Petofi Circle. It is true that, in the spirit of the Twentieth Congress, he attacked sectarianism, but he was quick to add: ". . . There are not only sectarian errors in our Party. There are also rightist errors, serious and brutal, and there exists even a deviationism of the right—a deviation represented, above all, by Imre Nagy."

The Party's insistence on maintaining Nagy's ostracism was even more strange in view of the fact that Mikoyan had wasted no time after his arrival in Budapest in letting its leaders know that the Soviet Party had not approved the exclusion of Nagy and had not been informed of the move in advance. Mikoyan even advised the Hungarian leaders to open negotiations with the ousted leader, with a view toward bringing him back into the Party. It is even true that this advice did not go unheeded; Nagy was called to the Central Committee and "negotiations" were opened; but they were carried on by such minor functionaries as Bela Veg and Sandor Nogradi, and not by the Party's real leaders. Both men were very courteous. Nogradi, with an eye on the future, even called Nagy "comrade," asked his views on Rakosi's fall, and made vague allusions to plans for Nagy's reinstatement. But the talks never got beyond generalities.

A few days later the responsible editors of the Communist press were called to a conference by the Central Committee. Many of these, having heard the details of the "Nagy affair," were his sympathizers, and they raised the question of his future, calling him "Comrade Nagy." Whereupon Lajos Acs, one of the secretaries of the Central Committee, rose and said: "Would you please take note of the fact that, to us, Imre Nagy is not a comrade. He is an expellee."

IX

The Russians, by all indications, would have considered Nagy's return to political life as highly desirable. But the leaders of the Hungarian Party continued to show their defiance. There were maneuvers and subterfuges. One day, Gero and Kadar summoned Nagy to talk with them. The atmosphere was constrained, to say the least, during this conversation. Gero showed himself less reticent than did Kadar, who returned constantly to the atttack, his purpose being to persuade Nagy to criticize himself, though stronger personalities than Kadar had not been able to achieve such an end.

At almost the same time, the Soviet Ambassador, Yuri V. Andropov, who had recently replaced E. D. Kisselev, invited Nagy to call at his office in Najza Street. Here a long and amicable conversation took place. This time it was not a question of making a confession of error, and, if the Ambassador's sincerity was open to question, Nagy was able to tell himself that what counted was the gesture. Andropov, he knew, had certainly not acted without Moscow's orders.

When Mikoyan again passed through Budapest, though for only a few hours between planes, he asked Nagy to visit him. At their meeting, Mikoyan overflowed with amiability. He repeated what he had already told the Hungarian Party leaders: that it was not the Russians, but Rakosi himself, who was responsible for Nagy's expulsion from the Party. He asked Nagy to cooperate in an effort to find a satisfactory solution to the situation.

Nagy was, on the one hand, calm because he had the impression that time was on his side. On the other hand, he was disturbed because he had already had one unhappy experience with the Russians, and he was not at all sure that he clearly understood their present motives. He was far too familiar with the mechanics of the Kremlin to have full confidence in these approaches. If they really wanted to reinstate him, their ability to do so should prove no more difficult than it had been to expel him, or than it had been to dispose of Rakosi. Perhaps, they simply wanted to hold him in reserve in case they should find no other solution? Then again it was possible that they sincerely wanted him back at the helm—though not right away, perhaps out of a desire to avoid too frequent changes. In any case, Nagy wanted desperately to establish good relations with the Russians, to clarify the situation, and to rebuild his confidence in their word.

His problem did not lie in the fact that he was anxious to know when he would be restored to Party membership, or to his post as Premier. Now, after the fall of Rakosi, he had plenty of time; and patience had never been lacking in him. The question was—and of this the Russians seemed unaware—whether the masses would wait. For, disquieting signs were appearing throughout the country as well as throughout the circle immediately surrounding him. New plans, new demands that he take some action, were laid before him almost every day. He went to every possible effort to restrain his partisans and to counsel them to patience.

Several days after Mikoyan left Budapest, a young Communist scientist named Istvan Zador called on Nagy. He brought a message from Attila Szigeti, President of the Gyor Departmental Council, who was also a non-Party deputy (representing the Peasants Party) in Parliament. Szigeti proposed to challenge the Government and thereby to provoke a debate. But, under parliamentary procedure, any question to the Government had to be submitted in advance. It was obvious that he would not be recognized and given the floor to speak his mind. He proposed, therefore, to submit an innocuous question and, once he had the floor, to speak out. He hoped he would not be interrupted and he was prepared to accept the responsibility for what he planned to do. However, he did not wish to act without consulting with Nagy himself. Knowing that the villa was watched by the secret police, he had sent Zador to speak for him.

Nagy listened to Zador's explanation, while sitting on the terrace overlooking his garden, sipping cold beer, and nibbling salt biscuits. He explained that he was happy to have word from Szigeti, whom he knew only slightly, but that, as far as his project was concerned, he not only would have nothing to do with it, but would oppose it with all his vigor. He regarded this as an attempt at a "putsch" and was opposed to any such illegal move.

"Do you believe, then, that you will be able to return to the Party leadership through legal means?," he was asked.

"This autumn, everything will fall into my hands," Nagy replied.

"Do you believe that the same Central Committee that expelled you would be capable of readmitting you?"

"They will have no other choice," Nagy replied, firmly. "The working class and the members of the Party will finally impose this decision on the leaders. We cannot resort to the methods of a Rakosi. Our strength lies in the fact that we are above reproach. We must remain that way."

With the utmost delicacy, Zador insinuated that this irreproachable attitude had previously not served Nagy well. If he had acted otherwise, he suggested, Nagy might have retained power.

Nagy replied that, although he would not go into detail, he was not unhappy at the turn events had taken, since otherwise the situation would never have been completely clarified.

"They are rushing to their doom," he said, insistently.

The visitor had the impression that he was speaking to that Kutuzov of *War and Peace* who restrained, with all his power, the young officers who were burning with desire to attack Napoleon. He was, in effect, convinced that the army of the emperor would succumb in the end and that a premature battle might be disastrous. Zador revealed some of his thoughts to Nagy and heatedly asked if he also saw an analogy between the two situations.

For the first time during the conversation, Nagy nodded his assent.

Before Zador left him, Nagy again asked whether he agreed that Szigeti's project would be a mistake. Zador replied that he would have to think about it. Thereupon, Nagy repeated that any attempt at a putsch would end in failure. It was his last word to Szigeti on the subject.

Knowing of the existence of so many plans and projects, Nagy was filled with anxiety. While he was convinced that he would come out on top and that the Party leadership as it existed was doomed, he was also aware that its fall might carry with it the entire country. It was not the future of Gero and Hegedus that concerned him, but that of the Party and of the people. The mutterings of the people—of the Party members and of his friends— beat, restless and impatient, like a stormy sea against the walls of his villa. Confident of the future, he was nevertheless fearful of an approaching catastrophe.

It was this fear that drove him finally to take a step toward rapprochement with the Party, although it was not up to him, as the injured one, to do so. On October 4, 1956, he wrote a letter to the Central Committee. The letter contained these essential passages:

"In addressing myself again to the Party, in putting aside all questions of personal interest, all considerations of prestige, and all rancor, I am obeying simply the convictions I hold as a Communist. . . . It is because I fear for the unity of the Party and because I desire to see myself back in its ranks as soon as possible that I have been moved to write this letter. I want to work beside the other members of the Party to build socialism, to uplift the country, and to give a peaceful and happy existence to our working people in order that they can assume and carry out the heavy tasks awaiting them. . . . For this task, it is necessary that every member of the Party mobilize his energies and present proof of his ideological strength.

"I believe it would be criminal to allow what has been called the 'Nagy Affair' to fester in the bosom of the Party, there to constitute an obstacle to its consolidation and its unity, and to the pursuit of a firm and homogeneous policy. By settling this affair, that obstacle can and must be set aside. I wish to emphasize that, for the purpose of settling this matter, I am ready to do anything that is compatible with my convictions and with my Marxist-Leninist principles, as well as with my honesty as a man. . . .

"I am of the belief that my place is in the heart of the Party, where I spent nearly forty years, and in the ranks where I fought with all the means at my disposal for the good of the people and of the country and of socialism, sometimes with arms, sometimes with a pen, sometimes with my work, sometimes with my words. . . .

"I demand, therefore, that the Central Committee reexamine my case, so that I can be reestablished in my rights as a Party member and, in putting an end to this matter, contribute to the most efficient accomplishment of the tasks that confront the Party and the country."

He could have done no more. Some of his friends thought that he had already gone too far. But, as he said in his letter, he was not thinking of himself. He wanted to avoid something that he sensed was coming and that he dreaded without knowing exactly what it was.

But, as he took the first step, the Party temporized. Nagy had to wait nine days for a reply. When it came, it restored him to the Party. But the document was so hedged with reservations and phrased in such a superior tone, that its publication, instead of dissipating the unrest, augmented it. It said:

"The Politburo has considered the letter of Comrade Imre Nagy, dated October 4, in which he asks to be restored to Party membership. The Politburo has decided:

1. To annul the resolution of November, 1955, excluding Comrade Imre Nagy from the ranks of the Party. If, in fact, he was guilty of political errors, these did not justify his expulsion. The personal control over the Party exercised by Matyas Rakosi played a considerable role in the vote on this resolution. Taking this fact into consideration, the Politburo restores Comrade Nagy to his rights as a member of the Party.

2. To propose that the Central Committee in the near future discuss the questions that remain unsettled in this matter. The Central Committee will have to detail the precise mistakes committed by Comrade Imre Nagy, as well as the excesses or the erroneous statements in the resolution excluding him from the Party.

"These measures will permit the Central Committee to clarify the ideological questions involved in the matter and to bring it to a close."

The day the letter was published, Erno Gero and Andras Hegedus left for Belgrade for a conference with Tito. The Party leadership hoped that a reconciliation with the Yugoslav leader would render the Nagy affair of minor importance. Their view was that, once he was back in the Party, there would be plenty of time to strike a balance between the mistakes of Rakosi and those of Nagy, after which a resolution would be passed providing Nagy with some kind of post. Thus, things would return to normal, all in good time.

But the people were not inclined to listen to such easy solutions. They had too much hatred for Gero, who had been the closest collaborator of Rakosi—the Premier who had fathered the Five-Year Plans that had pushed the country to the brink of ruin. The people were, in addition, far too attached to Nagy to accept any delay. Ten days earlier there had been an amazing demonstration during the celebration of a national funeral for Laszlo Rajk and for three of his friends who had been executed seven years earlier for the crime of treason. The temper of the people had been such that only chance and the presence of troops, and, no doubt, the presence of Imre Nagy and Madame Rajk, had saved the Party leaders from their anger. Every week there were announcements of other funerals for the rehabilitated victims of Stalinist wrath—for generals and for high police officials who had been executed by the Rakosi regime. In an attempt to calm the people, two men responsible for hundreds of executions and for hundreds of cruel tortures—Mihaly Farkas and his son Vladimir—were arrested. But these arrests served only as additional proof to the people of the regime's weakness, since these were men whom that regime had once entrusted with posts of responsibility.

In this situation it was the person of Imre Nagy, the man who had opened the gates of the concentration camps in 1953, who appeared to the people as the most certain—and, indeed, the only—guarantee against a repetition of such crimes. All the hopes of the nation now converged on him. All who desired a better life, more bread, more freedom, turned their eyes toward Nagy in the hope that he would bring an end to the terror. Contrary to all regulations, the newspapers, without waiting for permission from the Central Committee, published his photograph. One weekly unabashedly said: "The personality of Imre Nagy in recent times has, for reasons perfectly comprehensible, become the symbol of a policy opposed to the sectarian, dogmatic, Stalinist policy of Rakosi."

The entire country was of the same opinion. Only the Party kept silent. Its leaders thought they had plenty of time.

Then came the news of Warsaw. The workers, the students, and the writers of Poland had succeeded in reinstating Gomulka at the head of the Party. Why couldn't the same be done in Hungary with Imre Nagy?

This became the dominant question throughout the country. Only the Party remained deaf, convinced it had plenty of time.

The atmosphere became extremely tense. Everywhere, meetings were being held. The participants posed questions that they never would have dared to raise a few months earlier: How much longer would Russian troops remain in Hungary? What was happening to Hungary's production of bauxite and uranium? Why were not the assassins of Rajk being brought to trial? What was the reason for all the maneuvering around the question of Nagy?

At Nagy's home the news poured in, brought there by his friends. Time, no doubt, was on his side. But what a tragedy might await those who sought to stand in the way of history!

BOOK II

**The
Thirteen
Days**

Tuesday, October 23, 1956

The end of October is the season of the grape harvest in Hungary. During this season, on the volcanic slopes of Tokai, on the sands of the Alfold, on the downs of the northern shore of Lake Balaton, the clusters of grapes tumble into baskets, which the peasants then carry to the huge vats where the grapes are pressed by nimble peasant feet. Boys and girls sing, dance, exchange kisses; only the aged ask what the future will bring, or whether they will live to taste the new wine.

Late October, in that year of 1956, found Imre Nagy at Badacsony, north of Lake Balaton, in the Hungarian wine district where he had a small country home. He had left Budapest a few days earlier, partly to remove himself physically from the place in which he had become the focus of tension, and partly to take advantage of what he sensed might be his last days as a private citizen. On October 22, he was, after inspecting the local vinicultural institute, the guest of honor at the Badacsony wine festival.

On the morning of October 23, the radio brought the news that student demonstrators had, at an unprecedented series of mass meetings in Budapest's colleges and universities, demanded that "Comrade Nagy be restored to the leadership of the state and the Party." Nagy had known for a long time that it would be impossible to end the crisis without him. He was not hungry for power.

Indeed, he lacked the ambition that characterizes most politicians, and he saw the demands being made for his return as a burden that he was willing to accept for the good of the Party, the people, and the nation.

The news that morning convinced him that it was time to return to the center of activity, and so he started back to the capital. Toward midday he arrived at his villa on Orso Street. The road from Balaton entered the city through the reddish hills of Buda, a quiet residential district where there was no hint of the agitation evident in the streets of Pest, the center of the city.

Across the Danube, in Pest, the students that morning began preparations for a demonstration that had been decided upon at their meetings of the previous night. It was to be a silent demonstration in the streets of the city and in front of the sacred monuments of the Hungarian people in support of the Polish people's struggle for freedom. But, from the first, the issue of Poland's freedom was unmistakably connected with the rising demand of the students for freedom for Hungary.

At the meetings the previous night, numerous resolutions listing the students' demands had been adopted. No two had been alike in the order or in the phrasing of the demands, but all had set forth approximately the same points. After the meetings, the students had roamed the city seeking some means of making their demands public. They had been refused permission to broadcast them over Radio Kossuth and had ended by mobilizing typists in the universities and colleges to make copies of the resolutions.

On the morning of the twenty-third, these copies appeared throughout the city, tacked to trees or pasted to walls. By the thousands the people of Budapest read them, jostling each other around the improvised bulletin boards. Almost always there was one person close enough to read the demands aloud for those in the rear, an act of daring that would have been impossible a few days earlier. On the streets of Budapest the people were experiencing feelings similar to those that must have stirred the first Christians in the catacombs of Rome when they were at last able to pronounce the forbidden words of Christ. There was this difference, however: in the catacombs, the Christians were protected by the isolation and the darkness of their refuge. In Budapest, on the sunny, open streets that morning, it was the solidarity of the crowds that protected those who dared to read aloud.

This is what they read:

1. We demand the immediate evacuation of all Soviet troops, in conformity with the provisions of the Treaty of Peace.

2. We demand the election by secret ballot of all Party members from top to bottom, and of new officers for the lower, middle, and upper echelons of the Hungarian Workers' Party. These officers shall convoke a Party Congress as early as possible in order to elect a Central Committee.

3. A new Government must be constituted under the direction of Comrade Imre Nagy; all the criminal leaders of the Stalin-Rakosi era must be immediately relieved of their duties.

4. We demand a public inquiry into the criminal activities of Mihaly Farkas and his accomplices. Matyas Rakosi, who is the person most responsible for all the crimes in the recent past, as well as for the ruin of our country, must be brought back to Hungary for trial before a people's tribunal.

5. We demand that general elections, by universal, secret ballot, be held throughout the country to elect a new National Assembly, with all political parties participating. We demand that the right of the workers to strike be recognized.

6. We demand revision and readjustment of Hungarian-Soviet and Hungarian-Yugoslav relations in the fields of politics, economics, and cultural affairs, on a basis of complete political and economic equality and of non-interference in the internal affairs of one by the other.

7. We demand the complete reorganization of Hungary's economic life under the direction of specialists. The entire economic system, based on a system of planning, must be reexamined in the light of conditions in Hungary and in the vital interests of the Hungarian people.

8. Our foreign trade agreements and the exact total of reparations that can never be paid must be made public. We demand precise and exact information on the uranium deposits in our country, on their exploitation, and on the concessions accorded the Russians in this area. We demand that Hungary have the right to sell her uranium freely at world market prices to obtain hard currency.

9. We demand complete revision of the norms in effect in

industry and an immediate and radical adjustment of salaries in accordance with the just requirements of workers and intellectuals. We demand that a minimum living wage be fixed for workers.

10. We demand that the system of distribution be organized on a new basis and that agricultural products be utilized in a rational manner. We demand equality of treatment for individual farms.

11. We demand reviews by independent tribunals of all political and economic trials as well as the release and rehabilitation of the innocent. We demand the immediate repatriation of prisoners of war and of civilian deportees in the Soviet Union, including prisoners sentenced outside Hungary.

12. We demand complete recognition of freedom of opinion and of expression, of freedom of the press and of radio, as well as the creation of a new daily newspaper for the MEFESZ Organization (Hungarian Federation of University and College Students' Associations).

13. We demand that the statue of Stalin, symbol of Stalinist tyranny and political oppression, be removed as quickly as possible and be replaced by a monument to the memory of the martyred fighters for freedom of 1848-1849.

14. We demand the replacement of the emblems that are foreign to the Hungarian people by the old Hungarian arms of Kossuth. We demand for the Hungarian army new uniforms conforming to our national traditions. We demand that the fifteenth of March be declared a national holiday and that the sixth of October be a day of national mourning on which schools will be closed.

15. The students of the Technical University of Budapest declare unanimously their solidarity with the workers and students of Warsaw and Poland in their movement toward national independence.

16. The students of the Technical University of Budapest will organize as rapidly as possible local branches of the MEFESZ, and they have decided to convoke at Budapest, on Saturday, October 27, a Youth Parliament at which all the nation's youth will be represented by their delegates.

The comments of the people were brief and favorable. The older ones in the crowds were moved particularly by the points concerning the emblem of Kossuth, concerning the uniforms of the

Honved, and concerning the celebration of March 15 as a national holiday, all of which deeply touched their national pride. Of objections or criticisms, none was heard.

If, however, one of the students had posted a copy of these resolutions on the gatepost of Nagy's villa for the former Premier to read, that student's enthusiasm might have been dampened by the reaction. It is probable that Nagy would have removed the leaflet and would have explained patiently and with dignity which of the demands he could support and which he would have to oppose. For, the program of those who demanded that Imre Nagy return to head the government was not Nagy's own program, even though in some respects it paralleled his aims and contained some of his most cherished concepts—i.e., equality of political and economic rights, the revision of the economic structure by specialists in conformance with Hungary's needs and peculiarities, the rehabilitation of the victims of fabricated trials, and the demands for solidarity with the Poles in their struggle for freedom. But on other points the demands of the Hungarian students were different from the views of Nagy.

He could, for example, have accepted certain paragraphs, but they would have had to be phrased with more circumspection and tact—as, for instance, in the demands for the convocation of an immediate Party congress, for the publication of foreign trade agreements, for the trial of Rakosi, and for the return of deportees. But he would not have been in accord with the installation of a multi-party regime, nor with the demand for the immediate withdrawal of all Soviet troops. It was not that he wanted the Soviet troops to remain. It was simply that he was a realist and that he knew this demand would be impossible to fulfill. At that moment he again had confidence in the Party, and he believed that, under his leadership, the Party would be able to dominate the situation without Soviet help.

Given Nagy's beliefs, given his way of thinking, he would never have supported the program's anti-Soviet elements. He had no desire to defend the statue of Stalin, nor did he want Hungary's uranium to be sold to the Russians at prices they could dictate; but he believed sincerely in the necessity of Hungarian-Soviet friendship. He even believed such a friendship was possible.

At the moment when the burgeoning army of insurrection was assembling, its future leader was quietly eating lunch. Word of the tumultuous rumble and agitation on the streets had reached him only by telephone. He stayed quietly in his house, not because he disapproved of the demands, but because it was only ten days since he had been restored to Party membership, and, even apart from the fact that he was deeply imbued with Party spirit, he had no desire to lay himself open to any accusations of violating Party discipline or of "breaking the democratic centralism." He did not want to be the man who took the leadership of Hungarian youth against the Central Committee.

Within the Party itself, the developments in the street were spreading turmoil. An extraordinary meeting of Party members was called by the editorial staff of *Szabad Nep,* the principal Party newspaper. The atmosphere was both feverish and strained. Oscar Betlen, the assistant editor-in-chief, offered his resignation. The meeting went on to demand radical changes in the top direction of the Party. A delegation was dispatched to the Central Committee to urge the Party leaders toward immediate action to meet the demands of the people before it would be too late.

But there was no inclination at Central Committee headquarters to listen to such warnings. Party Secretary Erno Gero had come back that morning from Yugoslavia with the official delegation to Belgrade that he had headed. Now, although he had been kept informed of developments in his absence, it was apparent from the statement he issued at the railroad station that he expected the people's homage because he brought news of an accord with Tito. At the station he spoke in confident and optimistic tones of the meaning of the Hungarian-Yugoslav rapprochement and of the atmosphere of cordiality that had pervaded the discussions, unaware of how meaningless his words were in the context of the hour. It was apparent that he felt himself at the apogee of his career and that he believed he had strengthened his position both in Moscow and in Budapest. Now he was naturally furious at the stupid agitation stirred up by the students. They had spoiled his triumph.

In his office at Central Committee headquarters, Gero still smoldered over this anticlimax to his successful trip. He received the delegation from *Szabad Nep* coldly and arrogantly. With him were Jozsef Revai, former dictator of cultural affairs, and Janos Kadar and Gyorgy Marosan, both of whom had recently been freed after long years in prison, Kadar as a Titoist "heretic" and Marosan as a "social democratic spy in the service of Great Britain."

The head of the press delegation, Marton Horvath, who directed the editorial committee of *Szabad Nep,* explained his colleagues' point of view. It was their view, he said, that the demands of the masses must be given serious consideration. The twelfth hour had, he said, sounded, and there must be immediate action.

Gero brushed aside their warnings. They had lost their heads, he told them, and were underestimating the strength of the proletariat. The Party and the Government, he said, had at their disposal all the means necessary to control the troublemakers. The Party leadership had decided, he told the delegation, simply to forbid any demonstration.

One of the delegates asked what would happen if the students, deciding to ignore the ban, demonstrated nevertheless.

Gero, supported by Revai answered that the troops would in that event have to make use of their weapons. "We would fire!" Revai shouted. "We would fire! We would fire!" He repeated this threat over and over again in a rage that bordered on hysteria.

Throughout this scene Kadar remained quiet. Then one of the delegates touched fleetingly on the questionable attitude Kadar had taken in the Laszlo Rajk case, when Kadar had been Minister of the Interior. Kadar, troubled, replied in a low voice that things were not as simple as his interrogator believed.

At 12:53 p.m., the Budapest Kossuth Radio interrupted a program of gypsy music to broadcast a communique from Laszlo Piros, Minister of the Interior: "In order to assure public order, the Ministry of the Interior has forbidden any public meetings or demonstrations until further notice."

The effect of the announcement was quite the opposite of what was intended. Those who had previously been determined to demonstrate gave the announcement no heed whatsoever. And a great many of those people of Budapest who had not thought of taking part in any demonstration now decided to do so out of sheer bravado. Thus, the net effect of the Party's order was that what started out as a simple demonstration in support of the Poles was thereby turned into an act of hostility against the Government.

Though the order prohibiting the march had already been issued, the demonstrators moved rapidly, but in orderly ranks, toward the statue of Sandor Petofi, poet-hero of the 1848 rebellion, on the banks of the Danube. The young marchers came from every quarter of the capital—from Buda, from the suburb of Zuglo, from the Ulloi Avenue quarter. They marched in almost complete silence; one could hardly hear the commands of the leaders. Some held aloft the Hungarian national flag, red, white, and green; others carried the red flag of Communism. A few waved Polish flags until they crackled in the breeze. There were only a few placards or banners, and the slogans on these few all voiced homage to the people of Poland or to the people of Warsaw and Poznan, or they proclaimed the necessity of solidarity between the people of Sandor Petofi and those of Jozsef Bem, the Polish general who had fought on the side of Hungary in the 1848 war of independence.

At Central Committee headquarters, meanwhile, a certain irresolution began to manifest itself. Having firmly banned the demonstration, the Party leaders were now faced with the choice of taking action against the demonstrators or of seeking some means of saving face. At 2:23 p.m., which was approximately the moment when the march began, Radio Kossuth announced that Minister of the Interior Piros had lifted the ban on demonstrations. A gong was sounded after this announcement; then another official communique was read: "At eight o'clock this evening Comrade Erno Gero, First Secretary of the Hungarian Workers' Party, will deliver an address over the radio." This, the Party leaders obviously thought, would serve to calm the people.

They were quite wrong. At three o'clock in the afternoon, in Vaci Avenue which was the center of cosmopolitan life, autobus traffic was still proceeding normally. But at Petofi Square, the crowd of demonstrators overflowed its narrow confines and spilled over into the adjacent street.

The ceremony at Petofi Square was brief and quite simple. Young men placed wreaths at the base of the statue of the poet, who was shown holding one hand aloft as though taking an oath to his nation's freedom. Then Imre Sinkovics, a young actor from the National Theater, recited the Petofi poem that had inspired the Revolution of 1848. This was followed by a reading of the demands drafted by the students. The crowd then resumed its march in the direction of the statue of General Bem.

The monument to this revolutionary figure stood on the opposite bank of the Danube, in Buda, not far from the Margaret Bridge, and, as the crow flies, barely two kilometers from Petofi Square. But because the Elizabeth Bridge, which would have been the quickest route, was still in ruins from the war (it was the only bridge in Budapest which had not yet been rebuilt), the demonstrators were forced to make a wide detour by way of Lajos Kossuth Street, Bajcsy-Zsilinszky Avenue, and St. Stephen's Boulevard in order to get to the Margaret Bridge.

It is by such small chances that the fates can intervene, for it was on this long march through the busy streets of Pest that the demonstrators found their voices and chose their slogans. It was here, marching shoulder to shoulder and drunk with the feeling of power which their own numbers gave them, that the demonstrators, shouting their slogans more and more insistently, lit the flames of revolution. They called for freedom, proclaimed Polish-Hungarian solidarity and friendship, demanded restoration of the Kossuth emblem on the national flag, and, most insistently of all, they shouted: *"Ruszki, haza!,"* which is to say, "Russians, go home!"

Among the slogans there were many which were chanted in a rhythm and a rhyme (in Hungarian). These acclaimed Nagy as the leader of the masses.

> "We do everything, but always too late.
> Nagy to power, and without delay!"

This was the most political of the slogans. But there were others:

> "The leadership must change
> And Nagy shall be our leader."

Some slogans were clearly laden with hatred:

> "Imre Nagy to the Government
> Rakosi into the Danube."

Among the demonstrators were two of Nagy's closest friends and collaborators, Geza Losonczy and Miklos Vasarhelyi, both of whom were destined to play important roles in the events of the next few days. These were men who had never deserted Nagy, even in his darkest hour. They were his trusted advisors and his devoted friends. Upon being recognized, they were questioned by the other demonstrators:

"Where is Imre Nagy?" they were asked.

"At his home."

"Isn't he coming?"

"Certainly not."

"But why not?"

"Because, if he came, his presence here would be used against him."

Their viewpoint was easy to understand. After all, if Nagy were to join in the demonstration and if there should be a clash with the police, Gero and his followers would have no hesitation in blaming him, or in accusing him of plotting against the regime. Even if the demonstrators were to disperse peaceably, he would, under the circumstances, be vulnerable. And, in any case, he was a man of science, not one to join a mob of demonstrators or to seek to impose their views, even if he shared in those views.

Along the line of march the fever rose. One after another, the windows of apartment buildings along Bajcsy-Zsilinszky Avenue flew open. Streamers and flags were waved from them. Each building flew the official flag. In its center, in imitation of the Soviet emblem, was the emblem of Rakosi's Hungary—the Red Star surmounting a hammer and sickle, which, apart from its ugliness, was unanimously detested for what it represented. From the streets the demonstrators called out to the occupants of the buildings: "We want no more of that emblem." There were only two solutions: either to remove the stitches holding the emblems or to cut them out. The scissors proved the quicker. It was then that there appeared the first flags with holes in their centers.

It was after four o'clock when the demonstrators reached St. Stephen's Boulevard. This was the hour when the workers of the morning shift left their factories. Some of those who worked in the northern suburbs customarily traveled by streetcar to the terminal in Marx Place, and, as it so happened, it was shortly after the head of the column reached this point that the streetcars began disgorging these homeward-bound workers by the hundreds. The factory workers quickly made common cause with the demonstrators. At first, they stood on the sidelines, cheering and waving their hats. Then, as their numbers grew into the thousands, they began to join in the march. It was at this point that the phenomenon became that classic of revolutionary literature, a student-worker demonstration.

The ceremony at the statue to General Bem was not much longer than was the one at Petofi Square. Here the speaker was Peter Veres, the president of the Writers' Association, a man whose personality was such that he was incapable of arousing the enthusiasm of this audience. Although he had often taken a critical view of the country's situation, he was regarded by the public as essentially a representative of the regime. The speech he read in the name of the Writers' Association was a carefully measured one that demanded more liberty and the return of Nagy as a member of the country's leadership.

Veres' demands were clearly far more conservative than were the demands of the students. But, nonetheless, this stage of the demonstration was to have important repercussions, for on the fringes of the crowd a momentous event was taking shape. Adjoining the Square where the statue of Bem stood was a barracks of the Honved, the Hungarian National Guard. Here shirtsleeved soldiers who were off duty leaned from the windows to listen. Some produced flags and waved them outside the windows. Those nearest in the street cheered the soldiers. Sentries in front of the barracks left their posts and mingled with the throng. Suddenly, to those who witnessed these developments, the sight of soldiers smiling and waving encouragingly to demonstrators in Communist Hungary made it clear that the members of the Hungarian Army would not fire on the Hungarian people *no matter what orders they received, or who gave them.*

It was here, too, that eight hundred student officers of the Petofi Military Academy joined the demonstration. Almost all of the Academy students were the carefully chosen sons of workers and peasants or of the majority members—and even militants—of the Party.

Someone climbed the statue and placed a flag between the arms of the Polish general. Then a new column of students marched into the Square to swell the ranks of the demonstrators, carrying the Hungarian tricolor and the red flag. An elderly demonstrator called out: "Not the red flag!" Some students replied: "What have you got against the red flag?" He answered: "We have our own flag, the flag of Hungary!" The mood of the crowd took on an intense urgency; some of the soldiers, in response to demands from the crowd, tore from their caps the hated five-pointed star, emblem of the Soviets.

Quite forgotten was the fact that Petofi had just so imagined the people of Hungary joining in the last battle for the freedom of the world: "Red faces marching under the folds of the red flag." Forgotten, too, was the fact that Endre Ady, poet of the Revolution of 1918, had saluted the red flag with deep emotion and that Attila Jozsef, the idol of these very youths, had, during the Horthy regime, written a verse which hoped for the day when "the workers would raise above their factories the five-pointed star of free men."

To the Hungarians, the symbols that in other days had raised the hope of better times and the realization of humanity's dearest dreams had become, after ten years of Soviet occupation, the symbols of oppression. Even the idea of socialism had undergone a change in the first feverish days of tension. Many ceased to see in socialism the possibility of more social justice or the end of exploitation or the hope of more liberty. For them, the sullied word was now intimately linked with the only realities they knew: the realities of foreign occupation and control, of the curbing of their liberties, of their humiliation as men, of regimentation, and of an abnormally low standard of living. In times of revolt there is a tendency to simplify things. Once aroused, the people cease to consider subtleties. A people in revolt wants *something different,* a change, not the mere amelioration of their plight. And if their aims often remain somewhat foggy, they are always categorically clear about what they do not want.

The man in the villa on Orso Street obviously could not follow, moment by moment, the progress of these events. And, above all, he was necessarily ignorant of the little details that were to take on major significance. This villa, which had been the most sensitive spot in the country for a year and a half, was in the space of a few hours removed, so to speak, several light-years from that which, geographically speaking, was taking place two or three miles away. Nagy's strength, which differentiated him from the other Party leaders, lay in his always having listened to the heartbeats of the people and in his understanding of the complaints and of the hopes of the masses. At this point in the development of events he no longer understood; for the time being at least, he was cut off from his people. The ears which by habit were so keenly attuned to their cries were, for the moment, closed.

From Bem Square the crowd went, by way of the Margaret Bridge, to Parliament Square. On Maria Jaszai Place, the demonstrators passed by the Ministry of the Interior. The houses that once stood here had been burned to the ground during the war. In their place the government had erected a large building of greyish-white stone that was the headquarters of the political police, the AVH. There was no incident. From their windows the police officials and the office workers simply watched the tide of demonstration flow onto the large Square that lies before the Parliament Building. This next Square, where, in 1918 during another October Revolution, the Republic was first proclaimed, was now filled by the people of Budapest. According to various estimations, there were nearly 200,000 persons in the Square—that is to say, one out of every six or seven of Budapest's entire population. The people roared for Imre Nagy. But he was still in his house.

The ground floor of the Parliament Building was dark in the gathering dusk. On the first floor, a number of windows were illuminated. From the Square, those nearest the building could clearly distinguish the silhouettes of well-known political leaders. Among these were Istvan Hidas and Jozsef Mekis, both vice-presidents of the Council, and Ferenc Erdei, Minister of Agriculture. Hidas and Mekis were men without talent and without backbone. They could not stand the idea of being recognized by the people, whose presence in such numbers they deplored, and they finally drew the curtains so they could watch the demonstration without being seen.

It was undoubtedly these two who gave the order to cut off the lights that illuminated the Square. They hoped that the darkness would dampen the spirits of the people and that the crowd would then disperse.

But their order accomplished nothing. All at once, thousands of torches flared in the Square: the demonstrators had ignited their newspapers. They ignited leaflets, and all other paper which they could find. The leaflets were not those of the demonstrators. Thousands of Government leaflets had been handed out to the demonstrators when they were crossing the Margaret Bridge. These leaflets urged them to be calm and to listen to the radio address which would be delivered by Comrade Gero. Afire, the leaflets made a splendid spectacle. Not only was the crowd tasting the power of revolt. They were also savoring its beauty.

Suddenly, as if to signal a first victory for the demonstrators, the lights went on again. There was a steady chanting: "Where is Imre Nagy?" Then Ferenc Erdei, the Minister of Agriculture, appeared on a first-floor balcony. He wanted to speak, but the shouts from the crowd drowned his voice. He withdrew amid derisive booing. As head of the National Peasants' Party's left wing, Erdei had never been a member of the Communist Party, but only a faithful fellow-traveler. The fact that the people refused to listen to him showed that they were rejecting not only the leaders of the Communist Party but all those who had compromised with Rakosi.

A quarter of an hour passed. Then half an hour. It became evident that the people would not leave without having heard Imre Nagy. The throng, conscious of its power, sensed that such a movement as was now proceeding could not be set in motion every day. If they were to go home empty-handed, they would certainly not be given tomorrow what they would fail to obtain today.

Nagy's most faithful friends understood that his absence not

only was regrettable but that it could also result in serious consequences, for the throng was growing impatient and the impression
was spreading that Nagy wanted to be coaxed. At this, some members of Nagy's following, among them Geza Losonczy, Miklos
Vasarhelyi, the novelist Tamas Aczel, and others, went by automobile to the Orso Street villa.

Grudgingly, Nagy gave in to their insistence. He was happy,
true enough, to know that the people demanded his presence, but
he doubted that this was the time for him to go to Parliament
Square and he was far from sure that such an action would have
a favorable effect on the course of events. The more he listened to
their argument, the more doubts apparently came to his mind.
Would he be able to find the words by which to calm this wild
throng? To him the situation must have seemed extremely delicate.
He had no official position; he was not even a member of the
Central Committee. He was no more than a lowest-level Party
militant who had only recently been restored to Party life. In whose
name could he speak? Above all, in whose name could he make
promises?

In the automobile that was carrying him toward the Parliament
Building he was silent. When, at last, he spoke, it was to express his
astonishment at seeing a flag with a hole in its center. "What
happened to that?" he asked, puzzled; but in the moment of asking
he seemed to understand that what had happened to the flag was
exactly what he had foreseen for a year during moments of his
darkest presentiments. The Party's opportunistic policies had driven
the masses to the point of revolt and had plunged the country into
a grave crisis. The October night was chill; nonetheless, perspira-
tion poured down Nagy's forehead.

It was nearly eight o'clock when he arrived before the Parliament Building. On the balcony from which the throng had driven
Ferenc Erdei, the actor Imre Sinkovics, who had recited Petofi's
"National Hymn" early in the afternoon, was reciting other poems.
At first the crowd gave him an attentive ear; then it became bored
and restless. Once again the tension mounted, and the young actor,
popular though he was, was booed.

To reach the entrance of the Parliament Building, Nagy had
to part the solid rows of the demonstrators. They recognized him

and made way for him. The news of his arrival traveled quickly. Once inside, Nagy went directly to the office of Mekis, who regarded him not without surprise. Eighteen months before, Mekis had been one of those who had abandoned Nagy. Since then, he had never ceased to speak against him.

"You have no business coming here," Mekis now said. "You know very well that the Central Committee is going to meet next week to consider your case."

Miklos Vasarhelyi seized Mekis by the shoulders and shook him.

"Have you gone crazy?" Vasarhelyi asked. "Must you talk about next week when all of Budapest is clamoring at your door? We must act without delay. Imre Nagy must be named President of the Council. And immediately. Do you hear? This is a revolt. Don't you understand?"

Mekis paled. The shouts of the angry crowd seemed louder. Nagy stepped forward and walked out on the balcony.

At first, the throng did not recognize Nagy. There were several other people on the balcony and, in the uncertain light, faces were obscured. The demonstrators continued to shout for Imre Nagy even when he was already facing them and trying to quiet them so that he could speak. Then someone found a way to turn a lamp on the balustrade and to shine it into his face.

A roar, clear and prolonged, immediately burst from the throng. Nagy's appearance was their second victory. He raised a hand for silence.

"Comrades," he began . . . and there were protests and boos from all parts of the Square.

The demonstrators shouted back: "We are not comrades!" Their clamor swelled until it filled the Square. In reality, there were in the throng thousands upon thousands of Communists, all convinced members of the Party who could have had no argument with the form of address Nagy employed, and these were themselves surprised by the violence of the protests. At this moment all who had eyes must have understood that Hungary was rejecting not only Stalin and Rakosi, but all the dictates of the Party, whatever their manifestation. The Hungarian Workers' Party—the Communist Party—had encountered failure, and in an irrevocable way.

Nagy spoke. But there were few who either heard his words or had any disposition to heed them. No authentic text of this extemporaneous speech exists. But the Kadarist paper *Elet es Irodalom,* of May 10, 1957, gave this as the most accepted version:

"I affectionately salute those who are present here. All my esteem goes out to you young democratic Hungarians who, by your enthusiasm, would help to remove the obstacles that stand in the way of democratic socialism. It is by negotiation in the bosom of the Party and by the discussion of problems that we will travel the road that leads toward the settlement of our conflicts. We want to safeguard constitutional order and discipline. The Government will not delay in arriving at its decisions."

Instead of appeasing the people, Nagy's short speech only made them feel deceived. Those farthest away heard little, because no one had thought of providing a public address system. And those who were able to understand his words were no less dissatisfied. There were angry mutterings across the Square when, at the end, Nagy asked the demonstrators to return peacefully to their houses. There was no applause when he finished, only an embarrassed moment of silence. Then, in an attempt to save the situation, Nagy called on the crowd to chant the national anthem. He himself began in a sonorous voice.

Once the anthem was sung, the flood of the demonstration began to ebb. Some of its members were tired; others, thinking Nagy had sound reasons for speaking as he had, were shaken in their resolution by his words. Nonetheless, their hearts felt a vague sense of dissatisfaction. They had won nothing concrete. Tomorrow, things could fall back into the same old rut. And among those who remained in the Square, a new slogan ran swiftly: "Tomorrow, we strike."

Nagy reentered Mekis' office. No one told him that he should have spoken differently. He was perfectly aware of that. His words had been more conservative, more carefully chosen than those in the articles in the Party press in recent days. The reaction had been like a dash of cold water. Yet, those present in the office did not have the impression that Nagy was downcast by this setback. Although he seemed tired, he did not seem discouraged. It was as if he had known in advance that his words would not be well received. At bottom, it was the Central Committee to which he was speaking, not the throng in the Square. His allusion to negotiation within the Party and to the need for discussing the people's problems was revealing. He believed that the people of Budapest would return to their homes—no matter how disillusioned they felt—and that at the next meeting of the Central Committee he would be able to put across his conceptions of the way to liberalize the regime. Then the slight decline in confidence recorded that day would be compensated for to a large degree.

It was at this moment that the news of the firing at the Radio Building reached Parliament Square.

On the fifteenth of March, 1848, the youth of Pest went to the printing house of Landerer-Heckenast to publish their historic twelve points. The youth of 1956 separated from the main body of demonstrators and marched toward the building of Radio Budapest with the intention of making their demands known to the entire nation. This was quite natural. There was no need for making a plan in advance. It was quite natural, too, that the leaders of the political police would have thought of this before the demonstrators did. That is why, when the first groups of youths arrived within sight of the building, they found that the guard had been re-enforced two hours earlier.

The large block of antiquated buildings into which the editorial offices, studios, and technical departments of Radio Budapest were crowded, stood a few steps from the National Museum, which was the scene of the beginning of the Revolution of 1848. One might well believe there was an omen of destiny in this conjuncture of two revolutionary movements: it was in front of the statues of Petofi and Bem that the demonstrators had first gathered; it was Kossuth Square, before the Parliament Building, where they met in strength; and now they stood beside the National Museum. But in 1956 the fates wove, divided, and cut the thread much more quickly than they had a century earlier.

A hundred and eight years earlier, when the revolutionaries entered the Heckenast printing shop to set their manifesto in type, the owner, an old Swabian and a charming liberal, had said with a smile of complicity: "Gentlemen, I will submit only to force." Thereupon, one of the demonstrators had touched him lightly on the arm; force having been manifested, the work could go on. But now the directors of Radio Budapest, among whom there were none so courageous nor so astute, gave no such indication of solidarity with the young demonstrators. They refused to broadcast their demands.

The crowd, however, continued to flow into the narrow street. When the heavy door of the studios was closed, it was no longer possible to speak directly to the officials, and so the youths faced the building and began chanting: "A microphone in the street," a naïve demand which they repeated over and over. As a matter of fact, the demonstrators were simply demanding something which had supposedly been theirs for a long time. They had long been led to believe that the radio station belonged to the people and that they had a right to be heard over the air waves. The atmosphere became so tense that the station officials received a delegation of about twenty demonstrators. A long bargaining session ensued regarding which demands could be broadcast and which would have to be kept silent. Those supporters of Imre Nagy who were among the delegation did not fight for broadcasting the entire manifesto, but sought rather to arrive at a compromise. Having none of his authority, their experience was nonetheless the same as his; they were overwhelmed by the sentiments of the throng.

A record of this meeting was published by *Nepszabadsag,* the organ of the Kadar government, on January 23, 1957:

" 'What do you want with the radio?' asked Valeria Benke [who was the president of Radio Budapest].

"The majority of the delegation remained calm, but one snapped:

" 'We want the radio to belong to the people. We will not leave until we obtain satisfaction for our demands.'

" 'What do you mean by, "The radio must belong to the people?" '

" 'That a microphone must be set up in the street so that the people can express their opinions.'

"Peter Erdos broke in. [Erdos was the Petofi Circle delegate, and it was in this role that he took part in the negotiations.]

" 'The radio has been fighting a long time for more democracy,' [Erdos said]. 'Do you think that cause would be served by putting a microphone in the street? You yourself cannot provide guarantees for all the people you will find in the street. How do you know who would speak or what they would say?'

"The youth lashed out again:

" 'Enough of this empty and demagogic debate. It will get us nowhere.'

"Erdos reddened with indignation:

" 'How you dare speak to me of demagogy? I heard enough of that accusation in the prisons of the AVH.'

"One of the young men quieted his comrades by saying, calmly:

" 'We insist that our fourteen points be read.' "

Peter Erdos spent three years in prison after the trials of Rajk and Kadar. After he was freed, he criticized Rakosi so violently that he was the only one among those who had been rehabilitated to be returned to prison. In February, 1956, he was arrested and sentenced to eight months in prison for incitement against the regime. He was not released again until after the fall of Rakosi. The fact that in the early hours of the Revolution he was considered by the masses as being too moderate clarifies the fact that the so-called "rightist deviationists" lagged far behind the desires of the people.

The negotiations inside the radio building dragged on. Outside, the demonstrators began to ask themselves whether their comrades were not being held as hostages. As the time passed, this impression grew, arousing hot anger in those who watched detachments of the AVH arriving in a steady stream. The situation was aggravated by a stupid attempt by radio officials to fool the throng. An automobile equipped with a loud-speaker drew up in front of the door, assertedly to record the students' fourteen points. Was this not the microphone in the street that they had demanded?

A young woman in a coat the color of wine dregs perched herself on the roof of the car and began reading the manifesto into a microphone. Demonstrators called out to the people leaning out of nearby windows to turn on their radios in order to see whether what she was reading was really being broadcasted. When they learned it was not, the throng surged toward the men in the car, but these—five radio workers and a policeman—quickly reentered the building by a hidden door. Then the crowd began using the automobile as a battering ram against the heavy gates.

In the midst of this bubbling excitement, eight o'clock sounded and the radio began transmitting the speech of Party First Secretary Erno Gero. This speech is generally regarded as the fuse that set off the explosion. Gero's words, demonstrating the speaker's harsh inhumanity, his servility toward—and respect for—the Soviet Union, his lack of comprehension, and his aggressiveness would have exasperated the most patient listeners. And the demonstrators before Radio Budapest were not very patient. His obvious hatred of the people and his obstinate rejection of the overtures from the young demonstrators revolted them. Said Gero:

"We condemn those who seek to instill in our youth the poison of chauvinism and to take advantage of the democratic liberties that our state guarantees to the workers to organize a nationalist demonstration." This was the sole lesson that the Party First Secretary had drawn from the events, and he emphasized it with such reproachful formulas as: "attempts to make trouble," "hostile elements," "provocation," "nationalist subversion," etc. This was how Gero saw a demonstration that was destined to change the entire country.

It must be stated, however, that Gero's speech contained proposals that showed a certain progress by comparison with his previous declarations. "It is better to advance more slowly and, if possible, to make progress without harm," he said, in a statement that could be interpreted as a concession. With regard to the co-operatives, Gero said: "In the cooperative movement, we will not have to set down our goals in advance, either in percentages or in precise figures." Another retreat, another concession. But in this feverish hour, when it was the liberty of the nation and its whole way of life that was at issue, such innovations went unnoticed, drowned by his verbiage and his menacing phrases.

The demonstrators in the street heard the speech from radios placed in nearby windows. They were shocked by Gero's words as well as by the fact that their own views had not yet been broadcasted. Their indignation overflowed.

At last, the demonstrators made an organized attempt to assault the building and to force the broadcasting of their manifesto. A group of ten youths put the radio car into reverse and backed it repeatedly against the main gates. Some brought bricks from a nearby construction job and hurled them at the windows. Others tried to climb to the balconies, using the grillwork on ground-floor windows.

The defenders of the building were numerous: they numbered more than five hundred who, if the narrowness of the street is taken into account, represented a heavy concentration. While many of the soldiers who comprised the guard, including some of the officers, had no stomach for battle with this throng, it is evident that their arms gave them a sense of superiority. They became rougher and rougher in their attempts to disperse the mob.

The defenders at first hurled tear-gas bombs. But these proved a double-edged weapon, for the fumes swept back into the building through broken windows. Then they seized fire hoses and, with warning shouts, turned them on the throng. Soldiers posted in the corridors followed this action by fixing bayonets and hurling themselves against the people, shouting *"Hajra,"* which is to say, "Let's go." They forced their way into the demonstrators at two points and succeeded in clearing the street directly before the building. Here the soldiers deployed into firing position.

It was toward nine o'clock when the first shots were fired. Unfortunately, it will never be known who fired them. It is not impossible that they were fired into the air as a warning. It is certain, however, that, having cleared Sandor Brody Street, the AVH, who had taken up positions in the garden of the Museum and in Gutenberg Square near the big boulevards, opened direct fire across the two open squares as well as the nearby streets in order to prevent any more of the demonstrators from entering.*

---

* The Kadar Government press and propaganda organs understandably denied that the first shots were fired from the Radio Building. But they gave contradictory versions. In the second volume of that government's *White Book,* a Major N. K. stated: "Later [before 7:30] we fired some warning shots." Two pages further, in the same *White Book,* one can read: "Toward half-past ten in the evening, the soldiers received orders to fire some warning shots." In *Fighting the Counter-Revolution,* by Solyom Zele, appears this statement: "Colonel Orban gave the order to fire toward 11:30 p.m." In *Counter-Revolutionary Forces in the Events of October in Hungary,* the following statement appears: "The commander of the guard had asked his

Soon the dead and the wounded sprawled on the paving. The people's movement had been consecrated in blood for all time. The demonstrators carried one of the bodies to the street in front of the official newspaper, *Szabad Nep,* situated not far away. From the boulevard in front of the National Museum, two tanks arrived as reinforcements. The crowd, using these tanks as a screen, flowed back into Sandor Brody Street and there launched a real battle.*

In this battle the tide turned slowly to the side of the demonstrators. They had received weapons from policemen and from soldiers who did not want to fight against them. Later, the first trucks arrived, laden with light arms and ammunition and driven by workers from the arsenals.

Manpower reinforcements also continued to flow into the area.

---

superiors what he should do. At exactly 12:35 a.m., he received the order to open fire. . . . Toward 1 a.m., the various commanders, seeing that they had no other course open, gave the order to their units to open fire."

The last of these versions is the one most frequently cited. The same documents claim that the mob began to fire toward 9 p.m., and some say as early as 7:30. But even if one accepts this thesis, one might ask how it happened that the attacking throng did not succeed in taking the Radio Building, whose door they had forced, if the defenders held their fire for three or four hours.

* Where did the demonstrators get their arms? There have been various answers to this question: "From secret depots created by the imperialist espionage services," or "From arsenals buried under the ground, from which the weapons were distributed at an opportune moment," etc. Solyom Zele's work, *Fighting the Counter-Revolution,* admits, however, that "for the sake of historical accuracy, it must be frankly stated that among the throng were to be found a number of officers of the Home Defense Forces and many from the police. Before the Radio Building, one noticed, above all, a number of officers of the Petofi Academy. Part of these turned, in both words and deeds, against the AVH defenders of the Radio Building. Others, on the contrary, fought bravely to defend the building. The principal spokesmen of still other groups of demonstrators—before the East Station and elsewhere—were often also officers of the Home Defense Forces." The same work adds: "Among the counter-revolutionaries who were arrested were seven or eight young workers from Csepel. They were known to have received arms at their factory from the Association of Freedom Fighters (a paramilitary organization on the Soviet model). These young men lived in a workers' quarter in Csepel." And, in the second volume of the Kadar Government's *White Book,* one reads: "A truck loaded with soldiers entered the crowd; men clambered aboard and demanded or were given the weapons of the occupants."

Some of these men came from Parliament Square, most of them young men, discouraged and dissatisfied; the others, drunk with victory, came from the City Park, where they had toppled the statue of Stalin. They had first tied ropes to the dictator's neck, but could not budge the statue. Then steel cables, hooked to a heavy truck, were put to use, and now nothing remained on the pedestal but a giant pair of Russian boots.

The more the crowd increased, the more militant it became. The demonstrators wanted to avenge their dead. They redoubled the force of their attack. Some of the rebels had occupied nearby houses that provided them with firing positions. It was a fight to the death.

Informed of the battle, Imre Nagy decided to go to the headquarters of the Central Committee in Academy Street. He was accompanied by his son-in-law, Ferenc Janosi; by Gabor Tanczos, the secretary of the Petofi Circle; by Miklos Vasarhelyi; and by other friends.

There the confusion was at its height. After having broadcast Gero's speech, the radio had announced that the Politburo had called the Central Committee to meet *on the thirty-first of October*. A few minutes later the speaker issued a correction: "The Politburo, at its meeting today, decided to call the Central Committee to meet *at an early date*." Two hours later, a new correction was broadcasted: "The Politburo of the Hungarian Workers' Party has summoned the Central Committee to meet *without delay* to examine the situation and to discuss what decisions to take."

Between these announcements, the members of the Central Committee had been arriving, one after the other. The Minister of the Interior, Laszlo Piros, who, by grace of Rakosi, had been able to exchange a butcher's apron for a general's uniform, set up a defense for the building. He named as commander of the sector a colonel of the Frontier Guard and reinforced the defense, composed of police and Frontier troops, by a unit from the river brigades.

Nagy was taken to the office of Gero, where the Premier, Andras Hegedus, was also present. As soon as Nagy arrived, Gero attacked him violently. All that was happening was Nagy's work, said Gero. Now, he said, Nagy could cook in his own juice.

Nagy, however, protested vehemently. For a long time, he said, he had been trying to draw the attention of the Party and the Government to the danger that they faced. Then the bitter discussion disintegrated into a futile exchange of reproaches. At last, it was decided that Nagy would take part, in the role of a guest, in the meeting of the Central Committee scheduled for that night. However, his son-in-law and his friends were not to be admitted to the meeting-room, being forced to wait in an adjoining office.

The meeting of the Central Committee was stormy and dramatic and extremely confused. Word had arrived that it was not only at the Radio Building that a battle was raging. The insurgents had attacked the building of *Szabad Nep* and had gained a foothold there. With great difficulty, the newspaper staff had succeeded in spiriting Jozsef Revai, a member of the Politburo, out of the building by a secret door. Gero had sent Revai to *Szabad Nep* during the late afternoon to keep an eye on Marton Horvath, Party cultural leader, who was feared to have turned soft, and Revai had demanded repeatedly and dementedly that the rebels be fired on.

Now the Stalinists in the Central Committee demanded that the revolt be suppressed without mercy. They described the insurrection as "a fascist counter-revolutionary action" that must be mastered without delay. More moderate elements, however, raised the question of responsibility. In their eyes, Gero bore a large share of the blame. They insisted that Imre Nagy be named Premier and that the Politburo be reorganized.

Above all else, however, the representatives of the two viewpoints were indeed in agreement on the necessity of restoring order, and to this end it was decided martial law must be declared. Several speakers recommended that Soviet troops be called, but no decision was made on this question. Toward midnight, Andras Hegedus told three delegates from the Writers' Association who waited in an antechamber—Laszlo Benjamin and Zoltan Zelk, the poets, and Sandor Erdei—that a fascist counter-revolution had broken out and that it would be broken by force of arms. *In the event that it was not promptly suppressed,* Soviet troops would be called.

Nagy was trapped in a situation from which there was no way

out. He found himself facing a Central Committee which, two years earlier, had been unanimously ranged on his side *against* Rakosi and Gero. But it was also the same Central Committee which, six months later, had unanimously taken a position *in favor of* Rakosi and of Gero and against him—and which had brutally denounced his "machinations." These men, who would tear each other apart if they were so ordered, were the ones responsible for the existing chaos. Yet, it was with these men that Nagy would have to make the decisions. They had betrayed him, but, nonetheless, he was now the wisp of straw by which they hoped to be saved.

His participation in the meeting was brief. He agreed to declaring martial law. At that moment he did not know how broad the battle had become, and he was convinced that order could be restored in a few hours. He, too, believed that the first step was to reestablish order, after which there would be time to impose his own program. He made no allusion to any call for Soviet troops. That question was, in any case, not open to debate, for it had been mentioned only as a possible eventuality. On the other hand, in view of the repugnance with which he viewed such an eventuality, he thought that if he showed himself hostile to such a move, this would only aggravate the question instead of contributing to the peaceful solution that he hoped would result.

Again and again the meeting recessed while the opposing factions held secret meetings. Military information arrived constantly. In the early hours of the morning, the insurgents had succeeded in occupying the Radio Building. Fighting was going on in many parts of the city. A street-cleaning truck had dragged the statue of Stalin as far as the National Theater.

The Central Committee voted to declare martial law.

As a matter of form, a committee was named to go to Nagy for the purpose of proposing that he accept the post of Premier. He replied that he would accept and that he believed the swift development of a vast governmental program was now needed.

All his life, Nagy had fought and suffered to win the people's affection for the Party and to make the Party understand the people. But now, at the moment when he was called to head the government, the people, guns in their hands, were rising against the Party's dictates. It was less than a year ago that he had issued a passionate warning and prophecy: "It is to be feared that we will not understand the new errors we have made, until we are at the brink of the precipice—if not the bottom. This could be fatal to the country."

Now he believed that, by hurling himself like a bridge across the gulf, he would be able to save the Party from its inescapable fate.

The Intervention

At 4:30 a.m. on October 24, Radio Budapest broadcasted, in place of its usual musical program, the following communique: "Fascist and reactionary elements have launched an armed attack against our public buildings and against our forces of law and order. In the interests of reestablishing order, all assemblages, meetings, and demonstrations are forbidden. Police units have been instructed to deal severely with troublemakers and to apply the law in all its force. Signed: The Council of Ministers of the Hungarian People's Republic."

An hour later the same communique was broadcasted. This time the term "fascist" had been eliminated and replaced by that of "counter-revolutionary," a no less disparaging term. The crackle of rifle fire and the rumble of tanks through the city streets continued.

After four broadcasts of the communique, and after interminable military marches and confused noises, the radio announced at 8:13 a.m. the news that Imre Nagy had been named Premier. As though the carnage in the streets was not enough, the good news was phrased in a way that could only provoke disillusionment and bitterness. The announcement emphasized that the outgoing Premier, Andras Hegedus, would remain as First Deputy Premier and assistant to Nagy. It underlined the fact that the Central Committee had confirmed Erno Gero in his post as Party First Secretary.

To the people, it meant nothing that the communique had announced the removal of half the members of the Politburo and half the members of the Secretariat; it was the names of Gero and Hegedus which were important. Their retention was regarded by the people as a bad sign. Was it not the Government of Hegedus that had forbidden the demonstration and turned guns on the students? Was it not Gero who, as recently as the previous evening, had addressed the demonstrators as though they were beasts, his strident voice uttering threats filled with bitter hatred?

In a revolution, the failure to keep up with the pace of events is at least as dangerous—if not more dangerous—than is the distribution of weapons. Twelve hours earlier, the appointment of Nagy would have filled the entire country with joy, even though Hegedus and Gero had been kept at the head of the Party apparatus. Now the same news no longer satisfied anyone. A great deal of water had flowed beneath the Danube bridges and a great deal of blood across the pavements of Pest.

Yet Nagy saw only the fact that the new team was much to be preferred over its predecessor: Laszlo Piros, the Minister of the Interior who had opened fire on the people, as well as Istvan Bata, the Minister of War, had disappeared from the Politburo. Three Rakosi henchmen, Bela Szalai, Istvan Hidas, and Jozsef Mekis, had left the political stage, and with them had gone many of their followers. And, even if Gero had remained in the Secretariat, there were still three new members who were not Stalinists, and who had all served prison terms. These were: Ferenc Donath, Janos Kadar, and Gyula Kallai. Nagy also considered it a personal success that some of those close to him would henceforth be part of the leadership: men like Zoltan Szanto, who had become a member of the Politburo; and Geza Losonczy, who had become a deputy Politburo member; and Gyorgy Lukacs, who had become a member of the Central Committee.

It was the people who were less sensitive to these fine distinctions. Nagy, it might be said, was using a chemist's scales while the people were using a railroad freight weighing platform. The masses knew little of the ideological conflicts that raged within the Party; they were more or less familiar with the positions of Lukacs and Losonczy, but they knew almost nothing about Donath, who had just emerged from prison, nor about Szanto,* who had been in the political discard for years. Only the initiate knew that Ferenc Munnich, a new member of the Central Committee, did not worship Rakosi and that Gyula Kallai was perhaps a degree less sectarian than was his predecessor, Bela Veg. Who else today could be interested in such subtleties? The people knew that they had succeeded in restoring Imre Nagy to leadership, but they also knew that half of the new team was *not* new. The bloody tide continued to carry a political vessel that contained the Geros, the Hegeduses, the Karoly Kisses, and the Apros. The chemist's scales offered only soothing medicines for a patient who was urgently in need of drastic surgery.

To those with sharper political awareness, of course, it was evident that the new list of officials was not the work of Imre Nagy, but the result of a compromise. It is a matter for speculation whether it would not have been better if Nagy, risking everything to gain everything, had refused even the appearance of collaborating in any way with Gero and his colleagues and if, therefore, he would not have done better to have said, "Come what may," and not to have appeared before the people at Gero's side. Obviously it was not that he lacked the physical courage for such a move; after all, during the eighteen months when he had lived under the daily threat of prison, or worse, he had allowed no kind of pressure to make him waver. But unfortunately, in politics, weaknesses can be as serious as mistakes, and he did not anticipate the effect such an announcement would have on the public. No doubt, Nagy had overestimated the eagerness with which his appointment would be

---

* Zoltan Szanto had been Secretary-General of the Hungarian Workers' Party during the years of exile in Moscow. Under his successor, Rakosi, he became a diplomat. After having been envoy to Belgrade and to Paris, Szanto became President of the Office of Information in the Nagy Government. After Nagy's fall, he became Ambassador to Warsaw (from 1955 to 1956).

Ferenc Donath, former Deputy Minister of State and of Agriculture, and later Chief of the Secretariat under Rakosi, was arrested at the same time as Kadar. He was freed after three years in prison and, contrary to Kadar, did not accept another political appointment. Until October, 1956, he lived in retirement and dedicated himself to the study of agricultural problems.

received. A man more politically sensitive would perhaps have understood from the inefficacy of his brief appearance the previous evening before the excited populace at the Parliament Building that a compromise with Gero would solve nothing and that the time had come to break openly with him. But Nagy's appreciation of the events had remained oriented to the early hours of the demonstration, or even, more precisely, to the weeks that preceded it. He could not imagine that his name, acclaimed everywhere a few hours earlier, now no longer constituted a sufficient guarantee to the people.

Yet, his position, open though it was to criticism, would have been more defensible if it had not been for another maneuver by the Gero clique. This maneuver succeeded in undermining in a few minutes whatever confidence the people could still have in the new Government and in turning to anger what was left of their enthusiasm.

At 8:45, the radio announcer reported the first step taken by the new Premier. The step: Nagy's proclamation of martial law. Under this decree, all troublemakers were subject to the death penalty.

Thus Nagy, whom the people had carried to power and whom the demonstrators looked upon as one of their own, had inaugurated his term in office by brandishing the death penalty. He did not speak to the people—to *his* people. He did not ask them to stop fighting. He gave no explanation. He simply issued an order. Hardly had he been installed in the Premier's office than he took on the methods of his predecessors. Or, at least, so it seemed to the people of Budapest.

But this was not all. The radio, after having twice broadcasted the text of the Nagy decree, issued a new communique: "Government organizations have called for help from Soviet troops stationed in Hungary under the terms of the Warsaw Pact. Responding to the Government's appeal, Soviet troops will help in the restoration of order." Coming one after the other, the two communiques, of which only the first was signed by Nagy, created widespread confusion. Almost everyone believed that both were the work of Nagy. One would have needed a finely-tuned ear to have noted that the call for Soviet troops did not emanate, as did the other communique,

from the Government itself, but from "government organizations."
One would have had to be nursed on the intrigues of a seraglio to
have noted the fact that the name of Nagy did not follow the
announcement of the second communique. And, in their passion
and sorrow, in the anger and the blood, these were not men with
finely-tuned ears. Those who had handed the communiques to the
announcer and who had arranged the order in which they were to
be broadcasted knew perfectly what they were doing.*

Even if one of the points in the students' manifesto had not been
a demand for the withdrawal of Soviet troops, such an appeal
could only have been humiliating. Under the circumstances, the
Government decision was taken as an insult. To call on the armies
of the oppressors was, at this moment, treachery. Wounded in their
national pride, hungry for freedom and independence, the people
took to the streets.

The fact that this Machiavellian effort to compromise Nagy did
in the end run aground shows what an enormous reservoir of
popularity was at the disposal of the new Premier—and what confidence he enjoyed, and what hope he had aroused. His prestige,
to be sure, had been tainted. But most people, once the first
moment of surprise had passed, were simply incapable of believing
that the call for Soviet troops could have been issued at the initiative
of Imre Nagy. It was not that they understood the maneuvering
that was going on, or that they had sensed all the nuances of the
official communique; it was purely by instinct that they could not
believe it. That is why, in the streets of the capital, black with
their throngs in spite of the curfew, the demonstrators continued
to decry only Gero and his clique. Groups of students and workers
roamed the streets shouting: "Death to Gero!" and "Russians, go

---

* It is characteristic that the various publications of the Kadar Government, which showed little sympathy for Nagy and which were not always
squeamish in the choice of ways to compromise him, never went so far as
openly to charge him with responsibility for calling on the help of Soviet
troops. According to the third volume of that Government's *White Book,*
Nagy "approved" this step. According to *Nepszabadsag* (May 17, 1958),
Nagy had made "no remark against this proposal." The same source states
that Nagy did not accept the post of Premier until the early hours of the
dawn, when the Soviet troops were already in action.

home!" There was not a word against Nagy. On the contrary, a rumor quickly spread: "Imre Nagy is a prisoner, and agents of the AVH, guns in their hands, are putting pressure on him."

What was the truth?

At that moment Imre Nagy was to be found at Central Committee headquarters, on Academy Street, not at the Parliament Building, where the Government should have been meeting. From his windows he could see the street barricaded by Soviet tanks. The corridors of the building were thronged with militia of the AVH, all fully armed. Their role was ostensibly that of protector, and, when he passed, they saluted him. But it was evident that, if the situation deteriorated, Gero would be in charge, not Nagy. Nagy's telephone calls were being screened. There was no question of free contact with the world outside. In short, he was a prisoner.

He was a prisoner, also, in the political sense. He was not free to choose his own collaborators, nor to rid himself of those he did not want. He found himself in the state's highest office with a hundred-fold responsibilities, but with only a tenth of the real power he should have wielded. And not only was he a prisoner of the tanks and of the submachine-guns, of the telephone switchboard, and of the Stalinist apparatus of Party headquarters; he was held prisoner by his own ideas, too. This was to be seen, at ten minutes past noon, when he delivered over the radio "an appeal to the Hungarian people." His address before the Parliament Building had been heard by only a few thousand. This time, the entire country hung on his words.

"Order, calm, discipline. This slogan is addressed to all." His entire speech was a desperate effort at persuasion; here and there he was suppliant: the fighting must cease; it must not be permitted that "blood should soil our sacred national program." Here, too, the discerning ones might have noticed that the speech seemed to be composed of two parts, the one entirely different from the other. At one point, even the tone of his voice changed. The second part of the speech was more ordered and it was delivered more calmly than was the first, which sounded almost breathless.

The fact is that the beginning of the speech had been added at the last moment. In it, Nagy said that "the summary procedure [laid down in the declaration of martial law] would not be applied

against any of those who, to avoid further bloodshed, ceased their
resistance before 2 p.m." This was a concession which had been
wrung from Gero and the Stalinists. Since, by its first decree, the
new Government had given the impression that it was responsible
for the proclamation of martial law, Nagy was now trying to correct
that impression. Later on he actually succeeded in preventing any
armed insurgents from being brought before a court-martial, and,
furthermore, throughout the duration of his Government no one
was condemned to death.*

The speech was otherwise revealing by its omissions. It contained not a word on the call for intervention by Soviet troops.
Nagy had no other way to make the country understand that he
was not responsible for calling them. Had it been otherwise, he
surely would have tried to explain this move and to attempt to
justify it. His silence was, in short, a message, and he hoped that
it would be understood. He had good reason to count on the
people. And Nagy was not deceiving himself, as far as the people
were concerned, though on this score he was held in contempt by
the West. Even political practitioners, whose role it was to interpret
silences as well as words, could not, or would not understand. It was
from this moment on that a vehement radio campaign was launched
from abroad against Nagy—a campaign that had a fatal impact
on all that followed.

There was more to Nagy's predicament than even this. In spite
of its conciliatory tone and its imploring warnings, his appeal failed
to produce the desired effect because he was unable to put on
record the points in his program which paralleled the demands of
the insurgents. Obviously, he was not able to broadcast the slogan
"Death to Gero," which was being chanted everywhere by the
people of Pest. And, though he could have found lashing phrases

---

* This is precisely what Nagy is reproached for today by the Kadar Government in its press and publications. In Volume III of the *White Book,* one
can read: "In the first days of the Revolution, certain things were incom-
prehensible to the masses. They did not understand why they were not
called into combat against the rioting counter-revolutionaries, nor why
martial law was proclaimed only on paper. . . . To that extent, Premier
Imre Nagy had impeded the severity of military justice. . . . He gave instructions for the liberation of men taken with arms in their hands."

with which to denounce the crimes and the infamies of the past, he did not. He did not so much as even mention the name of Rakosi, for it was his opinion that this was a time to calm the people, not to incite them. And he did not perceive that it was precisely his attempts to quiet the people that made them even more excited.

The program which Nagy laid before the young rebels was also found to be wanting. "By all the means at our disposal," he said, "we shall realize, on the basis of the program which I presented to Parliament in June, 1953, the systematic democratization of our country in every sphere of Party, state, political, and economic life. . . ."

"On the basis of the program which I presented in June, 1953 . . . ," he was saying. But eighteen months earlier, in the solitude of his villa on Orso Street, excluded from the Party and threatened constantly with arrest, this is what he had written: "It is doubtful that tomorrow it will be enough to return to the program of June, 1953. . . . It is to be feared that the masses will turn away from the road of June, 1953, and also from the Party, and that we will have to go much farther back if we wish to remain masters of the situation."

The tomorrow he had foreseen had become today, but he remained in yesterday—in June, 1953. He was careful to make sure that his discourse would be ideologically irreproachable. He stuffed it with empty formulas stamped with the jargon of the Party. "Under the leadership of the Party," he said; or, "Line up behind the Party." But already the masses, as he had predicted, were separating from the Party—and his redundant phrases about the Party served only to cast oil into the fire. What the people wanted now was a program, even an improvised one, even a vague one, but one which would go beyond that of June, 1953. Instead, Nagy was giving them only a vague promise: "I will soon announce in detail the program of the Government, and it will be debated in the National Assembly, which will meet soon"—though the fighters for freedom, who saw their comrades falling beside them could not have cared less about a National Assembly elected under the sign of Rakosi. It was now, before lowering their arms, that these wanted to achieve their demands. A revolution is always distrustful, always impatient.

In the streets, meanwhile, it was as if a miracle were being enacted. According to all the rules of military art, the Soviet troops should—if one took into account the forces in action—have broken all resistance and have reestablished order within a few hours. But the fighting continued in many parts of Budapest, and it was even spreading.

The intervention of Soviet troops transformed the situation from both a political and a moral point of view. It had in some ways clearly defined the issues and it had drawn new lines of combat. No more was the question only one of the siege of various public buildings or of the fighting between the insurgents and the AVH. Now a Hungarian-Soviet clash was beginning. What had begun as an internal struggle was being transformed into a national battle —a battle that was at bottom a war of independence against a foreign oppressor. This transformation was apparent, above all, in the attitude of the Army. In the beginning, the great majority of Hungarian officers and soldiers had sympathized with the demonstrators, but this sympathy, in most cases, had gone no further than the supplying of arms to the civilian demonstrators. The soldiers themselves had not intervened in the fighting. It is evident that to turn against the authority whose uniform one wore required great audacity, and presented great risks to the soldier. But the Soviet intervention greatly facilitated the choice for those who were hesitant. The officers' corps, most of whose members were in the Party or in the Democratic Youth Federation (DISZ), which was otherwise known as the Young Communists, reached their moment of decision during these dramatic hours, and the majority favored the rebellion. The garrisons of entire casernes rallied to the revolt, among them that of the Zrinyi Military Academy under the command of Colonel Andras Marton.

By this time the young Hungarian fighters had succeeded in putting a large number of Soviet tanks out of combat. Though poorly armed, the rebels were animated by an ardent aggressiveness and they well knew the technique of partisan fighting, thanks to the lessons of "classic" Soviet literature: *The Young Guardsman,* by Fadeyev, *The Pure Conscience,* by Verchigora, and a number of other works that were actually part of the curriculum of Budapest schools. These stories by Soviet partisans had taught the young Hungarians how to fight effectively against an enemy which was vastly superior in number and in armament. For ten years, the necessity of imitating the Soviet example had been dinned into their ears. Never before had the glorious Soviet example been so carefully or so spontaneously copied.

Their first successes intoxicated the young fighters. The news that tanks had actually been destroyed swept the city, and the reputation for invincibility that the Russians had heretofore enjoyed was seriously questioned. New armed groups were formed, and the presence of the career officers who had joined the rebellion raised not only the level of these groups' technical proficiency but also the level of their strategy.

There is no doubt that a certain number of former officers who had served under Horthy were among those who contributed their aid, and that, here and there, through the military experience they had acquired on the Russian front, these were the ones who effectively directed the battle. But it is also not to be doubted that the great majority of those who directed the battle, as well as those of the rank and file, came from a totally different background. The students were almost all the sons of workers and of peasants, since the doors of the universities were opened with difficulty by the sons of the bourgeoisie. The officers' corps was even more carefully screened. To become a part of it, applicants, with rare exceptions, were required to produce an unassailable pedigree and to provide flawless proofs of loyalty. In addition, these officers had all been politically conditioned. They had been impregnated with Soviet ideology and socialist education. If, in spite of this background, so many went over to the insurgents, it was because they knew that the rebels were neither fascists nor so-called *Lumpenproletariat.* Nor were they the "valets of the bourgeoisie."

By the time Nagy went on the air to address the people, it was evident that the Government could no longer count on the Honved (the National Guard) to battle the rebels. Neither the exact number of soldiers who went over to the rebellion, nor the number who simply took off their uniforms and went home, was ever known.

But it is a fact that, toward midday of October 24, the only allies left to the Soviet troops were the AVH.

After the Nagy broadcast came a short speech by Zoltan Tildy, former President of the Republic. Tildy had the wisdom not to speak of counter-revolution; he expressed only his sadness in the face of the events and called for calm. "The nation must provide the calm, the order, and the peace necessary for action by our new Government," he said. "This is the first and most important task of the moment." But his words went unheeded. This little man, a Protestant pastor and the former head of the Smallholders Party, who now spoke so eloquently, was widely regarded as a suave politician who leaned toward the Communists and who had played their game. The fact that he had been under house arrest for eight years made him none the less suspect.

Radio Budapest's next broadcast added more fuel to the flames. During it, a vague organization known as the National Council of Hungarian Women poured out abuse against the "infamous counter-revolutionaries who," so they said, "were capable of anything." The National Council of Peace characterized the fighters as "pillars of fascism and bands of murderers." Epithets such as "provocateurs," "bandits," and "thieves" poured out over the air. The commentators warmed to their work. The rebels were not patriots, but rather a dismal rabble, or, at best, "spoiled children." "We salute the soldiers and the workers who are engaged in disarming them, as well as the Soviet fighters who have come to their aid," one broadcast said. The microphone was then given over to a popular sports commentator. "If the destruction and assassinations continue," he warned, in clinching the argument, "the football match between Hungary and Sweden, scheduled for Sunday, will have to be canceled."

The tone of the Government radio was quite different from that of the Premier. The broadcasts were no longer coming from the Radio Building, which was held by the rebels, but from the Parliament Building, which was under the protection of Soviet tanks. The content of these broadcasts was entirely under the control of men who had the confidence of Gero. While Soviet tanks fired on nests of resistance and while the blood of students and workers continued to flow, the Hungarian radio intermittently broadcast songs from operettas. Syrupy waltzes were followed by the rhythms of a French can-can and, in the street, the *danse macabre* went on.

Yet, in spite of these facts, the role of the radio was increasing hour by hour. All traffic was halted, newspapers were no longer being published, and the radio had become the vital communications artery for the country. The best thing Nagy could have done at this moment would have been to install himself before a microphone and to try to persuade the people to follow him. His rolling Hungarian delivery, voicing simple and humane arguments, could only have helped the situation. But he did not seem to recognize the importance of the radio. He had no time to listen to its broadcasts, and there was no one to report to him to what extent the radio was inciting the masses. Thus, he completely abandoned this weapon to his bitterest enemies, the Stalinists.

And that was not all. For the time being, Nagy was ignorant of the identity of those who were fighting on the other side. During the morning he received a delegation of five members from an armed group that was fighting near Barossa Square. The delegation informed him that the fighters were ready to lay down their arms if a total amnesty would be granted. Nagy accepted this proposal. For the space of a second he saw clearly that those who were fighting were not bandits but youths carried away by their enthusiasm. But the interview was too short. To have had confidence in the rebels, it would have been necessary to know them. Nagy would have had to stop thinking in abstract terms and to have faced up to the flesh-and-blood realities. True, there were among the young rebels some "hooligans" who were fascists and fugitives from justice. But these were isolated elements. What would have happened if Nagy had known something he was still ignorant of: that his own followers, his former students from the University, were fighting on the barricades or preparing "Molotov cocktails"? or if he had known that most of the resistance centered around Communist officers—all Nagy supporters—who had gone over to the rebellion with their troops? There is no doubt that events might have taken an entirely different course if he could have seen all this—and then he would have extended his hand to the people immediately.

The failure of the Party was total and irrevocable. The insurgents ordered a general strike, and it was obeyed throughout the capital. Almost everywhere, workers laid down their tools. It had been nearly twenty-five years since Hungary had experienced a serious strike. And if the Hungarian workers still had any idea of what a strike was, they owed it to the accounts given in the past by the Communist paper *Szabad Nep,* which had vibrated with enthusiasm for French, Italian, and English strikers. The Hungarian workers were enchanted to rediscover the right to strike and they entered upon it with all the pleasure of a baby taking his first steps. In vain did "the great Party of the working classes" publish its feeble appeals.

In the early hours of the afternoon the radio broadcasted the following appeal: "Communists! Militants! In these grave hours, when fighting is in progress against the counter-revolutionary bands that are attacking the working people, all members of the Party have the duty to protect and to defend peace and order, no matter what their posts are. You must convince the waverers, stop all disorder, and carry on the fight of the working people to a total and swift victory over the aggressions of the counter-revolutionary murderers." The terms were crude, but the contents lacked vigor. It was an admission of failure, poorly disguised. A Communist Party worthy of the name would, if its power had not been open to question, undoubtedly have armed its militants and called upon them to go into the streets to remove the barricades. In Hungary, the number of Party members exceeded 800,000; most of them were men able to bear arms. However, the Party had to think twice before putting guns into the hands of its militants: the danger of seeing the arms turned against its own leaders was too great.

At two o'clock in the afternoon, Soviet tanks appeared in front of Central Committee headquarters on Academy Street. Two civilians descended from them. One was a small Armenian with a large nose; the other was a tall, thin Great-Russian. They were Anastas I. Mikoyan and Mikhail A. Suslov, both Soviet Deputy Premiers.

The arrival of these two foreign guests was to put its mark on the course of events. In order to understand subsequent events and the attitude of Nagy, it must be remembered that these two men spent three or four days in Budapest during the Revolution.

Nagy knew them both. He had last seen Mikoyan three months ago at the Soviet embassy, where the Russian leader had asked him to call in order to explain to him that his exclusion from the Party had been ordered without the knowledge of the Soviet leadership. Mikoyan had also asked Nagy not to deny Gero his support. As for Suslov, Nagy's last interview with him dated back a year and a half. Suslov then had come to his bedside to ask him to draft a confession in favor of Rakosi. Nagy knew that Mikoyan was a man who followed the "new line." According to his experience and information, Suslov was a hardened Stalinist; along with Molotov, Suslov had been one of those who had most vigorously opposed any rapprochement with Tito; in addition, Suslov was one of Rakosi's defenders. The fact that these two men had arrived at the same time was important in Nagy's view; they personified for him the unity of the Presidium. Their decisions would be those of Moscow, and the agreements they would make would be agreements with the Kremlin.

This belief—future events would show whether it was sound or not—was the key to Nagy's future actions. Nagy had spent his best years in Moscow, and he knew, or thought he knew, how the Kremlin's gears meshed. The presence and the words of two emissaries of the Politburo had decisive weight for him. With the arrival of the two visitors at Central Committee headquarters, the room in which they carried on their negotiations became the heart of the building. And if Nagy was a prisoner, the presence of Mikoyan and his companion made him one even more than did the Soviet tanks on guard beneath his windows.

The two visitors arrived with rage in their hearts—against Gero. The accusations against Rakosi's successor literally poured out. Gero had shown himself to be a poor politician; he had not instituted the changes demanded by the spirit of the Twentieth Congress. In spite of Soviet advice, he had not called on Comrade Nagy. His unfortunate speech over the radio had only aroused the people. Suslov and Mikoyan, so to speak, carried Gero's walking papers in their briefcases.

So far as the general situation was concerned, it was these two

Russians' opinion that there remained only one thing to do: to crush the counter-revolutionaries by force of arms, and the quicker the better. The imperialists had already profited considerably from the situation. Once this affair was closed, Hungary, too, would receive the benefits inspired by the Twentieth Congress.

Gero would no longer be authorized to speak in public. In his place, it would be Janos Kadar who would address the people in the name of the Party and who would give support to the Nagy Government.

Kadar was, in fact, already the successor to Gero. But by his first speech he killed at the start any favorable sentiment that might have greeted his rise.

This speech by Kadar was nothing but a repetition of formulas that had become commonplace in the last twenty-four hours: reactionary and "counter-revolutionary" elements had committed aggression "against the power of the working-class"; these elements were "provocateurs working in the shadows," who would be obliged to "capitulate or be crushed." The Communists and their worker comrades must use every method to help the Government win, Kadar said. He said not a word about the essential question of the hour: national independence. On the contrary, he delivered a warm eulogy on the Soviet troops, whom he termed "allies and brothers."

Though his worker origin and his years in prison had conferred on him a certain prestige, no one, after this speech, looked to him for a solution.

On their first evening in Budapest, Mikoyan and Suslov thus had an experience they had not had since their early youth: they could listen to the sounds of a Revolution. Forty years ago, they certainly had not supposed—but now they certainly could not avoid the fact—that that revolution would ever lead to this new Revolution.

The Lonely Man

On the morning of October 25, the Hungarian Politburo—in the presence of Mikoyan and Suslov—attended to the formal replacement of Gero. His term had lasted exactly three months and eight days, and now he made a final attempt to hang on by making use of the argument previously used by Rakosi—that his departure would disorganize the Party. But Mikoyan silenced him with a gesture; the Party was already disorganized.

The deposed First Secretary nevertheless remained in the offices of the Central Committee. He behaved as though his downfall was nothing but a tactical move which signified neither the defeat of his policies nor a personal failure. He even tried something that could have historic consequences. He submitted to Nagy for signature a document by which the Government called on Soviet troops for help. The implication was that Nagy, confronted with a *fait accompli,* should now accept the responsibility for it. Gero hoped that, now with Mikoyan and Suslov in Budapest—now, in fact, that they were actually in the Central Committee's offices—Nagy would not dare refuse to complete this formality. But Nagy made no answer to this move. What purpose would it serve to become embroiled in a debate with Gero? He took the papers, at the bottom of which his name was already typed for his signature, folded them up with the copies, and put them into his pocket.

Today, Nagy seemed more calm and more confident than he

had the day before, though he did not know what kind of "household" he would be able to set up with Kadar. The political concepts of the new Secretary-General could not be very different from his own. But Kadar had the obstinacy of the mediocre, and he had authoritarian leanings. Nagy was not likely to forget their last meeting, when Gero and Kadar had summoned him to discuss his reintegration into the Party. On that occasion, Gero had been conciliatory and Kadar had been aggressive. Knowing how these matters operated, however, Nagy was sure that they had decided upon their roles and their attitudes in advance. And Kadar was a better bet than was Gero.

What was of more importance was the fact that the situation had improved. The fighting seemed to be abating. Fatigue had claimed some of those who were still resisting, while others had begun to see the hopelessness of their situation; still others were running short of ammunition. Some had gotten rid of their arms, hiding them carefully, and had then gone quietly home. The groups who sought the protection of the amnesty—an amnesty which had already been extended twice to them, were becoming more and more numerous; they were raising the white flag and ceasing to fight. Centers of resistance were still holding out at the corners of the big boulevards and on Rakoczi Avenue and Magdolna Street, as well as in the Ferencvaros district. The military leaders of the Government were agreed that the fighting would end by nightfall at the latest. Bata, the Minister of Defense, issued an order of the day which directed the military forces to liquidate before midday "all revolutionary elements still to be found in the capital" by "increasing their own activity and employing the utmost firmness."* The reports that poured in were so optimistic that, at 6:30 a.m., the Government issued an appeal for the resumption of normal traffic: workers must return to their factories, clerks to their offices, and stores were to be reopened; in short, except for the schools, life in the capital must resume its normal course.

However, the situation was not quite so simple. In no way had the people gained any impression that they had won a single one

---

* Order of the Minister of Defense, broadcasted over Radio Budapest at 9:13 a.m.

of their objectives. The news of Gero's disgrace was not yet known. The communiques which invited the people to go back to work meant to them only that everything must begin again as it was before—and under the authority of the very Gero whom they hated so bitterly. They were, in fact, not yet ready to renounce the struggle. If armed resistance were to become too difficult, it was certain that they would find other means to fight.

Implicit in the back-to-work call was the end of the curfew, and tens of thousands of people milled into the streets, not to go back to work but to find out what the situation was, to exchange opinions, and to talk politics. (The newspapers, of course, were still not being published, and the radio was still lying.) These street-gatherings of students and workers and white-collar employes soon took the form of a new demonstration that entered the boulevards and marched from the National Theater, the demonstrators still crying, "Down with Gero." This demonstration proved, once more, the ends to which temporizing can lead in a revolutionary period. If the downfall of Gero had been made public immediately and if it had been known to those who formed this rapidly growing column of demonstrators, the catastrophe which gave a tragic course to subsequent events might not have occurred.

From the long queues which had formed before the bakeries, many of those waiting in line left to join the line of the marchers. The demonstrators were unarmed. They followed a red, white, and green Hungarian flag. They were heading in the direction of the Parliament Building, hoping they would find Nagy there. It was to him they wished to speak and it was to him they would listen.

On the way, the column was joined by Soviet tanks. The throng showed no hostility toward the soldiers who manned them. On the contrary, they began to fraternize with them. Some of the young demonstrators spoke Russian, the study of which was obligatory in secondary schools. With stumbling grammar, but with passion enough to compensate for their errors, they tried to explain to the young Russian soldiers that they were neither fascists nor counter-revolutionaries, that they were not looking for a return to the old regime, but that they aspired toward liberty and independence as their right. The Soviet soldiers listened and smiled; at bottom the soldiers would probably have been content if the matter could have been settled without their being involved. The young Hungarians clambered over the Soviet tanks and planted Hungarian flags on them. Then the demonstration arrived in front of the Parliament Building. It was a particularly moving moment, making clear as it did that simple people can understand each other and that the Hungarian people were not the enemies of the Russian people.

In Parliament Square the people continued to raise their hostile cries against Gero. An officer of the AVH ordered them to disperse immediately. He reminded them that all assemblages and all demonstrations were forbidden, and in doing so, he betrayed his own conviction that the demonstrators intended to attack the Parliament Building.

This gratuitous assumption irritated the crowd. They had marched along without provoking the slightest incident and they had no intention of attacking the seat of the National Assembly. They began hurling insults at the officers. "Pig!" they cried. "Assassin! Down with the AVH!"

Opposite the Parliament Building, on the roofs of the Ministry of Agriculture, there was stationed a detachment of AVH troops whose mission it was to control the Square and the approaches to the Parliament Building. The scene of confusion that followed aroused them to the point of opening fire on the crowd.[10]

Frightened, the demonstrators panicked. Some ran as fast as their legs would carry them; others threw themselves flat on their bellies. Many of them sought shelter under the arcades and behind the pillars of the Parliament Building. Some vaulted through open windows into the Ministry of Agriculture, from which the firing was coming. A hundred or two finally succeeded in forcing open the two main doors of the Parliament Building, and these took refuge inside. Indignation mingled with terror.

This bloody confusion had reached its height when the Soviet tanks opened fire against the AVH men on the roof. The Russians, not knowing who the men were who had fired into the Square, thought they themselves had been the target of this assault. They thought they had been ambushed—that the fraternal appeals and embraces to which they had been subjected were aimed at disarming their vigilance and laying them open to a surprise attack at the moment when they least expected it. Accordingly, they fired mainly at the AVH, but also into the crowd of demonstrators.

The Square was soon strewn with the dead and wounded. According to many witnesses, the dead alone must have numbered between 170 and 180. According to the report of the AVH guard at the Parliament Building, however, there were no more than twenty-two dead, of whom four had been policemen. In addition, there were several dead and wounded among the Soviet soldiers.

The news of the massacre, which took place between eleven o'clock and noon, spread quickly, poisoning the entire atmosphere of the city. There had been thousands of witnesses to spread the story. The news not only traveled swiftly, but it was amplified with the telling. Soon, as the radio and the authorities kept their silence, the rumor spread that there had been thousands of casualties. But the event itself was sufficiently revolting to make exaggeration of the number of victims unnecessary. New anger filled the hearts of the people. From now on this anger was concentrated against the AVH. The idea of armed resistance imposed itself even on the minds of men who previously had not even thought of such a thing.

Hardly an hour after the massacre, the radio announced that Gero had been superseded and that Kadar had been appointed to his post. But the news passed almost without effect. Had it come two or three hours earlier, it might have been decisive. In vain, speakers on the radio tried to capture their listeners; in vain, they broadcasted appeals to patriots, though not without a certain clumsiness. "Hungarians!" the announcer proclaimed (no longer did he address them as "comrades"), "Deck your windows, raise the tricolor flag!" But the tricolor had already been flying for a day and a half from the windows of Budapest. And, with the news of the massacre, black flags appeared beside them.

In the afternoon, Kadar and Nagy spoke over the radio. Kadar said nothing new; he repeated the gist of his discourse of the previous evening, giving a sketchy picture of the situation and larding his speech with vague promises. The Nagy speech, on the other hand, contained some new elements. Nagy was no longer satisfied with speaking of counter-revolutionaries; instead he spoke of the bitterness of the workers and the errors of the past. He promised that, at the next session of Parliament, a reform program would be presented and that the Government would be reorganized along the lines of a national and democratic assembly of the patriotic popular front. Even more important, he announced that the Hungarian

Government would open negotiations with the Soviet Government on relations between the two countries, and particularly on the question of the withdrawal of Soviet troops stationed in Hungary. These negotiations would take place on a basis of "Hungarian-Soviet friendship, of proletarian internationalism; on a basis of equality between Communist Parties and socialist countries, and on a basis of national independence."

According to all the evidence, Nagy must have wrung some concessions from Mikoyan and Suslov—important concessions which he considered a personal success. Nevertheless, the insurgent people attached little weight to them. Why? Perhaps because the over-all tone of the speech did not find a favorable echo in the masses. The peroration, "Forward, then, under the leadership of the Communist Party . . ." irritated rather than appeased. On the other hand, Nagy had promised that, as soon as order was restored, he would recall the "Soviet troops whose intervention in the fighting had been made necessary by the vital interests of our socialist order." The same listeners who the evening before were unable to discern the nuances of Nagy's speech suddenly had more sensitive ears and concluded from this last phrase that the call for Russian troops must have been the work of Nagy. The truth was that the presence of Mikoyan and Suslov made it impossible for Nagy to pass over the Soviet intervention in silence; nonetheless, it was on the withdrawal of the troops that he placed the emphasis.

The thing that disappointed the people the most was the fact that Nagy did not name a single member of the new Government, nor did he fix any date for the departure of the Soviet troops. His promises were still general in their terms, and they were conditional regarding the restoration of order. The situation was characterized by a reciprocal defiance, a common development under such circumstances: The Government said, "Order first, concessions afterward"; the people said, "Concessions first, order afterward."

In the course of the day, the tension again increased, not only in the streets, but also in the offices of the Central Committee. After the massacre in Parliament Square, Geza Losonczy and Ferenc Donath, who had been summoned by the Party leadership at the same time as had Nagy—and whom Nagy regarded as his two most dependable supporters—demanded a firmer policy toward the Stalinists. Losonczy insisted that those responsible be brought to account and that the leadership of the Party be purified. He held that the developments since October 23 were not a counter-revolution, but a movement in favor of independence, even though there were reactionary elements involved in it. He voiced indignation at seeing the Central Committee still peopled by Rakosi's creatures, by men without talent, obtuse and limited, and by careerists without scruples and by inveterate Stalinists who had only hatred for the new regime and who were concerned only with a means of saving their own skins. Losonczy and Donath were not concerned with personal rivalries, but with principles; they felt that it was impossible to restore order in the country by means of this group and that any collaboration with them was doomed. They also saw in these men a grave threat to Nagy's leadership.

Nagy did not ignore the fact that Losonczy and his other followers had reason on their side. But he felt that it was still too early to act. It would be time enough, he thought, when order was restored and when the question could be examined with a clear head. For the moment, he felt, internal disputes would only be harmful to the Party, would destroy its unity and paralyze its leadership. He would not listen to the arguments of Losonczy and his friends: that it was essential at this juncture for him to break openly with the Stalinists, both on the questions of principles and of personages. These men did not want to be used as a screen by such leaders. And, since they were unable to convince Nagy, they withdrew and left the Central Committee building. Thus Nagy lost his best friends, his wisest counsellors, who had stayed at his side during his worst moments.

That evening a delegation looking for Nagy arrived at the Parliament Building. The delegation consisted of the young men who had occupied the *Voros Szikra* printing shop, where the sixteen-point manifesto had been printed. The four young men had come to present a copy of this document to the new head of the Government. The Cerberuses of the Central Committee immediately led them to the cellars and proceeded to interrogate them. Who were they? Why had they come here? They replied that they were workers from the suburbs of Ujpest and Angyalfold and that they wished to speak to Nagy.

After a while, the Premier went down to the cellars. He took up a position in front of the delegation, accompanied by fourteen or fifteen armed guards.

The leader of the delegation read the sixteen points.

Nagy responded to each of their demands. The delegates should be reassured, he said. They should go back to their suburbs and try to calm the population. Then their demands would be satisfied.

The young men were not satisfied. They demanded that Nagy be specific as to whether his program provided for the withdrawal of the Soviet troops before the end of the year.

It appears that Nagy at that point became impatient. He replied to the effect that they would have to show gratitude toward the Soviet authorities and that the withdrawal of the troops was not so simple an affair. To demand that he fix a date for the troops' departure was to provide proof of their own naïveté.

The delegates then asked when the AVH would be dissolved and the guilty among them brought to trial.

Nagy replied that the AVH would have to be reorganized and that this reorganization was a part of his program. However, he added, it would be altogether useless for the delegation to present such a demand. They could have confidence in him. He was just as good a Hungarian as were they.

At this stage, Nagy showed signs of losing patience. Everyone who came looking for him wanted to give him advice. There had been Mikoyan and Suslov. There had been the bureaucrats who swarmed through the corridors of the Central Committee office. There had been Losonczy and Donath. All the responsibility rested on him, and he was being pulled in all directions. Everyone wanted to give him instructions, to advise him of what was a good Hungarian, a good Communist, a responsible official. But who among these was ready to share with him the burdens of responsibility?

During the night, the crackle of shots sounded again. It was the same as the evening before and the night before that. How much longer would it go on? How would it all end?

Nagy was a man standing alone, very much alone.

The Blessing of the West

Encouraging news from abroad was being beamed to the Hungarian people by Western radio stations by day and by night. Editorials in Western newspapers, liberally quoted on the radio, saluted the heroic people of Hungary. President Eisenhower was quoted as saying, "The heart of America goes out to the people of Hungary." The U.S. State Department reported that the United States had opened discussions with Britain, France, and other friendly countries on the problem of submitting the Hungarian question to the U.N. General Assembly, which was not then in session. A spokesman for the State Department said that the question could be raised by invoking Chapter Seven of the Charter of the United Nations, which deals with any "threat to the peace, breach of the peace, or act of aggression," or by invoking Chapter Six, which recommends that nations seek peaceful solutions of disputes menacing peace and international security. In addition, it was pointed out, the U.N. Charter also includes clauses covering the rights of man and the rights of peoples to self-determination and self-government. The employment of Soviet troops against the Hungarian people could be considered a violation of these principles.

The various statements that the Western radios broadcasted ceaselessly to the Hungarian people exercised considerable influence in Hungary. Obviously, any people enjoys being the subject of world solicitude. For the people of little Hungary, the news that the United Nations might take up their case was a powerful stimulant. The tide of revolutionary sentiment rose again. Most Hungarians were, in any case, suffering from a nostalgia for the West—in a divided world, this was a natural corollary of anti-Soviet sentiment. They also had vague aspirations for liberty, for a better life. The twisted propaganda about the West, to which they had been subjected by the Russians for years, had an effect precisely the opposite of that which had been intended: it had made them think of all the richness, the pleasure, and the gentleness of life to be found in that forbidden world.

The fact that the leaders and the press of the greatest countries in the West were rendering homage to the people of Hungary had an extraordinary effect on events. The mere possibility that the United Nations might put the Hungarian question on its agenda was taken as an assurance that this international organization would take Hungary under its protection. No responsible Western statesman had promised aid of any kind to the Hungarian revolt, and the United Nations was not even in session. But a people that has taken up arms in a struggle for liberty is not composed of diplomats, and, for such people, possibilities become confused with realities.

"It is not possible that so many hearts should bleed in vain." This line by a Hungarian poet of the last century seemed to lend itself marvelously to the situation. In the eyes of the Hungarian people, it was not possible to imagine that, after so many ardent words of praise, the West should abandon Hungary and allow its quest for liberty to be crushed. The Hungarians could not have shown more confidence in the West if Hungary had been linked to it with treaties. Even though, on the contrary, such treaties did not exist—and even though she did have treaties with the Russians—the people of Hungary were convinced that the world could not be disinterested in the outcome.

There was another factor which had an important bearing on the Hungarian dream. After a decade of ostracism from international political life, Hungary had just been admitted to the United Nations. The Hungarians did not yet understand sufficiently either the mechanics or the limitations of the world organization, and they harbored certain illusions as to its possibilities of action. Their confidence in the West and their hope for U.N. action were responsible for the demonstrations that took place before the foreign embassies in Budapest, and before those of the United States and of Great Britain in particular. Delegations went in search of the heads of diplomatic missions to urge that they make an effort to see that the Hungarian question was placed on the U.N. agenda with the least possible delay.

Breaking out of the framework of Hungarian-Soviet relations, the Hungarian situation assumed, little by little, a predominant role on the international stage. The more the interest in its international aspects grew, the more the purely Hungarian aspects of the situation faded. The rules of international diplomacy, the ambitions of the great powers, and the interests of their alliances came more and more to the foreground. The more resolutely Hungary fought for her independence, the more her problem shed its national implications. Hungary found herself becoming a pawn on the international chessboard.

Understandably, little of this was apparent, even to the politically acute, on October 26. What was apparent was that the Soviet Union had suffered a tremendous propaganda setback and an enormous loss of prestige. Its slogans of ten years—dedicated to the indestructible affection of the Hungarian people for the Soviet people, to the desire of the Hungarians to follow the inspiring example of Russia, and to the disinterestedness of the Moscow Government in its dealings with the Hungarians—had almost overnight faded from the view of the world. Little by little, the monuments erected in memory of the Soviet soldiers who had fallen in the struggle against fascism had become the detested symbols of a new and harsher oppression. Now they were overturned and mutilated. The demonstrators had broken the doors and the windows of the Soviet bookshop, the "Horizont," and they had thrown the books and phonograph records into the streets. They were fed up with the "leading Soviet Culture," with "socialist realism," and with the melodies of the *Stalin Cantata*. (But it was extremely painful to see that, together with the rubbish, the books of Tolstoy and of Gorky, as well as the broken records of Moussorgsky and of Khachaturian, burned and smouldered on the streets for several days.)

The day began with a curfew, imposed at 4:30 a.m. Budapest Radio broadcasted warnings to all to stay off the streets or face the risk of being shot on sight. Factories were ordered to remain closed. Then, as the task of blotting out resistance progressed, the curfew was modified. The people were told they could be on the streets during the middle of the day to obtain food and perform necessary tasks. Few took advantage of the offer. Those who were on the streets were driven from the sanctuary of their homes by another hunger—the need for news.

The radio was confusing and unsatisfactory. Threats, warnings, appeals to reason, optimistic reports of the progress of fighting against the rebels followed one upon the other.

"Soldiers! Remain loyal to your Government," the radio pleaded. "Please help us."

"Party members! Say to the insurgents: Your demands are being fulfilled. We have a new Government. All members of the new Party leadership were in prison under Rakosi."

"Hungarian youth! Your wishes have been attained. Gero is gone. Nagy is back. He will create a New Order. Why are you fighting?"

"Workers, go back to your jobs. Help clear the ruins of our capital. Damage is increasing hour by hour."

"Old Communists, everything now depends on you, you old and proven fighters."

In the provinces, the soldiers responded to such appeals by handing over their tanks and guns to the rebellion and joining the revolutionary forces.

The general strike was effective throughout the country. There had been several skirmishes at Szolnok. The people of Nyiregyhaza had held a great demonstration in favor of the rebellion. At Magyarovar, where the people had tried to penetrate the barracks of the AVH, the political police had opened fire on the throng, leaving eighty-seven dead. Three AVH officers had been lynched in the street by the enraged crowd.

All these factors increased Nagy's anguish. Not only were his sensibilities shocked by the mounting evidences of the people's hostility toward the Soviet Union, but so was his sense of the political realities. He had spent fifteen years in the Soviet Union and he was sincerely convinced not only of the desirability of Hungarian-Soviet friendship but also of its absolute necessity. More, perhaps, than anyone else who was still in Hungary, Nagy knew the power of the Soviet giant. And if for a moment he should be tempted to forget, there were always Mikoyan and Suslov at his side to remind him where Hungary's interests and security lay. There is no doubt that these men wanted to find a solution as quickly as possible, but there was also no question in their minds of allowing Hungary to follow the will of its people and thus to leave the Soviet orbit.

A Western commentator said during this period, in tones that were somewhat disparaging of the Hungarian leader, that Nagy was no Gomulka. This was quite true. Gomulka was certainly more accustomed to political infighting than was Nagy, whose preference lay in the agricultural sciences. Then, too, Nagy was more a man of peace than a man who would choose to lead an insurrection. The chief difference between the situations in which the two men operated, however, lay in the fact that Gomulka had at his side, strengthening his hand and lending him every support, men like Ochab and Cyrankiewicz, who helped him literally boot the Soviet delegation of Khrushchev, Mikoyan, Bulganin, Molotov, Kaganovich, among others, out of Warsaw. By contrast, Nagy was surrounded by enemies, by men who sought only a return to the days of Rakosi and Gero and who saw in each development merely the opportunity to hasten his downfall. Gomulka made his first steps on rather solid ground; Nagy made his on swampland, and the first steps had already determined everything.

Paradoxically, Nagy was at that moment better able to count on Mikoyan than on the Hungarian Party clique that surrounded him on Academy Street. Mikoyan and Suslov were intent only on consolidating the situation, on bringing the juggernaut to a halt, and they looked upon Nagy as the only Hungarian who could bring this about. They were more supple, less petty, and less unyielding than were the bureaucrats of the Hungarian Party. Since their own status and privileges were not at stake, it was easy for them to abandon Gero and the other followers of Rakosi.

The Central Committee, still dominated by Nagy's foes, was called to meet on Friday morning, October 26, to consider the state of events. Before the meeting, a workers' delegation from the

Borsod District arrived at Party headquarters to see Nagy. The delegation was led by a man named Rudolf Foldvari, a typical Party turncoat who had gone from Horthy's air force into the Party as a Rakosi man, and had switched allegiance to Nagy, while he was in power, then back to Rakosi. Now, having switched once again, here he was, filled with professions of friendship and leading a workers' delegation from Borsod with a complete list of recommendations for Nagy.

Some turncoats are at once comical and disgusting. Nagy's first impulse was to tell Foldvari off and show him the door. But he reminded himself that it was better to see a Party Secretary at the head of a workers' delegation than it was to find such a delegation being led by fascist or reactionary elements. Then again, Miskolc, the capital of the Borsod district, was a long distance from Budapest, and Nagy's first problem was to restore order here. So he listened to the delegation's proposals and appealed to its members to give him their confidence and their support.

After his meeting with the Borsod delegation, Nagy went directly to the Central Committee meeting. Gero and Hegedus were not present. Deeming it prudent to accept Mikoyan's offer of transportation out of the city in Soviet tanks, these two had left the country. It was wise for them to leave. Obviously the people would sooner or later insist upon knowing who had called in the Soviet troops, and they would be held accountable. Gero had been a member of the Communist movement for forty years. A tireless worker who spent sixteen to eighteen hours a day at his desk, he concentrated on the realization of his distorted aims with the fanaticism of a madman. Sitting in his tank, he carried away nothing but the hatred of the people, a stomach eaten by ulcers, and eyes nearly blinded from overstrain. If his record had not been smeared with so much blood and so many crimes, his ignominious flight might have seemed pathetic.

The departure of Gero and Hegedus did not, however, rid the Central Committee of its complement of Stalinists. Those who were able to remain at the helm still felt strong enough to take the offensive. Ignoring the fact that there was still fighting in the street and that the Central Committee was, because of the disintegration of the Party, in command in name only, they presented a resolution denouncing "the treason that is being perpetrated in the country, a treason whose nerve center is to be found in Academy Street." Though he might here have found an issue on which to test his strength against his foes, Nagy, who had himself so often been punished for disagreeing with the majority, preferred now to let the matter pass without debate rather than to strike out at those who were in disagreement with him.

Another matter which was brought up for discussion was the question of the Workers' Councils, whose organization in each factory was under way as a result of Yugoslavia's influence. The Hungarian workers knew little of what was actually going on in Yugoslavia, but they did know that the situation was better than in Hungary and that they had Workers' Councils. Their Communist leaders had told them repeatedly that they were the masters of the factories; now they wanted to be the masters in actuality.

Nagy saw the Workers' Councils movement as a measure that would polarize authority and help bring some order out of the chaos. As a result, the statement that was issued at the close of the meeting took a position in their favor. It differed from previous Central Committee communiques in other respects. It no longer spoke of counter-revolution or of imperialist forces. Instead, it took note of the tragedies of the past days, of the flow of blood, of the entire fratricidal struggle. It promised a new national government and, following the example of Polish-Soviet relations, negotiations with Moscow on a basis of full equality and non-interference. It again extended the amnesty, to 10 p.m. that night. It also warned that those who continued to resist would be "pitilessly annihilated." The communique emphasized that the "cause of socialism" would be defended, and it proclaimed the necessity of drafting "a broad national program for a democratic, socialist, independent, and free Hungary."

But this communique was still a document hedged with reticences. What it added up to was that the Party was now prepared to take the initiative in trying to give the people some of the things they wanted—and yet to retain what it could of its power, lest the people take everything.

It was on this somewhat equivocal platform that Nagy had to build a government. If he were to achieve results, he would have to move quickly. But his efforts at negotiation dragged on. He wanted to bring into his Cabinet the leader of the Smallholders Party, Bela Kovacs, who had for some years been a prisoner of the Russians. But Kovacs was in Pecs, and Nagy was unable to reach him in order to ask him to come to the capital. There was a similar problem with Miklos Ribianszky, whom Nagy regarded as the leading Hungarian expert in agrarian matters and whom he also had difficulty in reaching.

Another twenty-four hours slipped away between the time of Friday's Central Committee meeting and the hour when Nagy was at last able to announce his Cabinet. It was almost midday before the radio broadcasted the list of Government members. On Friday, it might have been a heartening list. By noon on Saturday, it was only another artifice in a long series of deceptions.

By Saturday noon, the people were no longer disposed to notice that the names of Andras Hegedus and Erno Gero were not on the list, or that Laszlo Piros, the former Minister of the Interior and thus the head of the hated AVH, and Istvan Bata, the Minister of Defense who had ordered Hungarian troops to fire on the Hungarian people, were among the missing. Nor did they notice that such personalities as Hidas and Marosan and Mekis—and as Lajos Szijarto, the hated Minister of Construction; Andor Berei, President of the Planning Office; and Jozsef Darvas, dictator of arts and letters—were also absent.

Of all the new ministers, Bela Kovacs was perhaps the only one whose name the people received with pleasure. The former Secretary-General of the Smallholders Party, who enjoyed great popularity among the peasants, had consistently refused to capitulate before Rakosi. Framed by fabricated accusations, he had been deported by the Russians. After years in prison, he had returned from the Soviet Union only a few months before the rebellion, worn by sickness and privation. But he still stood by his opinions, refusing any compromise, and for this reason he was more important and more valuable to Nagy than was Zoltan Tildy, the other leader of the Smallholders Party, who also was part of the Government. As for the others, there were some highly regarded specialists: men like Professor Antal Babics, a well-known urologist; Gyorgy Lukacs, the Marxist philosopher, and Miklos Ribianszky, the agronomist. Their names, however, were not such as to rouse great popular enthusiasm.

But that was the best of it. The trouble with the new Government was that it appeared to the discerning ones among the people—and there were many at this moment—to have been constituted after a formula that was just a bit too clever, with one old Cabinet member for each new one. Like a river with its burden of mud and flotsam during a flood, the Nagy Government carried along its dead weight. Among the members of the Nagy Cabinet were Imre Horvath, Minister of Foreign Affairs; Janos Csergo, Minister of Metallurgy and Machine Industry; Sandor Czottner, Minister of Mining and Electricity, and, in addition, Antal Apro, and Lajos Bebrics. All these were men who bore the stigma of the Rakosi regime.

Thus, again, Nagy failed to win the support of the people—and this at the crucial moment when his time was running out. It seemed that he had still not learned the lessons of the past—that he still failed to comprehend how the names of these men would resound in the ears of the people, drowning out the sound of all others.

At the time when he had been driven from the leadership— and then from the Party itself—his friends had hoped that, if he ever returned to power, he would avoid the pitfalls that had brought about his downfall. They had hoped that he would surround himself with men whom he could trust, with men who would not let him be delivered, bound hand and foot, into the hands of his Stalinist enemies. A few months earlier he had written in his memoirs: "If, in this connection, I am responsible for something, it will be only because we have not been able to break this opposition in time by firm and energetic measures. However, it would be impossible to achieve this by means conforming to the spirit of the Party, without the help and support of its apparatus."

Yet his Government was again burdened with old Stalinists. With the exception of Antal Gyenes, a young politician and a former student of the People's College which had been closed down by Rakosi, he had not a single follower, not a single personal friend at his side. He could not be accused of pursuing a policy of personalities, or of surrounding himself with friends. At a time when the Party was disintegrating, with its former leaders hastening toward the airports in Soviet tanks and its former militants fighting the Party's dictates with guns in their hands, Nagy could still visualize only those measures which conformed to the ideals of the Party that had banished him, vilified him, and dragged him through the mud. . . .

A Cease-fire is Proclaimed

All the news that reached the capital was of a nature calculated to encourage, rather than to still, the rebellion. From the "free" radio stations of the western provinces came a report that troops wearing the Soviet red star had melted away along 160 miles of Hungary's Austrian border, and that the rebellion seemed in firm control of western Hungary, with Soviet troops showing no disposition to intervene and Hungarian troops joining the revolt.

The radio of Gyor, while reporting that Soviet tank forces were being concentrated between Gyor and Komarom, said the Soviet commanders had pledged they would take no action unless they were attacked. One after another, provincial towns proclaimed themselves "free"—there was Vac, Hatvan, and Szolnok, the news of each being broadcasted in tones shaking with emotion. The roads from Vienna to Budapest were crowded with vehicles bringing food and medical supplies to the rebellion.

From abroad, by radio, came word that the United States, Great Britain, and France had formally requested a meeting of the United Nations Security Council to take action on "foreign military intervention" in Hungary. But from Radio Moscow came the charge that the rebellion was incited and financed by the United States and other Western powers.

In the capital, the struggle went on. Little by little, the Soviet troops were winning the day. Still, there was one strong center that gave no indication of any inclination on the part of the insurgents to surrender. This was Kilian Barracks. On Saturday, an Austrian journalist of Hungarian origin succeeded in making his way to the Barracks. He was taken before the man who was commanding its 1,200 defenders, a tall, thin officer already greying at the temples, whose defensive positions were under siege by Soviet tanks.

"For us, there is no choice," said the officer. "Either we win or we fall. There is no third possibility. We have confidence in Imre Nagy, but we will not give up our arms except to Hungarian troops, and we will put ourselves immediately at the disposal of the new Government, if there is one truly worthy of the name." The officer introduced himself to the journalist under a *nom de guerre*—Colonel Acs. His real name was Pal Maleter. Until word of the heroic defense of Kilian Barracks spread through the country, Maleter's name had been known to very few outside the armed forces and the Government. From time to time he was to be seen at a meeting of Party functionaries, or in dress uniform at an opera. There were few who knew anything of his background or of his career.

Pal Maleter had begun his military career under the Horthy regime. Captured by the Russians in World War II, he had volunteered as a partisan against the Nazis. After the war he had attended the Soviet Military Academy, and, before the rebellion, he had served in the Armored Corps. He explained briefly how he, an officer of the Communist regime's army, had become a military leader of the insurgents:

"Early in the morning of Wednesday, October 24, the Minister of Defense, in the course of his duties, gave me the order to lead a formation of five tanks against the insurgents in the Eighth and Ninth Districts. Once I arrived there, it quickly became clear to me that those who were fighting for their freedom were not bandits, but loyal sons of Hungary. As a result, I informed the Minister of Defense that I was going over to the insurgents."

By Saturday, word of the resistance at Kilian Barracks had spread through the country. Although there were other isolated groups who were still fighting, the defenders of Kilian Barracks became at this stage a symbol of the continuing struggle. Its defenders numbered only 1,200, many of them boys; but, from behind the thick walls of the Barracks, they were secure against any but the heaviest Soviet artillery available. One by one, Soviet tanks were leveling the houses that shielded it, but not without cost. Dozens of burned-out tanks could be counted in the area as proof that the defenders were not without resources.

Isolated groups of revolutionaries still held out in the squares of Buda, barricaded behind walls of rubble and stone and steadily refusing to surrender either to Soviet or Hungarian troops. They replied, "We will stay here and die, if necessary, until the Russians agree to leave our homeland."

By dawn, on Sunday, the resistance had been quelled at several centers of insurrection, all of them, however, less important than that commanded by Colonel Maleter. There could be no question of a unified command; the various insurgent groups were able to communicate with each other only occasionally. Each of the rebel movements operated independently, reflecting the spontaneity of their origins.

Whoever was on the streets of the capital at that hour could see that the Russians were almost completely the masters of at least the military aspect of the situation. The principal arteries of the city were lined with tanks; armored cars stood before public buildings. Soviet soldiers searched the passersby. To an observer, it was evident that only political measures could thereafter balance the military superiority of the Russians.

According to the third volume of the Kadar Government's later-published *White Book*, a common plan of action had been drawn up at the Ministry of War to coordinate the efforts of the Hungarian Army and the Soviet units. In actuality, the plan provided only for Soviet action, since the Hungarian forces had been reduced to a shadow by defections to the rebellion. According to this actual plan, a final attack was to start at 6 a.m. Its mission was the total destruction of Kilian Barracks and of the buildings surrounding the Barracks on Corvin Passage.

Nagy was informed of this plan at dawn. It was obvious that there would be an enormous loss of life if Soviet tanks, backed by Soviet planes, concentrated their fire on the Barracks. Thus, the

Premier faced a grave decision. The plan gave him the means of establishing order, but the silence that would follow the thunder of battle would be the silence of death; and if the blood-bath before the Parliament Building were now to be followed by a massacre at Kilian Barracks and at other centers of resistance, the agonizing memory of such a Soviet attack would cost him the confidence of the masses forever. On the other hand, if he should succeed in bringing an end to the fighting by negotiation, and in so doing recognize the patriotism of the insurgents and the positive aspects of the rebellion, he would win the confidence of Hungarian youth; and then the work of reconstruction could begin.

In the *White Book* one may read that, half an hour before the attack was to begin, Nagy telephoned the military leaders and informed them that he would resign if they launched their offensive. Thus he saved the lives of several hundred young Hungarians, and he opened the way to a peaceful solution.

It was this series of exchanges at dawn which, above all, made him understand that the time had come for him to take a firm hand. Mikoyan and Suslov had left the Hungarian capital, assuring him up to the moment of their departure of their entire confidence in him. Kadar had also seemed to be unreservedly backing him. To Nagy, at this hour, it seemed incredible that plans for an offensive should be drafted behind his back, thus blocking his own plans. The military leaders, in defense of their plan of action, had cited the last resolution of the Central Committee—a resolution which had threatened with annihilation all those who failed to lay down their arms by Friday at 10 p.m. This deadline was, in fact, long past. But how many times over the last twelve years had the Central Committee failed to implement its resolutions? How many delays had there been in carrying out plans for raising the living standards of the people, or for increasing their socialist liberties, or for any other projects for the benefit of the people? In any case, the Central Committee, or what remained of it, seemed to be an anachronism. It no longer exercised authority; it commanded no respect; it had no power. It was nothing but a dead weight. Its newly-appointed First Secretary, Janos Kadar, was himself of this opinion.

On Sunday morning the Central Committee of the Hungarian Workers' Party met for the last time. During the meeting, a number of resolutions, through which Imre Nagy hoped to stabilize the situation, were adopted. One of these resolutions made the point that, although certain counter-revolutionary elements were involved in the uprising, it was far from being a counter-revolution, but was, in fact, a movement of popular and democratic origin, embodying the entire nation. It was a movement which had been provoked by the crimes of the previous period. Its aim of independence and of democratic national sovereignty was set forth as the only possible basis for socialism in Hungary. The Government, the resolution said, must immediately set for itself the task of satisfying the legitimate demands of the people.

This resolution ordered an immediate cease-fire. The armed forces would be given an order not to fire unless they were the victims of an attack. No one was to be persecuted for having taken part in the fighting. A new force would be set up to maintain order, with the cooperation of the armed workers and youths. Once order had been reestablished, a new national police would be organized and the old political police, the AVH, would be disbanded.

By other resolutions the emblem of Kossuth replaced the Soviet Star in the national flag, and the March 15 anniversary of the Revolution of 1848 was again proclaimed as a national holiday. The Soviet troops would begin to leave Budapest at the moment the new militia was organized. The Government would open negotiations with the Soviet Union on the question of withdrawing Soviet troops stationed in Hungary.

In regard to the Party, the Central Committee was delegating its powers to a group of six members. This group was composed of Antal Apro, Karoly Kiss, Ferenc Munnich, Imre Nagy, and Zoltan Szanto, and it was to be presided over by Janos Kadar. The group would remain in power until the Fourth Party Congress, which would be called into session as quickly as possible.

When Nagy announced these decisions to the country, he had the feeling that, although his road would still be difficult, it was at least passable, since neither barricades nor more bodies would be there to block the way. Inasmuch as he was a Party man and inasmuch as he was incapable of ignoring this fact, he attached particular importance to the disappearance of the Central Committee, in fact if not in form, as well as to the formation of the Presidium of six members. In addition, he believed, Stalinism had thereby suffered a decisive defeat, for the old Central Committee had consisted chiefly of unshakable sectarians, of climbers and yes-men and sycophants, of men without honor, of men who lacked all sense of initiative, of men who trembled for their privileges. True enough, the composition of the new Presidium was not perfect. It included Antal Apro and Karoly Kiss, both of whom had supported Rakosi to the very end and whose names were enough to produce a feeling of queasiness. But, in spite of this fact, Nagy thought that he could count on Kadar, Munnich, and Zoltan Szanto—a circumstance which would give him a majority. No longer would he need to fear that the careful plans and projects launched by the state would be undermined by the Party leadership and its devoted functionaries.

Nagy was satisfied. For the first time since October 23, he would be able to sleep in peace.

That afternoon, at the same time that Nagy was making his statement, a meeting of leading intellectuals, both students and faculty members, was taking place at the University, on Pazmany Square. Here the Revolutionary Committee of Hungarian Intellectuals was formed. Those who took part in the meeting were mostly Party members who, as followers of Nagy, had taken a firm and open position against Rakosi and his supporters. Their stand had brought them a certain prestige. Within the Petofi Circle and during the struggle of the Writers' Association they had more or less erased the stain of the past. They were under the impression that their names would carry some weight, that their arguments were sound enough, and that their plans were precise enough to exert some influence on the country.

These men knew that neither Nagy's latest speech nor the program he had announced would assure the peace and order which were so necessary. On the one hand, his speech had not, in spite of its positive aspects, been delivered in tones capable of stirring the hearts of the people.* On the other hand, its content, even if it had been delivered with consummate ability, would not have been enough to calm a people who had already gone far beyond him in their demands. From all over the country, there came more and more frequently—and with growing insistence—two demands: namely, the demand for a multi-party Government and the demand for an immediate renunciation of the Warsaw Treaty.

The intellectuals who met at the University tried to draft a platform that would be acceptable both to Nagy and to the masses. For them the point was not whether the multi-party or the single-party system was superior, and it was even less the point, as far as they were concerned, that they would be sorry to see a Hungary free of all military blocs. For them the point was that they must face up to the realities in Hungary and, simultaneously, to the realities of international politics. They wanted to try by all possible means to avoid the catastrophe they felt was threatening the country.

After a discussion of several hours and after having weighed the pros and cons as carefully as possible, they drafted their proposals in ten points. Those dealing with domestic politics and social questions went considerably beyond Nagy's program. The direction of industries and of factories must be given to freely-elected Workers' Councils. A free system of agriculture must be guaranteed, and the system of mandatory deliveries to the state must be abolished. There must be complete freedom of press and of public assemblage. These were the principal points on domestic matters.

As far as the two essential demands being voiced by the people were concerned, the intellectuals did not go so far as had the increasingly intransigent masses. To be sure, they favored general

---

* The promises made in this speech about the social situation were generalities. The others, regarding Hungarian-Soviet relations or the dissolution of the secret police (AVH) were limited by such qualifications as "simultaneously with the formation of new forces of order," or, "after the reestablishment of order." Nagy ended his speech by recalling "the results, historic, durable, and ineffaceable, of the last twelve years" obtained "under the direction of the Hungarian Workers' Party." As he was speaking these words, the people were exhibiting their opinion of the Party—and of its activities of the last twelve years—by strikes and armed combat.

elections by secret ballots—not, however, in the framework of a multi-party regime, but only on the basis of individual, free candidacies. They thought in this way to avoid a division of the nation and a rivalry of opposing parties and clans.

As for the state of relations between Hungary and the Soviet Union, the intellectuals demanded that these be immediately reexamined on the basis of complete equality. They demanded also a reexamination of all secret trade treaties, and added: "Soviet troops must begin to withdraw from the nation's territory." That was more than had been proposed by Nagy, who promised the withdrawal of Soviet troops only from Budapest. But it was less than a renunciation of the Treaty of Warsaw, which the people were demanding so insistently.

The intellectuals hoped to win Nagy's support for their program. With his backing, they would undoubtedly be able to convince the masses that blind haste would bring dangerous consequences. At the same time that they would present their demands, they planned to circulate proclamations among the insurgents—the students, the young workers and peasants, the members of the Petofi Circle, and the others—to join the ranks of the militia that was being formed. Thus, they hoped to be able to bring to the Government the support of a sizable Hungarian armed force capable of maintaining order, of reenforcing the prestige of the new leaders, and of repelling "all attempts to restore Stalinism or to provoke a counter-revolution."

Late that evening, having polished up their "declaration," the intellectuals sent a delegation to present the text of their proposals to Nagy and to arrange its broadcast over the radio. This delegation was composed largely of writers and journalists who, during the years of his trials, had supported Nagy and had remained on excellent terms with him.

Shortly before midnight, the delegates succeeded in reaching the Parliament Building, which was encircled by a heavy screen of Soviet troops. They were taken to the office of Sandor Ronai, President of the National Assembly. There, several Cabinet ministers welcomed them warmly, recognizing among them a few men with whom they had previously had dealings. These ministers told the delegates that Nagy was not at the Parliament Building and that he was staying at the Central Committee headquarters. Nagy, they said, was tired, and it would be in their best interest to wait until the following morning.

Most of these ministers seemed lost. They looked as if they feared that even the earth might cave in under their feet. They were frightened. They reticently said "Yes" in answer to questions which, in their hearts, they were answering with a categorical "No." The one among them who knew best what was going on in the country was Zoltan Tildy, a man whose ears were very sensitively attuned to the reactions of the people. Tildy spoke calmly and clearly, and with the authority of a true statesman. He listened sympathetically to the "declaration" of the intellectuals, showing an understanding of its *raison d'etre* and its pragmatic approach. The others contented themselves with comments on details of the statement. Ronai, the Assembly President, said, for example, that since the Central Union Councils had not taken a stand on the question, there was no reason the intellectuals should demand broader rights for the unions. Prudently, he went no further. Another minister tried to convince the members of the delegation that, if all the factors involved were weighed, the Hungarian-Soviet trade agreements would not seem to be disadvantageous. He also tried to convince them that all the clamor over the Hungarian uranium that had fallen under the control of the Russians was clearly "exaggerated." Imre Horvath, Minister of Foreign Affairs, offered no opinion at all, preferring to play the modest role of an efficient secretary by lifting the telephone each time it rang. It was Ferenc Erdei who closed the debate: the statement of the intellectuals could not, he said, be read over the radio or otherwise circulated, and, personally, he was not at all certain that Nagy would accept it.

The members of the delegation spent the rest of the night at the Parliament Building, some stretched out on the rugs, others curled up in chairs.

On Monday morning they were informed that Nagy was awake. Then they went to the headquarters of the Central Committee on Academy Street. This building, situated close by the Parliament Building, was similarly guarded by a ring of Soviet tanks. Inside, Soviet soldiers carrying submachine guns, and frontier troops and members of the AVH stood guard. The delegates were told that Nagy had left his office and was coming down to the lobby.

The delegates waited. In the vestibule they saw the former dictator of Hungarian letters, Erzsebet Andics, head sunk between her shoulders and eyes riveted on the ground, pass by on her way to the street. Leaving on her heels, guarded by a platoon of AVH police, was Gyorgy Marosan, the Social Democratic leader who had presided over the death of his Party by helping along its merger with the Communists. A curious, somewhat cynical smile flickered across Marosan's lips. It was the smile of a man who has known something for a long time, but who had been waiting for his hour to come.

A few minutes later, Nagy came down the steps. He seemed rested and refreshed, although he was visibly impatient. A delegation of armed insurgents, with whom he would have to negotiate, was awaiting him at the Parliament Building. He listened impatiently to the delegation's proposals.

"In any case," he said, in a loud voice, almost as though he were speaking from a tribunal, "there must be an end. Neither you, comrades, nor any others can keep coming to the Government with constantly changing demands. A truce on your demands. They are worthy only of hot-heads. . . . The Government has its own program, which I made known last night on the radio. . . . We will go just that far, and no farther. You are writers, journalists, Party men; your task is to apply and to popularize this program. That is what I demand of you. I repeat, the time for hot-heads has ended. If you do not agree with me, we are no longer friends. . . . It is intolerable that the authority of the Government should constantly be sapped by demands that are constantly changing."

The delegates were nonplussed. His cutting tones, his bizarre welcome left them speechless. His arbitrariness awakened unhappy memories for them. Having broken with Rakosi years earlier, they would no longer allow themselves to be swallowed up in the ranks of the "vulgarizers" of a Governmental program, unless that program reflected their own views. That they were being asked to act in behalf of the Nagy Government changed nothing.

But the fact that caused them even greater consternation was that Nagy still lacked a clear understanding of the situation—that he remained isolated from the people and from the events which were taking place all around him. That he should categorically order an end to their demands when, in reality, the entire country was knocking at his door! Clearly, Nagy was confusing his success in having taken over leadership of the Party with his role as leader for the country as a whole—a role in which he had yet to prove himself. He was interpreting the formation of the new six-member Party Presidium as a compelling personal victory, while, in fact, the people remained completely indifferent to this achievement. It was no longer a question of their rejecting certain leaders. They were rejecting the entire Party!

The delegates tried hurriedly to explain to Nagy that their statement was intended to sustain, not to undercut him, and that the impatience they were demonstrating was their best means of supporting him. Nagy then promised a speedy response to their demands and headed for the Parliament Building. Though he did indeed invite his friends to accompany him there, these sensed that their presence was not really wanted. Obviously, he was afraid that, in leaning on those who were devoted to him personally, he would be accused of practicing favoritism. He was still incapable of surmounting his old obsession. He had an enormous fear of what the Party bureaucrats would say of his acts.

Having told his chauffeur to precede him in the car, Nagy started on foot along the short distance to the Parliament Building. Though he had to pick his way among the debris and broken glass that littered the sidewalk, this little walk in the crisp October air along the sunny streets of Pest gave him pleasure.

By the Kossuth Bridge, which had just been reopened, there were other pedestrians, most of them going toward Pest. Nagy was recognized and quickly surrounded.

"What is going to happen, Comrade Nagy?"

"Will there be a cease-fire soon?"

"Will the Russians be leaving the country?"

The questions poured out and Nagy listened to them with a smile. It was clear that he was regarded with deep affection by the man in the street. He had not lost his popularity.

An attractive, rather distinguished-looking woman, her eyes filled with tears, spoke haltingly:

"It is good to see you, Comrade Nagy. Everyone was saying that you were a prisoner."

Nagy's smile broadened.

"You see how much I'm a prisoner!"

He looked about him. He was surrounded by his friends, the little people of the capital. He spoke as though his personal liberty had not been subjected to the slightest restraint during the days just past.

A man in working clothes asked him what was going to happen.

"Go back to your work, Comrade," Nagy replied, in a tone of encouragement, "and have no fear. . . . Return to your work. . . . Everything will be arranged in the end."

"That's really somebody," the young workman said, as he left. "That's the man we need!"

Nagy strolled gaily on toward the door of the Parliament Building nearest the bridge. Never before, perhaps, had he been so sure of what he was doing as he was on this morning of the twenty-ninth of October. He had read the demands of the Revolutionary Committee of Hungarian Intellectuals. He had found them excessive and had become angry. Instead of helping the Government, these hot-heads were pressing it at the wrong moment. It was not such improvised demands which were needed at this moment. What was needed was a program whose points would stand the scrutiny of an objective and scientific analysis. It was his intention to proceed calmly and reasonably, and to get to the bottom of the problems.

In the midst of a revolution, he still saw himself as a man of science.

A Visit from Mikoyan and Suslov

It sometimes happens in history that a whole country becomes the victim of an optical illusion. That was what happened in Hungary. Nagy's announcement of the cease-fire order, which he linked this time to a promise that the Soviet troops would leave the capital, spread drunken joy throughout the country. The little people of Hungary, who had fought with such indomitable courage, now thought that they had triumphed over the Soviet Union, not only morally but also militarily.

Just as the masses were wrong in their estimation of the situation, so it seemed to them that their demands could be transformed into rigid ultimatums. Judging the situation on the basis of the nation's complaints, one would not be surprised at this reaction. The experience of the past eleven years prompted the Hungarian people to demand—if not vengeance—at least reparations from their Soviet oppressors.

Now, throughout the country, it was the turn of the provinces to try to right their injustices. The large provincial cities, which during the early days of the uprising were content to wait and see, suddenly became the centers of action. Not only did they want to catch up with Budapest, but they also wanted to surpass it.

The people of the provinces were no longer satisfied with simply denouncing the Warsaw Pact. The workers at the Lovasz oil fields urged the immediate withdrawal of the Soviet troops, and the miners of Balinka went even further: they called on Nagy to tell the Soviet troops to withdraw under the protection of white flags of truce! The workers in the automobile repair shops at Szombathely announced that they would not resume work as long as a single Soviet soldier remained on Hungarian soil.

The situation deteriorated even further as the people began to criticize not the man Nagy himself, but the composition of his Government. It became absolutely clear to the intellectuals that Nagy, in speaking of the "authority" of his Government, was living under an illusion. The demands for the removal of men like Bebrics and Kossa, both survivors of the Stalinist era, were comparatively mild demands; but in its voicing of these demands the National Committee for the Department of Vas no longer spoke of the *Hungarian* Government but instead of "the government in *Budapest*." And the Workers' and Students' Council of the Department of Borsod declared itself in disagreement with the line of a Government that "rests on a foreign power."

The situation was at its worst in Gyor. The radio station in that town had—even before Radio Budapest had done so—gone over entirely to the cause of the Revolution. This fact is to its credit in history, and yet even at this time it was broadcasting ultimatum after ultimatum to the capital. In Gyor, too, a provisional National Council was formed, with Attila Szigeti at its head. He was a member of the Peasants Party and of Parliament, and the fact that he was able to have himself elected the head of a revolutionary organization would have seemed to be outlandish if it had not actually happened. Szigeti was a sincere partisan of change and a sincere partisan of Imre Nagy. He was the same man who, in the summer of 1956, had planned a surprise move in the Parliament. Far in advance of events, he wanted to control their development and to conserve the masses' loyalty to Nagy.

Szigeti's situation became more and more delicate. In the presence of a number of Western journalists, the corpulent deputy with the bristling red moustaches had been forced by his colleagues on the Council to call Budapest on the telephone and to ask the Government the date of free elections—they insisted that they be held within three months—and to demand an immediate cease-fire and the start of the Soviet evacuation. If the Government refused to comply, tens of thousands of demonstrators from Gyor would go to the capital to give their aid to the uprising. Szigeti phoned;

but for his colleagues this was not enough. A member of the National Council who had also been a former worker on the town council under Horthy announced to an American journalist: "The Council is not satisfied with Szigeti's action. He was the Number Two Communist in Gyor. We naturally cannot have full confidence in him. He is too moderate. . . ."[11]

In the capital the atmosphere became more joyous and at the same time more tense. It was in vain that the last issue of the Communist Party's principal newspaper, *Szabad Nep,* published on its front page the Kossuth banner and saluted in its lead article the victory of the young revolutionaries.[12] For, in the street, the demonstrators burned the papers without even reading them.

There was a change on the radio, too. The chief Budapest station broadcasted a message from its reporters and announcers. The principal part of the message read:

"The tone of our radio announcements on October 24-25 did not conform to the best interests of the nation. These announcements were in conflict with our national honor, and they insulted the memory of those who had sacrificed their lives. In our opinion, no editor, publicist, or technician can collaborate any further with the authors or organizers or instigators of such broadcasts. . . . It is the desire of the honest workers of the radio station that these announcements shall, in the future, be truthful. They must speak in the name of truth, without that truth's being discolored by past events; they must denounce as traitors those who, like the snipers who opened fire before the Parliament Building on the crowd which was peaceably demonstrating in favor of democracy, have endangered the life of our country."

Following this declaration, the Government removed all Stalinists from their posts as directors of the broadcasting system, and the effect of this action was immediately apparent: instead of lagging behind the Premier, the station's announcements took the lead and outdistanced him. The Budapest transmitter even broadcasted this slogan: "Work will not be resumed until Soviet troops have been evacuated from Hungary." The repercussions from this announcement were enormous.

Not only was there a spontaneous joy evident in the people, but so, too, was there a spontaneous defiance. The entire history of Hungary, and, particularly, that of the last dozen years, had taught the people to trust only in hard facts. The demands presented to the Government by the miners of Balinka and by the metal-workers of Gyor—of which the first was that the Government rid itself of the soldiers of the leading workers' state in the world—constituted a brutal criticism, not only of the Soviet Union but also of the so-called socialism which had been built up in that country. In formulating these demands, the workers needed no outside pressure; they had resented in their own flesh the methods of the so-called dictatorship of the proletariat—a dictatorship in which they were supposed to be the masters.

Still, the people's defiance and the demands formulated by the revolutionaries were not purely spontaneous. The importance of the influence of the press and of radio—and, particularly, of Radio Free Europe in Munich—was far from negligible. Radio Free Europe performed an important service to history by publishing an almost complete text of broadcasts over Hungarian transmitters from the twenty-third of October to the ninth of November. It is regrettable that it has not as yet published the text of its own broadcasts, for, under these conditions, one cannot precisely weigh the effects of its broadcasts on the development of the events of the Revolution. But its role cannot be passed over in silence. Since Radio Budapest had been almost completely discredited and since it had opposed the insurgents during the early part of the rebellion, the orientation and the opinions of the Western radios, and particularly those of Radio Free Europe, which were broadcasted around the clock in Hungarian, took on a prime importance. One example will suffice:

On Monday, October 29, the military expert of Radio Free Europe said of the cease-fire order of the Nagy Government: "Imre Nagy and his supporters want to revise and modernize the Trojan horse episode. They need a cease-fire so that the present Government in power in Budapest can maintain its position as long as possible. Those who are fighting for liberty must not lose sight even for a minute of the plans of the government opposing them. Otherwise there will be a repetition of the Trojan horse tragedy."

It is easy to see what repercussions such a statement would have on a people already aroused to defiance of the Imre Nagy Government.

Another incident of a totally different character helped to enhance the resolution of the Hungarian people. The special session of the Security Council of the United Nations, in which the Hungarian situation was to be discussed, had been called in New York for Sunday night. Western broadcasts underlined the fact that not since June, 1950, when the Korean War had begun, had the Security Council met in special session on a Sunday. The Hungarian question had been placed on the agenda at the request of the United States, the United Kingdom, and France, under the U.N. Charter's Article XXXIV, which deals with situations that could endanger international peace and security. On its part, the Soviet Union had invoked Article II of the statutes, an article which prohibits interference by the United Nations in the internal affairs of a member state. Nonetheless, the Security Council had decided to take up the Hungarian question, nine votes being cast against the Soviet proposal, with one abstention. As it so happened, the Soviet Union, after six hours of intense debate, made use of its veto power, thereby blocking any concrete action: in a word, the session ended in expressions of sympathy from the Western world for little Hungary, without giving her the slightest effective aid, and the statements of the delegates, calling as they did on the Security Council to "take measures" or "not to remain inactive," could only be, as their authors well knew, empty phrases. Yet, in a rebellious Hungary still gripped by tension, the reaction to this meeting was quite otherwise.* The fact that the Security Council had felt that it was its duty to call a special session to consider the situation caused a widespread feeling among the Hungarian people —a feeling which was enhanced by the praises heaped on them by the Western press and radio—that the United Nations was on their side and would help them. If the adjournment of the debate *sine die* was disillusioning to many—and we speak here of those who understood this action—the eloquence of the delegates and the comments

---

* There was, from the first, a wave of indignation against the Hungarian delegate who was permitted to speak at the Security Council session. The delegate, Peter Kos, a young Stalinist who was in reality a Soviet national named Leo Kondouktorov, had opposed consideration of the question by the Security Council. In Budapest, the people demanded the recall of Kos and his replacement by a delegate who would be capable of speaking the truth to the world and who would be dedicated to the defense, not of Soviet interests, but of those of the Hungarian people.

of the Western press helped to counteract the disillusionment. The great majority of Hungarians thought that the Soviet veto was largely a matter of form, constituting no great obstacle, that the will of the great majority of states would finally triumph, and that, therefore, the United Nations would not remain inactive for long. Almost all the foreign journalists who were in Hungary at the time wrote of the Hungarian people's immense hope for action by the United Nations, a hope that in some minds went so far as to count on the imminent arrival of international troops to liberate the country.[13]

In spite of the ultimatums coming from the provinces, in spite of the attacks by Radio Free Europe, and in spite of the blocking of action in the Security Council, Imre Nagy was optimistic. He was more resolute, and he was more sure of himself than at any time since the start of the Revolution. He was also in a better humor. At last, he had been able to leave the headquarters of the Central Committee and to get back to Parliament, where he knew every corner. In former President Zoltan Tildy he had found a friend who gave him intelligent and discreet support; at his side was Jozsef Bognar, who had been with him during his first term as Premier and whose clear view and understanding of the techniques of governing Nagy prized highly. Ferenc Erdei, another member of his entourage, would do anything to serve him. Ferenc Munnich was there to sign the decrees calling for a cease-fire, for the organization of a new national police, for the appellation to be used henceforth for members of the armed forces (brothers-in-arms instead of comrades), for changing the uniform of members of the Honved (removing from their caps the Rakosi emblem, which recalled that of the Russians, and replacing it with a tricolor ribbon). At his side also was the youthful and active Zoltan Vas,* who was

---

* Zoltan Vas was one of the veterans of the Hungarian Communist movement. He spent sixteen years in prison in company with Matyas Rakosi. Named mayor of Budapest in 1945, his sense of humor and his dynamic leadership, particularly in the organization of food supplies and reconstruction, won him a certain popularity. Later, he was thrown into the discard. During the period of the "doctor's plot" in Moscow, he was arrested. Politically, he had—though hesitantly—sympathy with Nagy. Having also demanded asylum at the Yugoslav Embassy, he was arrested with the others on leaving that building and, since then, there has been no reliable information as to his fate.

President of the Food Supply Commission and who was bestirring himself to supply the capital with bread, potatoes, and milk, just as he had done after the siege of Budapest in 1945. Yes, one might say that the atmosphere of 1945 had been revived. There was an aura of new beginnings after so much sorrow and so much blood, and it was exciting.

The results of the understandings now reached through several meetings with the various insurgent groups were also serving to put new heart into Nagy. The negotiations encouraged him, and he was pleased. Maleter, Marton, and the others seemed to him brave men, honest, enthusiastic, and loyal. He ascertained with no small pleasure that a good many leaders of the insurgents were Party members and that they were his devoted followers; he would be able to count on them in the future. The principal condition they were setting forth was that they not be required to surrender their arms to the Russians. Their point of view was entirely comprehensible. By the terms of the agreement being revealed, formations of the Honved would replace the Soviet troops by sectors throughout the city, and it was to the Hungarian troops that the insurgents would surrender their arms. It was evident that, in most cases, this would be a mere formality, since the new democratic army of Nagy's Government would have need of men like Maleter and Marton.

Nagy had also received telegrams from Gomulka and Tito. These were encouraging. Both were stamped with the same note of anguish: just so the Hungarians did not go too far; just so long as they did not abandon the way to socialism, for then they would strengthen the position of the "bureaucratic groups" which would play into the hands of the Stalinists. At the same time, both political leaders assured the Hungarian people and the Nagy Government of their sympathy. This would have weight, Nagy thought, even with the Russians.

These testimonials of friendship were even more satisfying to Nagy because of the attitude evidenced by the other people's democracies—by Rumania, Czechoslovakia, Bulgaria, and East Germany —where the events in Hungary were met with open hostility. That this hostility should exist was, of course, easily understandable. The Czech, Rumanian, Bulgarian, and East German counterparts of Rakosi and of Gero were far from sure of their own popularity.

They trembled at the thought that their turns might also come soon. Their radio stations spewed forth a constant stream of insults against the "counter-revolutionary bandits" and denunciations against the "imperialist maneuvers." But these attacks were simultaneously stupid and dangerous, for they could only give birth to chauvinism among the people of Hungary and increase their irritation. Up to that time, the insurgents had foregone any demands for the return of those provinces, such as Transylvania, which had been lost after World War I.[14] This campaign of hate—especially on the part of the Czech and the Rumanian Communist leaders—could lead to a revival of such demands. The support of Gomulka and of Tito could be extremely useful in opposing the attacks of Radio Prague and Radio Bucharest.

Above all, however, the optimism of Nagy was nourished—and, in this case, justifiably so—by an important fact. Mikoyan and Suslov had returned from Moscow, and these two came bearing a gift that went far beyond the hopes of the most audacious. The gift: an official declaration by the Soviet Government regarding the matter of relations among the socialist states.

This document is, at least insofar as it concerned the events in Hungary, of historic importance, and it cannot be passed over in silence. Neither can it be quoted in fragments if one wishes to compare the words of the Soviet Government with the acts that were to follow. And it is also a document of capital importance, because, without it, an understanding of either the attitude of Imre Nagy or the events that were to follow is impossible. This is the document:

> The unchangeable foundation of Soviet foreign relations has been and remains a policy of peaceful coexistence, of friendship, and of collaboration with all other states.
>
> The most profound and the clearest expression of this policy is to be found in the relations between the socialist countries. Linked together by the common goal of building a socialist society and by the principles of proletariat internationalism, the countries of the great community of socialist nations can base their relations only on the principles of complete equality of rights, of respect for territorial integrity, of political independence and sovereignty, and of non-interference in the internal affairs of one state by the

other. This does not preclude, but on the contrary assumes, a close fraternal collaboration and a mutual assistance between the countries of the socialist community in economic, political, and cultural matters.

It was on this foundation that, after World War II and the collapse of fascism, the democratic people's regime leaped ahead. It was on this foundation that the regime was strengthened and that it was enabled to demonstrate its vitality throughout numerous European and Asian countries.

In the course of establishing the new regime and in the course of establishing deep revolutionary changes in socialist relations, there have come to light several difficulties, several unsolved problems, and several downright mistakes, including mistakes in the relations among socialist states. These violations and these mistakes have demeaned the principle of equal rights in socialist interstate relationships.

The Twentieth Congress of the Communist Party of the Soviet Union strongly condemned these violations and errors and decided that the Soviet Union would base its relations with the other socialist countries on the strict Leninist principles of equal rights for the peoples. The Congress proclaimed the need for taking into account the history and the individual peculiarities of each country on its way toward building a new life.

The Soviet Government has systematically applied the historic decisions of the Twentieth Congress in creating the conditions for strengthening the amity and the cooperation between socialist countries. It has based its application of these decisions on the firm foundation of complete respect for the sovereignty of each socialist state.

As recent events have shown, it is apparently necessary to declare the position of the Soviet Union concerning its relations with the other socialist countries, and, above all, concerning its economic and military relations with such countries.

The Soviet Government is prepared to examine, along with the governments of the other socialist states, the measures that will make possible the further development and reinforcement of economic ties between the socialist countries, in order to remove any possibility of interference with the principles of national sovereignty, of reciprocal interest, and of equality of rights in economic agreements.

This principle must also be extended to cover the question of advisors. It is well known that during the period just past, when the new socialist regime was being formed, the Soviet Union, at the request of the governments of the people's democracies has sent into these countries many specialists, many engineers, and many agronomists and scientists and military advisors. Recently, the Soviet Government has frequently proposed to the socialist states the question of withdrawing those advisors.

Inasmuch as the people's democracies have trained their own personnel, who are now qualified to handle all economic and military matters, the Soviet Government believes that it is necessary to reconsider, together with the other socialist states, the question of whether it is still advantageous to maintain these advisors of the U.S.S.R. in these countries.

As far as the military domain is concerned, an important basis for relations between the U.S.S.R. and the people's democracies has been provided by the Warsaw Pact, under which the signatories have made political and military commitments with each other. They have committed themselves, in particular, to take "those concerted measures which are deemed necessary for the reinforcement of their capabilities for protecting the peaceful employment of their people, for guaranteeing the integrity of their frontiers and their territories, and for assuring their defense against any aggression."

It is well known that, under the Warsaw Pact and under agreements between the governments, Soviet troops are stationed in the republics of Hungary and Rumania. In the republic of Poland, Soviet troops are stationed under the terms of the Potsdam Agreement with the other great powers, as well as under the terms of the Warsaw Pact. There are no Soviet troops in the other people's democracies.

In order to insure the mutual security of the socialist countries, the Soviet Government is prepared to review with the other socialist countries signing the Warsaw Pact the question of Soviet troops stationed on the territory of the above-mentioned countries.

In doing so, the Soviet Government proceeds from the principle that the stationing of troops of one member state of the Warsaw Pact on the territory of another state shall be by agreement of all the member states and only with the consent of the state on the territory of which, and on the demand of which, these troops are to be stationed.

The Soviet Government believes it is essential to make a

declaration regarding the recent events in Hungary. Their development has shown that the workers of Hungary have, after achieving great progress on the basis of the people's democratic order, justifiably raised the questions of the need for eliminating the serious inadequacies of the economic system, of the need for further improving the material well-being of the people, and of the need for furthering the battle against bureaucratic excesses in the state apparatus. However, the forces of reaction and of counter-revolution have quickly joined in this just and progressive movement of the workers, with the aim of using the discontent of the workers to undermine the foundations of the people's democratic system in Hungary and to restore to power the landlords and the capitalists.

The Soviet Government and all the Soviet people deeply regret that these events in Hungary have led to bloodshed.

At the request of the People's Government of Hungary, the Soviet Government agreed to send Soviet military units into Budapest to help the Hungarian People's Army and the Hungarian Government to reestablish order in that city.

Being of the opinion that the continued presence of Soviet units in Hungary could be used as a pretext for further aggravating the situation, the Soviet Government has now given instructions to its military commanders to withdraw their troops from the city of Budapest as soon as the Hungarian Government feels that they can be dispensed with.

At the same time, the Soviet Government is prepared to engage in negotiations with the Hungarian People's Government and the other signatories of the Warsaw Pact regarding the question of the presence of Soviet troops elsewhere on the territory of Hungary.

The defense of socialist gains in the Hungarian People's Government is at the moment the primary and sacred task of the workers, the peasants, the intellectuals, and all the working people of Hungary.

The Soviet Government expresses its conviction that the people of the socialist countries will not allow reactionary forces, whether foreign or domestic, to undermine those foundations of the democratic People's Government which have been won and strengthened by the struggle and sacrifice and work of the people of this country. These people will, it believes, employ all their efforts to eliminate any obstacles in the way of strengthening the democratic foundations, the independence, and the sovereignty of their country. Such actions will, in turn, strengthen the socialist foundations of the economy and the culture of each country and will continue to increase the material well-being and the cultural level of all the workers. The Hungarian people will strengthen the brotherhood and the mutual cause of the socialist countries in order to consolidate the great and peaceful aims of socialism.

What could this statement mean to Imre Nagy? What could it mean in the eyes of this man who had studied the problems of Marxism-Leninism with the meticulous care of a scientist, and who would seize on each nuance of this eloquent but forbidding text—on even those passages which, to the eyes of the undiscerning, would appear to be empty and commonplace generalities expressed in an ideological jargon?

It gave him, above all, a feeling of triumph, and, for him, nothing could have been more normal, since, right at its beginning, the declaration contained this phrase: "The countries of the great community of socialist nations can base their relations only on the principles of complete equality of rights, of respect for territorial integrity, of political independence and sovereignty, and of non-interference in the internal affairs of one state by the other." Was not this phrase, in every detail, an admission by Moscow of the soundness of his theories? Was it not the very same theory that he had drafted ten months earlier during his lonely retreat, when he had been under the permanent threat of arrest and of death? At that time, it had still been a heresy to hold that the Five Principles accepted at the Bandung Conference were needed not only to regulate relations between socialist and capitalist countries but also to govern relations between socialist countries themselves.

Clearly, the Soviet Government was now subjecting itself to self-examination. It was recognizing that mistakes had been committed in the relations between the socialist countries. The Soviet leaders were recognizing that "these violations and these mistakes [had] demeaned the principle of equal rights in socialist interstate relationships." Was not this the spirit, if not the letter, of what he had once written: "The heavy heritage of the Stalinist era, its influences and its offspring, must be eliminated from the breast of the socialist camp." It was clear that Moscow was recognizing that the chief responsibility for the events in Hungary did not rest either with fascists or with the imperialists, but that it grew from flaws in Soviet foreign policy itself. All in all, the declaration constituted a self-criticism, and, when the Russians placed their seal on such a text, they had a reason for doing so.

The statement also contained important promises. Soviet troops would be withdrawn from Budapest, and the Russians had even agreed to withdrawing them from the entire country. Perhaps they were already regretting their intervention in Budapest. They were extending a friendly hand; they were themselves suggesting the withdrawal.

The formula according to which "the Soviet Government is prepared to engage in negotiations . . . regarding the question of the presence of Soviet troops . . . on the territory of Hungary" amounted to a precise plan. The Russians were, in a manner of speaking, doing half the work; it remained only to pose the question, and then they would press the matter. At the Kremlin, too, they had reached the conclusion that the tanks embedded in the muddy Hungarian roads would be able to roll again in only one direction— toward Moscow. Obviously, the Russians wanted to see matters put back into shape—honorably and with dignity, if such a thing were still possible—and they were ready to make concessions, and, indeed, were offering to do so.

Could anything be more explicit? Obviously not. The Soviet statement gave homage to Nagy the theoretician, and gave virtually a free hand to Nagy the politician. The only condition, the one limit, was the protection of socialist gains in a democratic People's Hungary.

All Nagy's efforts thenceforth must be concentrated on maintaining these gains: on safeguarding the agrarian reforms, the nationalization of industry, and the other socialist institutions. He would have to prevent the restoration of the old regime of landlords and capitalists. And, if he succeeded, then Hungary could indeed become an *authentic* socialist country. This would benefit both Hungary and the U.S.S.R. The country had run a fever. It had become prey to confusion and trouble. The task Nagy faced would not be easy. But the fact that Moscow had made this friendly gesture toward him greatly simplified things. He would have elbow room in which to achieve the necessary reorganizations. Mikoyan and Suslov were showing great cordiality and were encouraging him to proceed calmly and firmly. The Kremlin was behind him. On Monday evening, Marshal Zhukov, in replying to questions from journalists at a reception in the Turkish embassy in Moscow, said: "In Hungary, the situation has improved. A Government has been formed in which we have confidence. . . ."

These were the reasons why Imre Nagy was so optimistic.

The End of the One-Party System

Nagy had a sense of greater freedom than he had ever known before. He was well aware that the concessions he had won from the Soviets were not a reflection of their particular affection for him. It was, Nagy undoubtedly knew, by force of circumstances that these concessions had been granted. There had been the events in Poland, the reaction of world opinion, and the decline in Soviet prestige. All these were a part of the picture, and now Khrushchev and his followers were trying to put a good face on the situation in Hungary. They were trying to get out of the mess peacefully and at the least possible cost. How different things would have been if Moscow had announced its policy on the satellites five days earlier!

For the first time Nagy sensed, and with good reason, that he had become an independent political leader. Yes, he would bring order to Hungary's affairs, no matter how complicated and how poisoned they might appear. He was still being accused by the people of Budapest and by the foreign radios of being a step behind events. But, he believed, the time had come to establish a full understanding with the people—to establish an agreement which had not yet been reached.

The first week of the Revolution had been a week of purity. Frequently, a rare and precious article of merchandise had been left undisturbed behind broken store windows. There were many

stories of such occurrences that were absolutely true. Although
Stalinist radio announcers spoke of "bandits" and "pillagers," no
one touched the jewels and the watches in the wrecked windows
of the shops. A placard that read, "THIS IS HOW THE HUNGARIAN
PEOPLE STEAL," was enough to protect them more effectively than
a cordon of police. There were other windows, emptied of their
displays, in which signs read: "INVENTORY: THE ARTICLES LISTED
BELOW HAVE BEEN DEPOSITED WITH THE CONCIERGE OF THIS
BUILDING."

In the later days of the Revolution, however, many common-
law criminals had been freed from their cells, along with the
political prisoners. Some of these were able to obtain weapons.
Armed robberies, pillaging, and other acts of violence multiplied.
Most of the insurgents still held their weapons. Many of these,
with weapons in their hands, turned their thoughts to the crimes
of the past decade. In the absence of any real military function for
them to perform, they began looking for other work.

They began to hunt for members of the dissolved security
service. These former AVH men either took off their uniforms
and donned civilian clothes, or else they removed their insignia so
they would look like ordinary police. They kept close to their homes,
or hid out in cellars. When one would be recognized on the street,
it was the end. At one corner, a hanged man dangled from a rope.
He had been lynched by the mob. Suspended from his neck was a
placard that read: "SO WILL END ALL THE MEMBERS OF THE AVH."
In its issue of November 3, the revolutionary daily *Magyar Honved*
gave this description of a lynching: "Already the slip-knot was
tightening around the man's neck. His head fell back and the
cold November wind set his body swaying. Death was imminent.
At this moment, someone in the crowd called out: 'Quick! Let
him down. He is not of the AVH. His name is Kelemen and he
lives in Kobanya.' By good fortune, it was in time. Kelemen, still
alive, was taken to a hospital. . . . There were other incidents
in which the anger of the people was vented against innocent victims who were accused in error. Members of the air force and of
the entertainment branch of the Honved were attacked by fanatics
who took them for members of the AVH because they, too, wore
blue collars on their uniforms. Frequently, there were 'people's

trials,' followed by lynchings in which the identities, much less the activities, of the victims were never verified."

The most serious incident took place on the morning of the thirtieth, in Republic Square. There, in front of the Erkel Theater, was the headquarters of the Greater Budapest Federation of the Hungarian Workers' Party. On October 23, at the time of the first demonstration, a detachment of the AVH, consisting of forty-five soldiers commanded by a lieutenant and a sub-lieutenant, had taken up positions there. The soldiers were twenty-one- or twenty-two-year-olds who had been trained in the AVH by order of the recruiting boards. They were young recruits who had been drafted into the AVH without their own consent and who had nothing in common with the torturers of that infamous organization. No further orders having reached them, the detachment had remained in the Party headquarters, not daring to venture into the streets, where the fever ran high.

On the morning of the thirtieth, a truck arrived, bringing meat for their mess. A short distance away, housewives were lined up in a queue before a meat store that had little to sell. Within seconds, word spread that the meat was destined for the AVH troops, and, since there were many armed rebels in the area, the people in the queue spread this word to them.

The insurgents streamed toward the door of the building housing the Party offices. These doors were still guarded by the same police who had been stationed there before the Revolution began. They asked whether it was true there were AVH men inside, and they tried to force their way in. They got as far as the vestibule. Then they were forced back and the doors were closed. The lieutenant of the AVH succeeded in capturing the leader of the attackers and took him before Imre Mezo, secretary of the Budapest Party organization.

A veteran of the Spanish Civil War, then of the French Resistance, Mezo was one of the Party's leaders who was possessed of great integrity. He had been opposed to the policies of Rakosi, and that one, being afraid of him, had kept him in the background as much as possible. With Jozsef Kobol, he had been the only Party functionary who had dared to protest in writing against the removal of Nagy from the Party leadership. He had distinguished himself among the revolutionaries by organizing that national memorial celebration in honor of Rajk which had been a prelude to the rebellion.

That morning Mezo was negotiating with a delegation from the Ministry of Defense, with a view toward organizing an armed workers' militia for the purpose of defending industrial plants for the support of the Government. The delegation was headed by Colonels Asztalos and Papp.

Mezo questioned the insurgent who had been brought before him and, in doing so, was told that the building would probably soon again be attacked. He ordered the prisoner kept under guard.

All these factors—the AVH soldiers inside the building and the arrival of a truck laden with meat, plus the arrival of the two high-ranking officers who were also taken for AVH members and the arrest of one of the insurgents—contributed to the rise of tempers. The building was surrounded and again brought under attack.

The defenders returned the fire. The siege lasted three hours. Mezo and his friends telephoned everywhere in search of aid. The telephone was working, but their appeals for help were futile. Neither the Premier nor, for better reason, the Party had forces available in that area capable of assuring the security of the building's occupants.

Finally, the Ministry of Defense sent three tanks to clear the area around the Party building. They were to protect the withdrawal of the defenders, but the insurgents surrounded the tanks and persuaded the tank crews to come over to their side. At this, the two officers from the Ministry of Defense advised Mezo to cease fire, but the tank guns were already aimed at the building.

The summing up was atrocious. The victorious insurgents and the mob in the square gave no quarter. Foreign reporters who were present photographed the scenes of horror. The young recruits of the AVH were beaten to death by their assailants. Imre Mezo, gravely wounded, died later in a hospital. Colonel Asztalos was also killed. Colonel Papp, after having been beaten and spat upon, was strung up by his feet from a tree. Some soldiers poured gasoline on him and set him afire. The paper *Magyar Fuggetlenseg* (meaning "Hungarian Independence"), which had appeared during the rebellion, described in detail in its November 1 issue this "people's judgment." It gave its approval, but not without remarking: "This was a spontaneous act by an irresistible force. But, to be faithful to the truth, we must raise our voices against those who stoked the fires of anarchy, who circulated slogans of fascist inspiration, who incited the throng to press this fratricidal struggle, and who took delight in the devastation and the destruction that resulted."

Premier Nagy should now have realized that he lacked the forces necessary to put his program into operation, for, after the departure of the Russians and the dissolution of the AVH, the armed forces had been represented in Budapest only by irregulars. Among these were to be found perfectly disciplined and completely honest students, but among them were also to be found fascist elements and even common-law criminals who had recently been freed. The attitude of these formations was often as undependable as it was unpredictable. Under these conditions, the organization of a force capable of maintaining law and order—a force that could be counted on to reestablish peace and order in Budapest— was a matter of extreme urgency.

Sandor Kopacsi, Budapest chief of police, played a large part in the effort to organize such a militia. In 1944, when he had still been quite young, Kopacsi had joined the partisan brigades in the Miskolc region and had fought the troops of the Nazi occupation. He sympathized with Nagy's views. He had quickly sensed the revolutionary character of the insurrection and had refused, from the beginning of the rebellion, to stigmatize the insurgents as counter-revolutionaries. During the fighting, Kopacsi's policemen had largely taken a passive attitude, refusing to fire on the insurgents. Many policemen had gone even further and had given their arms to the rebels, thereby winning for themselves a certain popularity with the people.

Kopacsi had succeeded in protecting police headquarters and his armory of weapons. One day, several thousand demonstrators had appeared before the cream-colored building in which the police headquarters was housed and had demanded that they be admitted, charging that a number of AVH members were in the building disguised as ordinary policemen. Kopacsi had appeared on the balcony and calmed them, averting an attack that would have caused considerable bloodshed.

Since October 28, Kopacsi and his friends had been engaged in organizing the new militia. It was their opinion that the only solution was to find some means of fusing those members of the armed forces who had not been soiled by the spilling of Hungarian blood with the honest and disciplined elements of the insurgents. On this basis, the militia would then recruit members of the police, as well as students. Of the latter, those whom their comrades could answer for were armed and given tricolor armbands and militia identity cards. In the days that followed, more and more members of this militia could be seen directing traffic at congested inter-sections, patrolling against looting, and preventing the people from taking the law into their own hands.*

On October 30, at the headquarters of the People's Army, a Revolutionary Council was formed. The hard-shell Stalinists—Generals Lajos Toth, Istvan Szabo, Jeno Hazai, and Ferenc Hidvegi—were superseded. The Revolutionary Council declared: "The Army is on the side of the people in their defense of the gains of our glorious Revolution."

Through all this time, Imre Nagy, Janos Kadar, and Ferenc Munnich were holding conversations with the leaders of the various insurgent groups. In the course of these negotiations, they became convinced that these men, these leaders, who, for the most part, were quite young, had no intention of undermining the gains that had been made under socialism. On the other hand, they succeeded in convincing the insurgent leaders that, by firing their guns in all directions and by allowing summary executions, they were harming the rebellion.

That evening of the thirtieth, at 10:43 p.m., the insurgents broadcasted the following appeal to the people: "After the end of the fighting and the beginning of the withdrawal of Soviet forces, Comrades Kadar and Munnich met in a conference with the leaders and representatives of the revolutionary youth. After

---

* Sandor Kopacsi, one of those tried with Nagy, was condemned to life imprisonment for having participated in the "mutiny."

three hours of discussion, it was decided to form a Revolutionary Committee of Youth for the Ninth District,[15] representing the defenders of Kilian Barracks, Tompa Street, Corvin Passage, Tuzolto Street, and Berzenczey Street. . . . This is the first step toward restoring order and security, and toward assuring peace and creating the basis of a sovereign Hungarian republic. The directors of the armed groups have adopted this resolution because certain pillagers and bandits are: 1.) endangering the results obtained at the cost of heavy sacrifices of human life; 2.) threatening the lives of those fighters for freedom who are returning to their work; and, 3.) threatening the existence of all working people, of all personal well-being, of public property, and of the swift constitution of a free and sovereign Hungarian republic. An agreement has been reached in which it is stipulated that all members of the AVH will be sent home, that the protection of public buildings as well as of Party headquarters will be assured by members of the Honved, reenforced by the Revolutionary Committee of Youth. . . ."

One of the signers of this proclamation, which placed public and Party buildings under the protection of the armed revolutionaries, was Colonel Maleter.

The formation of the militia, the decision of the Honved to go over to the Revolution, and the adherence of the majority of the revolutionary organizations to the Government created the basis for the consolidation of the situation along military lines. To head all these forces, a Revolutionary Committee for the Maintenance of Order was created at the Ministry of National Defense. During the night, Nagy issued a declaration in which he recognized this new Revolutionary Committee and gave it his approval.

For the moment, these new forces were actually more in the realm of an objective than a reality. However, their organization was accomplished far more quickly than one would have thought possible. During the reinforcement of the new forces within the succeeding forty-eight hours, there continued to be summary executions and attempts by some elements to keep the turmoil alive. But, hour by hour, the balance hung more and more on the side of order and discipline.

Obviously, Imre Nagy was not ignoring the fact that a purely military solution would solve little. For, at the same time as the demonstrations and the strikes and the summary executions in the capital, the situation in the provinces was also becoming grave. It was at Gyor that the situation was the most critical. This city, close to the western frontier of Hungary, had become a center of the provincial uprising. In it, a National Transdanubian Council had been formed, which had invited other National Councils in the country to join it. Delegates from not only the various towns in Transdanubia, but also from such centers as Miskolc, Csepel, and the cities of the pusta, responded. From these delegates, a group was sent to Budapest. Its members announced: "If the Government does not give satisfaction to our demands, we will refuse to recognize it under any conditions."

It was evident, then, that there existed the threat of the formation of a dissident government. A proposal to this effect had, in fact, been made during a meeting at Gyor, and it was clear that such an action might lead to a tragic split within the country. Thus, certainly, a political solution must be quickly found.

But, in order to find such a solution, it would be necessary for Nagy to be reconciled with his own friends—the friends who had been the most dependable. Nagy sent a message to Geza Losonczy, asking his support. Losonczy's reply was to join him immediately. In those troubled hours, anger flared quickly, but, just as quickly, it died. Nagy had need of his friends. In his antechamber was installed a tall, brown-skinned, vigorous man named Jozsef Szilagyi, who was the son of a peasant. He was an old partisan of Nagy's whom neither the tortures of the Horthy regime nor the disgrace under Rakosi could break. He became Nagy's personal secretary, handling all his telephone calls and disposing of importunate visitors—a routine job, true, but he had resolved to remain at Nagy's side and to protect him with his person.

Nagy also sent a message to the Revolutionary Committee of Intellectuals, those writers and journalists whom he had so recently classified as hot-heads. He told them, quite simply, not to hold rancor against him, for he now realized that they were right.

Nagy's aim was to restore order everywhere, quickly, very quickly. To do so, he would have to deny the charge that it was he who had called for help from the Russians. Therefore, on Wednesday evening, the radio broadcasted this communique:

"Hungarians! To our sadness and shame, two measures have caused hundreds of our citizens to shed their blood and have unleashed the anger of the people. The first was the appeal to the Soviet troops to intervene in Budapest; the second was the infamous proclamation of martial law against the fighters for liberty. Fully conscious of our responsibilities, we declare before history that Imre Nagy, President of the Council of Ministers, had no knowledge of these two measures. Neither the resolution of the Council of Ministers, which asked the help of Soviet troops, nor the decree announcing martial law carried the signature of Imre Nagy. The blame for these decisions rests on Hegedus and Gero. It is they who must carry the responsibility before the nation and before history."*

But this communique did not raise the most important question, which was the need for replacing the authority of the Party— a Party which had crumpled lamentably—by the creation of a new political organization. It was such a move which would not only fall in line with demands of the people, but which would also be in the interest of order. The fact was that the Communist Party had collapsed and that it would not, in any case, provide a healthy political base on which to build. The fact was, also, that there were those who thought it would be wise to channel the passions of the people toward the political struggle and away from the armed battle in the streets. These thought it would be much better to have the people pronounce their judgments by ballots, not by bullets. It was clear that a return to June, 1953, would not be enough. In some respects, it might even be necessary to go back to 1947–1948—though only in some respects.

The Moscow Declaration of October 30 had urged Nagy to

---

* The drafters of this communique went beyond the facts. They discharged Nagy of all responsibility as far as the martial law proclamation was concerned, when actually he was not kept in ignorance of this measure. The contrary was the case regarding the appeal for Soviet troops. It should have been made clear, however, that this decree was never put into effect. It is, evidently, always difficult to remain within the bounds of truth.

defend the victories of socialism. But, must a multi-party regime necessarily be dangerous for socialism? It was only six months since the Twentieth Party Congress of the Soviet Communist Party had recognized the rights of each country to go on its own road towards socialism. Why could not a multi-party regime be the Hungarian way? Why could it not be agreed that all parties would respect the victories of socialism—a democratic Hungarian socialism, free of all violence? An agreement with the wise and thoughtful leaders of the other parties would, in itself, constitute a defense of socialism against the extremists. To refuse a multi-party regime would result either in a return of Stalinism or in a counter-revolution of the Right.

On the preceding afternoon Imre Nagy had announced over the radio that the Government, acting in complete accord with the Presidium of the Hungarian Workers' Party, in order to allow a more complete democratization, had abolished the one-party system and had decided that the country must return to a system of government based on the cooperation of those coalition parties which were in existence in 1945. Following this announcement, a limited Cabinet was formed within the Government. Its members were Imre Nagy, Zoltan Tildy, Bela Kovacs, Ferenc Erdei, Janos Kadar, Geza Losonczy, and a representative of the Social Democratic Party to be nominated by that Party.

The formula used was a wise one. The parties that had participated in the 1945 coalition were the Smallholders, the Social Democrat, the National Peasants, and the Communist. But there had been one revision of the formula: this "democratic collaboration" would not be one of unrestrained rivalry; instead, it would be a kind of "popular front." Otherwise, the composition of this limited cabinet was such that even the most bitter Stalinist could not believe that it would endanger the gains of socialism.

Kadar was fully supporting him in everything. True, that one was a little regretful in announcing on Radio Kossuth the renunciation of the Party's monopoly rule. "It is with a deep sense of responsibility for sparing our nation and our working masses further bloodshed," Kadar had said, "that I declare that every member of the Presidium of the Hungarian Workers' Party agrees with today's decisions by the Council of Ministers." Every member. That meant Munnich, Apro, Kiss, Szanto, and Kadar himself.

The Soviet leaders Mikoyan and Suslov were giving their full support to Nagy, too. They were still in the Central Committee's building on Academy Street. It would be unthinkable to make decisions of such importance without their full approval. As a matter of fact, they were also ready for even further steps. They agreed with Nagy and Kadar that the Soviet troops must be evacuated from Budapest—as had already been promised in their statement of October 30—and they had begun negotiations for the evacuation of the Soviet troops from the whole territory of Hungary. The authorization for their action lay not only in the above-mentioned statement. The fact was that Khrushchev, too, had authorized the action.

Thus, a few minutes before five o'clock on Tuesday afternoon, Nagy was able to send the following message to the people: "My Hungarian brothers! I inform you that the evacuation of the Soviet troops, initiated by the Government, has already been started."

At 7:20 that evening, Radio Miskolc in northern Hungary announced: "Attention! A few minutes ago our correspondent in Nyiregyhaza phoned to tell us that the evacuation of Soviet troops through Nyiregyhaza is proceeding continuously. He even told us of an episode during that evacuation. Soviet armored cars stopped in the center of the city, and their personnel asked the people: 'Which road leads to Zahony?'—that is, to the Hungarian border. The men of Nyiregyhaza answered the question with understandable joy, showing the direction to the Zahony station."

On the same day, British Prime Minister Anthony Eden had announced in Parliament that the British and French Governments had asked the permission of the Egyptian Government for British and French troops to occupy temporarily some key military positions in Port Said, in Ismailia, and in Suez. The Prime Minister had added that the Government of Israel had also been informed about this step and that both Egypt and Israel had been requested to reply within twelve hours. President Eisenhower had sent an urgent personal message to the Prime Ministers of Great Britain and France, requesting them to try to solve the crisis in the Middle East by peaceful means and not by armed force. He had asked them to renounce their ultimatum and to abandon their plan for landing troops in Egypt.

Not much later the Associated Press reported that British and French troops had begun to occupy the Suez.

The Move Toward Consolidation

As to the events of October 31, *Igazsag* (Truth), which was edited by the journalist Gyula Obersovszky, the dramatist Jozsef Gali, some university students, and several left-wing intellectuals, published this account by a reporter:

"Within the last few hours, I was able to penetrate the inner sanctum of the Party office on Academy Street. The Hungarian Workers' Party, which is to be reorganized before long, will soon move its offices to Nador Street. Janos Kadar, who was in the midst of all the important negotiations that were going on, had still found time to issue a statement on the reorganization and on the Party's position. He was speaking in his official role as a member of the Presidium. . . .

"The reception hall, bordered with tall marble columns, was plunged in deep silence. Sitting about were vigorous-looking young men, all wearing the same dark blue overcoats and the familiar Russian caps. They were members of Mikoyan's and Suslov's entourage. Otherwise, the building was more or less under the protection of members of the revolutionary Honved.

"Janos Kadar sent me word to be patient. He was in conference, I was informed. 'With whom?' I asked one of the functionaries. 'With Mikoyan and Suslov,' I was informed. 'They are discussing the withdrawal of Soviet troops.' After a few minutes, Imre Nagy came out of the conference room. The negotiations must not have been fruitless. Then Gyorgy Lukacs entered the building, accompanied by the poet Istvan Eorsi and a student.*

"Suddenly the door of the conference room opened, and Mikoyan and Suslov emerged. Suslov's face wore a smile. Mikoyan was not as dark as one would expect. His hair and moustache were streaked with grey. Both men wore dark blue overcoats.

"I had just learned that they had been here the previous week for only a few hours and that they had now come back to get a precise picture of the situation in Budapest and in Hungary. People around me believed that the information Mikoyan had earlier provided to his Government had resulted in that Government's expression of regret that events in Hungary have led to bloodshed.

"I found myself in their path, and the Russians—was it by habit or did they take me for a Party official?—shook my hand. . . . Then, rapidly descending the stairs, they took their places in a Soviet tank, and the armored procession started for the airfield."

The writer did not consider this short item worthy of his signature. He was not aware that destiny had made him a witness to the final scene of an episode that was of prime importance to the future of Hungary.

Having concluded a satisfactory agreement, Mikoyan and Suslov had parted with the Hungarian leaders on the best possible terms. Taking part in the negotiations on the Hungarian side had been Nagy, Kadar, and Tildy. Tildy had posed the problems bluntly: the formation of a multi-party regime, the withdrawal of Soviet troops from Hungary, and the withdrawal from the Warsaw Pact on the part of Hungary. He had explained that these solutions would be the best way to calm the anger of the people. He assured the Russians that they could have faith in what he was saying. The Hungarians, he went on, had no intention of following an anti-Soviet policy. Indeed, they wanted to tighten the bonds of Hungarian-Soviet friendship. It must be a friendship, however, that would not be based on force, but on understanding; not on suspicion, but on confidence.

---

* Lukacs had been stopped on the street and asked to show his identification. He had to give his word of honor that he was the new Minister of Culture. In all the confusion he had not had time to obtain proper credentials.

Mikoyan had agreed with each of the points. He had declared that the Soviet Government and that he himself had faith in the Hungarian leaders. It was clear to him, he said, that the situation had greatly deteriorated. In no event, he assured them, would new Soviet forces be sent into Hungary. Moscow took its responsibilities under its declaration of October 30 very seriously. The Soviet delegates said they did not want to go into details; indeed, they said, they would not be capable of doing so. It was up to the Hungarian comrades to act for the best as they saw it. All Mikoyan would ask was that the gains made under socialism be protected and that the old regime should not be permitted to return to power. He was intransigent on only one point: Hungary must not become an anti-Soviet base.

On that point, too, all had agreed with him. None of the Hungarians who were present saw any reason to doubt Mikoyan's sincerity. Furthermore, *Pravda,* as well as Radio Moscow, had by now changed its tune. Moscow supported the Nagy Government and spoke less and less of counter-revolution.*

The military commander at Miskolc announced that, at the frontier station of Zahony, steps were being taken to provide trains for the Soviet evacuation. The radio station at Szabolcs-Szatmar, which was in the hands of a Workers' Council, announced that a Soviet division had already crossed the Tisza; that another was waiting between the Tisza and the artillery caserne at Zahony in order to cross the river in its turn; and that the other divisions farther south were on the move. "Do not be disturbed at seeing Soviet troops taking roads other than those by which they arrived," the announcer said reassuringly. "The withdrawal will take place in many directions."

Before the Hungarian negotiators had adjourned, Tildy had said with conviction: "We can negotiate with the Russians. We can get along with them well, as long as they are convinced that we are sincere." He recalled incidents from the period when, as Hungary's Premier, he had negotiated with Voroshilov, pointing out that he was able to say the most disagreeable things to the

---

* Radio Moscow said: "Reports pouring in from all over Hungary show that the workers support the new Government and approve its program." *Pravda* said: "The Nagy Government has won the support of the people."

Russians as long as they were aware of his basic goodwill. Rakosi and his group had spoiled everything, he said, by their lies and by fawning on the Russians.

The Soviet leaders had apparently been deeply influenced by the fact that China had reacted very quickly to the declaration of October 30. Peking had agreed, as had Warsaw and Belgrade, that the Hungarians had justice on their side. Almost bluntly, the Chinese had accused the Russians of following a policy of "bourgeois chauvinism" and "of not taking the principle of equal rights into account in their dealings with other Communist states." These errors, said the Chinese, had unfortunately "seriously damaged the solidarity of the socialist states and their common objectives. In spite of the intrigues of reactionary elements, whose number in any case was small, the demands of the Polish and the Hungarian peoples were entirely justified. . . . The Chinese People's Republic also believes that the relations among socialist countries must be based on the Five Principles [enunciated at the Bandung Conference]."

Those words might have been lifted from Imre Nagy's book. What once were heresies had now become part of the Marxist-Leninist vocabulary, and, no doubt, they would soon be put into practice. Nagy could have hoped for no greater satisfaction. His pleasure as a man of science who had reached the proper conclusions surpassed that of the man of politics.

He had the same feeling he had had three years ago: the Russians had confidence in him. True, he had been bitterly deceived later on when the Soviet leaders had replaced and abandoned him. But now, he felt, the situation was completely different. Today he was the only "Muscovite" acceptable to the Hungarian people. He was not a danger to the Russians. He was a guarantee.

He forgot the precarious state of his health, his weariness. He forgot everything but the need to consolidate the situation and to break the wave of anarchy sweeping the country. He threw himself into this task with a youthful vigor that was astonishing. The twenty-third of October was declared a national holiday. Peter Kos, the Hungarian (or pseudo-Hungarian) delegate to the United Nations, was recalled. The system of compulsory collections from the farms was abolished.

Happily, the countryside was quiet, and, not without reason, Nagy saw in this phenomenon a sign of his personal influence. The peasants had confidence in him, and it was not from them that his difficulties arose. But actually the quiet in the countryside had come about for another reason. Farmers don't strike during the fall sowing season, when the bread for the following year is at stake. It was not that the editorials in *Szabad Nep* were calling on them to sow their fields, but that they were observing a way of life a thousand years old. A century and a half earlier, the French had discovered that people make love even during a revolution. The Hungarians were now learning that peasants sow their fields even during revolutions.

Still, there were also other reasons for the quietness. The peasants are always more prudent than are their brothers in the city, and they react more slowly. Always, they have a tendency to wait and see what happens, and they do not seize their forks and mattocks until the last moment. For the time being, they were content to send provisions to the people of Budapest. On the streets of the capital, there could be seen the unusual spectacle of farmers giving the people chicken and eggs; at the factories, trucks arrived loaded with potatoes, apples, and onions. If they were not fighting for the Revolution, the farmers were giving it sustenance.

The situation was different wherever the workers were concerned—quite different and more delicate. The Marxist theoretician who wanted to study such subjects as "The Role of the Working Classes in a Revolutionary Period" or "The Workers' Struggle for Independence and Against Foreign Oppression" would have found rich source material in the capital at this moment. For the strike continued. Not even the barbers could open their shops (the streets were full of unshaven men) without running the risk of a blast of gunfire. If they did open, they would be regarded as scabs. The workers refused to work until they had received guarantees that their basic demands would be satisfied—an understandable attitude, even though at times they made such exorbitant claims as did the workers at Csepel, who wanted to be paid during the strike.

The continued strike and the sporadic fighting could be costly. But the word was spreading that the West was going to send help. And, actually, medical supplies, clothes, and food were being sent from Austria, Switzerland, Britain, and France. It is a fact that similar gifts were also arriving from Poland, Czechoslovakia, and Rumania. The people in the streets showed their solidarity by their response to collections organized for victims of the rebellion. Governments, too, were hastening to their aid. President Eisenhower offered $10,000,000. All this, though it was very well, was, however, nothing the Government could base its policies on. It was more important to persuade the workers to go back to their jobs.

Nagy received delegation after delegation, one after the other almost without interruption. He listened to their demands. He tried to reassure them and to make them listen to reason. Kadar, at his side, supported him. A delegation arrived from Szolnok. Nagy told its members that the Russians would, within twenty-four hours, evacuate not only Budapest but also Szolnok. The leader of the delegation demanded that Cardinal Mindszenty, Primate of Hungary, be freed and be allowed to enter into direct communication with the Holy See. Nagy replied that the Cardinal was already at liberty and that the Government would put no obstacle in the path of his resumption of the direction of the Hungarian Catholic Church.

During the meeting, Kadar scribbled a few words on a piece of paper: "Dear fellow workers of Szolnok," these words read. "On this last day of a difficult era, which is also the first day of a new era, we send you our greetings through the delegate from your city, Comrade Ferenc Bujaki. Let us all join with all patriotic Hungarians of goodwill to reestablish order and to resume the work that is the basis of life. We urge that the partisans of the Communist ideal, delivered from the ashes of the past, show confidence in the future. Hungarian socialism will triumph in the service of a just ideal—and by the proper methods. With my Communist salutations. Janos Kadar." He handed the paper to Nagy, who read the closing lines. Perhaps he added to himself that the road to the future would also be long and hard. But Kadar had written these lines with all his heart. And Nagy wrote his name next to that of Kadar.

In the capital, the atmosphere was even more feverish than it had been during the previous night. The people, who were not working, crowded the streets. They stood in little groups, discussing the situation. The walls were plastered with leaflets, tracts, manifestos, appeals, demands. Worse yet, several Party offices were sacked, the furniture broken, the books burned—and the man hunt, too, continued. Throughout the city, members of the AVH were hunted down, and those who were only taken into custody and held under guard were lucky. Lynchings were frequent.

It was not only a question of spontaneous demonstrations of hatred, as in the earlier days. The hatreds nurtured by the events of the last ten years were artificially kept alive. Over the air there were appeals from abroad exhorting the people to beware of their government, to watch that they would not be lured away from their goals by it, and to continue their strike. On October 31, Radio Free Europe proclaimed: "The Ministry of Defense and the Ministry of the Interior are still in Communist hands. Do not let this continue, Freedom Fighters. Do not hang your weapons on the wall. Not a lump of coal, not a drop of gasoline for the Budapest Government, until Interior and Defense are in your control." And another voice cried: "This little Government [the limited Cabinet] offers no guarantee. The actual situation is such that it must not be accepted even on a provisional basis. It is urgent, as the free radios have demanded, that a new National Provisional Government, capable of facing the situation, be formed immediately."

In the face of so much incomprehension and hate, it was difficult to hold out. Unfortunately, the organization of armed forces in support of the Government had only been begun. Nagy took a number of steps aimed at speeding the process. He named Pal Maleter as first Deputy Minister of National Defense, Istvan Kovacs as Chief of Staff, and Bela Kiraly as commander of the forces in Budapest. Maleter, a man whose name had become enormously popular in recent days and a man whom Nagy saw that he could trust, told the press: "We have full confidence in the Provisional Government. We approve each of its acts because it is trying to reestablish order and restore peace. We know Zoltan Tildy and Imre Nagy, their way of thinking and their steadfast honesty; and we know that they will fight with tenacity for the people. They represent Hungary's interests. We are not laying down our arms, but will assure order in Budapest, thanks to the formations of the Honved and the help of the police who have remained faithful to the people."

But Nagy knew that fine words would not solve political problems. He had been accused several times—and now he understood that the accusations had not always been wrong—of having lagged behind events. The facts, regardless of excuses and explanations, were that he had been slow to understand on October 23, when he stood on the balcony of the Parliament Building, that he had been slow in ousting Gero, in reorganizing the government, in cleansing himself of the accusation that he had called in the Russians, and in leaning on his friends. Someone has said, "This was the revolution of the lost forty-eight hours."

Now the moment had come to catch up. There was no longer any reason to hide from the people the agreement he had reached with Mikoyan and Suslov. One of the purposes of this agreement had been to reassure the people. It would be criminal to be late once again.

In the afternoon, demonstrators again appeared before the Parliament Building. They demanded the withdrawal of Soviet troops from all of Hungary, the removal of Minister of the Interior Ferenc Munnich, and freedom for Cardinal Mindszenty, of whose release the people were still largely ignorant.

Nagy realized that he could not delay another minute. He flung his overcoat over his shoulders and stepped out onto the balcony.

The demonstrators gathered beneath him. Nagy spoke:

"I speak to you once more, Hungarian brothers, from my heart. The revolutionary struggle in which you have been the heroes is won. These glorious days have given birth to our National Government which will fight for the freedom and independence of our people. We will tolerate no foreign interference in Hungarian affairs. We are for national sovereignty and for equal rights. We will found our policy firmly on the will of the Hungarian people. My dear friends, these are the first days of our sovereignty and independence. We have driven the band of Rakosi and Gero from the country. They will answer for their crimes. They tried to smear me—me, too. They spread the lie that it was I who called in the Soviet troops. This is a shameful lie. Imre Nagy, who has fought for Hungarian sovereignty, Hungarian freedom, and Hungarian independence, did not call in these troops. On the contrary, it was he who fought for their withdrawal.

"My dear friends, today we have started negotiations for the withdrawal of Soviet troops from our country and for the abrogation of the obligations imposed on us by the Warsaw Pact. I only ask you to be a little patient. I think the results will be such that you can place that much confidence in me.

"My dear friends, stand by us. Help us to reestablish normal conditions of life and to begin our creative work. We want the people to know peace and order and to have confidence in the future. We ask you to have confidence in our Government, to allow the return of order and calm so we can realize our broad democratic program.

"Long live the Hungarian Republic, independent, free, and democratic! Long live Free Hungary!"

Nagy had the impression that he had said what needed saying. His address was warmly received. He was finished with being too late. Now he was on the right road.

This was early in the afternoon, toward three o'clock.

At approximately the same time, the airplane carrying Mikoyan and Suslov touched down on the airport at Moscow.

The Face of a New Hungary

Hungary has democratic traditions, but, in practice, it never had had a real democracy. During the democratic Revolution of 1848-1849 the Hungarian people were so burdened with battles that it was impossible for democracy to strike deep roots into the nation's life. In the next half century (1849-1918), the country became Europeanized, but the semi-colonial situation of the country—plus the basically feudal structure within it—overshadowed everything from the Parliament to daily life to public opinion and to public institutions. The Revolution of 1918 lasted for only a few months, and, later on, the Horthy regime succeeded in amalgamating it, as far as popular opinion is concerned, with Bela Kun's dictatorship of 1919. In Hungary's quarter-century under Admiral Horthy (1919-1944), the country had a Parliament (and even an opposition party in Parliament); the country also had a kind of freedom of press and of speech, but at the same time the system of great estates was retained, the peasants were landless (they were the so-called 3,000,000 beggars), the workers were looked upon by the Government with contempt, and chauvinism and racial prejudices made Hungary an unhealthy and anachronistic region of the world. This path led straight to Hungary's outright fascism of 1944, and, after 1945, any genuine democratic procedures were limited—even in the first and comparatively free years—by the Soviet occupation which was, in turn, soon replaced by the dictatorship of Rakosi and Gero. In Hungary, democracy was measured by days, and oppression by decades.

The burning question of these days was how the nation would be able to use its newly-gained freedom: would not political prejudice or economic selfishness squander those achievements which were worth keeping, or would not these revive the mistakes of the past, thereby bringing about a new anachronism? What kind of a country would the new Hungary be? What forces could be counted upon for the creation of a progressive country? And what forces should be feared?

The parties of the 1945 coalition were in the process of reorganization. Nagy could see in advance that it would be the Smallholders Party that would be numerically the most important, as it had been in the past. The former Secretary-General of that Party, Bela Kovacs, was quoted at a meeting held in Pecs for the purpose of reconstituting the Party:

"No one, I believe, wants to reestablish the world of the aristocrats, the bankers, and the capitalists. That world is definitely gone. A true member of our Party can no longer think in terms of 1939, or even of 1945. These last ten years have been bitter, but they have taught us a useful lesson. It is now up to us to profit from this lesson. We must modify our program and our way of thinking."

Everyone believed that the Smallholders Party would take a position in favor of such fundamental changes and gains as the agrarian reform and the nationalization program. Of course, some of the leaders of this Party were in the West, and none knew whether they would return and, if so, what their attitude would be. But, according to all probabilities, the voice of those at home would prevail, and the most important personalities among the emigres would not want to reverse the tide of history.

Another member of the coalition, the National Peasants Party, which had just been reconstituted as the Petofi Party, represented without any doubt a "popular trend of the left." Ferenc Farkas, Provisional Secretary-General, had said in a broadcast: "We shall retain the gains and conquests of socialism to the fullest extent that they can be useful in a free, democratic, and socialist country, following the will of the people." The Party had just elected a council, some of whose members were such well-known writers as the poet and dramatist Gyula Illyes, the novelists Laszlo Nemeth, Peter Veres, and Janos Kodolanyi, and the poet Lorinc Szabo.

The Social Democrats found themselves in a rather delicate situation. The Rakosi regime had made unpopular such expressions as "socialism," "international proletariat," and "comrade"—terms which for twenty years had been the key words of the Hungarian Social Democrats. It might therefore have been supposed that, out of fear of being assimilated by the Communists, the Social Democrats would be the most anti-Communist of all the parties in the coalition. Their first statements spoke of "liberty" and of the "noble ideals of the workers' movement," finding no occasion to use the word "socialism." This is not to say that they had renounced their principles. Gyula Kelemen, the Provisional Secretary-General, had very unambiguously declared that his Party was in favor of maintaining the nationalization and of safeguarding the rights of the workers' councils.

However, the announcement of the reestablishment of most of the parties had aroused the determination in some groups to demand the right of all the other parties which had not been members of the 1945 coalition to exist. There were, among others, the Popular Catholic Party, the Popular Democratic Party, the Hungarian Independence Party, the Young Hungarians' Party, and the Federation of Christian Youth.

These were the parties in which Catholic inspiration was of importance—even, sometimes, of considerable importance. The Catholics were in the majority in Hungary, and ten years of persecution had, in the end, only strengthened the Church's popularity and increased its prestige. Cardinal Mindszenty had just been freed from Felsopeteny Castle, where, in these last months, he had been under constant surveillance after several years of imprisonment. Officers of the Honved had escorted him to the capital and had reinstalled him in his episcopal palace in Buda.* The position he would take would carry great weight because the masses listened to his voice. On Wednesday evening, he made a brief statement over the radio, but he did so without expressing his political views.

---

* Major Antal Palinkas, who freed Cardinal Mindszenty, was later condemned to death and executed by the Kadar regime.

"We must find a solution later," he said. "For the moment, I shall inform myself. Two days from now, I shall address an appeal to the nation in the hope of leading it toward that solution."

The president of the Catholic Party, Endre Varga, who had also made a declaration "in the spirit of Mindszenty," had said among other things: "We demand the maintenance of the social victories which have been realized since 1945 for the benefit of the people, and we even insist that they be expanded. Our program?—Social evolution, respect for legality, and liberty. Our slogan?—'With Christ for the people, and with the people for Christ.' " It was almost certain that the Catholic movements would not seek to restore the old regime of pre-1945, or, more exactly, to erase all that had happened since that time. However, there was no doubt that they stood farther to the right on social as well as ideological questions than did all the parties of the old coalition. On some issues, their views recalled those of the Catholic and nationalistic trends which characterized the Horthy regime.

In striking a balance under these fluctuating conditions, one would be tempted to say that the existing political forces tended to polarize toward two points: the first being a progressive center whose axis would be the Smallholders Party, supported by the Social Democrats, the National Peasants Party, the radicals, and the Communists; and the second being a conservative center based on the influence of the Catholic Church. The relations between these two forces would be hard to define, but the first force would probably be the stronger.

In regard to the "social conquests" whose retention the various parties favored in their declarations, Nagy could count on their being defended above all else by the masses—the peasants and the workers themselves. In spite of the failure of the Communist Party and the discredit that had become attached to the word "socialism," no politician in his right mind would go into the factories or into the countryside and tell the workers and peasants to return their land and "their" factories to their old owners. The peasants, after many years of an instability and an uncertainty which had been marked by state requisitions that sometimes stripped them of all their produce, as well as by their compulsory entrance into *kolkhozy* (called in Hungary "production cooperatives") now

wanted only to become the real owners of the land they cultivated—
and to work in security and in peace. As for the workers, these
wanted to see "their" factories, over which they had so long been
harangued without ever being able to profit from them in the
slightest, really become their collective property.

In a way, the situation was that the majority of the people
would prefer a Hungary which—as far as the economic "substruc-
ture" was concerned—would resemble most closely that of Yugoslavia or of the new Poland, and which, as far as the political
"superstructure" (and human rights and national independence)
were concerned, would be similar to Austria or Sweden or Finland.
Whether this was at all possible (i.e., whether the political and
economic factors of these two systems would not be in such sharp
contradiction that they would clash, and whether foreign influences
would not try either by material loans or by political pressures—
or by both of these—to change this structure of the new state)
was an undecided question. The answer depended, as the Hungarians say, on "the music of the future." The only certainty was
that the new Hungary would be one of the most interesting, as
well as one of the most exciting, countries in our changing world.

Was there any danger of the revival of fascism? In the days
of the Revolution, one could also observe some fascist tendencies.
It was impossible to deny that fascism had roots in Hungary. The
leaders of the Horthy regime had more than once said proudly
that the first fascist country of the world had not been Germany,
nor even Italy, but the Hungary of the 1919 counter-revolution.
There were still former members of fascist parties and former supporters of fascist ideas in the country. Others of their persuasion
had gone to the West or to South America, but a part of these
would certainly return, and, in fact, some had already crossed the
frontiers.[16] The fiasco of Communism had persuaded some fascists
to believe that their anti-Bolshevist ideas had been proved correct.
The decade of national oppression under the Soviet Union had
given new birth to an over-wrought Hungarian nationalism. And
then, too, the question of anti-Semitism was important. For twenty-
five years anti-Semitism had been the official policy of the Horthy
regime. It was a prejudice fostered in the universities and cul-
minated in the gas chambers. The fact that the majority of the

leaders of the Rakosi-Gero era had been of Jewish origin had served only to preserve—if not to increase—anti-Semitic feelings. As a matter of fact, Rakosi and the others had been so busy hiding the fact that they were Jewish that they had never allowed an open and honest fight to be waged against anti-Semitism. On the contrary, they had even encouraged prejudices.[17]

Still, the danger of fascism could be overcome in Hungary. First of all, fascism had been forsaken by the whole world. Though it had flourished in Hungary during the time that it had flourished in Western Europe, it was now out of fashion even if it had not completely disappeared from practice. Now the majority of the Hungarians wanted to match the most important achievements of Western progress: they wanted to achieve greater freedom and a better life. They did not want to replace one dictatorship with another one; after more than thirty years they were fed up with excesses. Those who were thoughtful realized that the immense sympathy aroused throughout the world by the Revolution could be quickly forfeited if fascist tendencies arose. And even those who were personally inclined to the extreme right wing well understood that—to be completely blunt about it—fascism was actually a bad business maneuver. If the country wanted to obtain moral and material help from the West, it would be absolute insanity not to follow the road of a moderate democracy.

The whole picture was naturally sketchy, and in many ways it was simply speculative. Yet it tried to be as realistic and as exact as it is possible to be in the midst of a revolution.

One more question had also to be answered. This was a question of extreme importance to Nagy personally. The question: What would happen to the Communist Party—i.e., the Hungarian Workers' Party?

As for the Hungarian Workers' Party, it had literally been reduced to nothing. Its central organ had ceased to appear. Some of its offices had been sacked by the people. Its militants were burning their Party membership books. One of them had fastened his to a wall with a sign that read: "A testimony to my stupidity. Let this be a lesson to you." It would be impossible to continue this Party. It would be useless to try to explain to the people that its militants were not responsible for its crimes. The only solution would be the establishment of a new Communist Party. Kadar was in agreement on this. In fact, he went even further in his thinking. An Italian journalist had asked him several questions:

"What kind of Communism do you represent, Mr. Kadar?" he asked.

"The new Communism," Kadar replied. "One born of the Revolution and which does not want or have anything in common with the Communism of the Rakosi-Hegedus-Gero clique."

"This new Communism," his interrogator continued. "Would it be of the Yugoslav or of the Polish type?"

"This new Communism will be Hungarian," said Kadar. "It will be a sort of 'third line' that will have no connection with either Titoism or with the Communism of Gomulka."

"And what will it consist of?"

"It will be Marxism-Leninism applied to the particular requirements of our country's problems and difficulties as a nation. It will take its inspiration neither from the Soviet Union nor from other types of Communism, but, I repeat, will be a Hungarian National Communism. This 'third line' is the child of our Revolution, in the course of which, as you know, many good Communists fought on the side of the students and the workers."

"Could one say that your new Communism will take a democratic form?" Kadar was asked.

"Your question is well put. There will be an opposition and no dictatorship. This opposition will be heard because the new Communism will have the national interests of Hungary at heart and not those of international Communism."

Some of Kadar's phrases, vague and exaggerated, had nothing in common with socialist dialectics. Nagy would never have expressed himself in such terms. Nevertheless, the basic ideas were approximately in line with his own.

The question that had to be answered was whether, after all that had happened in Hungary, such a Party would be able to attract a following. It was useless to nurse illusions. If there were really free elections, the Party's vote would be considerably reduced. If it won six to eight per cent of the vote, it would be doing well.

Still, the Party would not be a negligible one. The Hungarian Communist movement was not solely a movement of Stalinism and

Rakosism. Nor was it solely a movement of terror and of spineless-
ness, nor of oppression and treason. Honesty and courage, and love
of freedom and patriotism, too, were also inherent in the movement. If this had not been so, there would have been no revolution
in Hungary.

The obvious question is: Why, out of all the satellite countries,
was it in Hungary that a revolution broke out? Was it perhaps
because of the standard of life in Hungary? But the standard of
life in Rumania or Bulgaria was lower than in Hungary. Was it
perhaps because the national feelings of the Hungarians had been
hurt? But so had every other nation's feelings. Was it because of
the presence of Soviet troops in the country? There were Soviet
troops in Rumania and in Poland, too. Was it because of the bloody
purges? The Slansky trial in Czechoslovakia or the Kostov trial in
Bulgaria were little better than the Rajk trial. Because of the
servility, the stupidity, and the guilt of the Hungarian leaders?
Chervenkov in Bulgaria was no less servile and Gheorghiu-Dej in
Rumania was no cleverer, nor was Enver Hodia in Albania less
criminal than were Rakosi and Gero. Perhaps as a result of Hungary's traditional ties to the West? But this tradition was much
stronger in Czechoslovakia than it was in Hungary. Was it because
Hungary was not a Slavic country? Neither are Albania and
Rumania Slavic countries, and Yugoslavia, which had broken with
the Soviet Union ten years earlier, is a Slavic country. Was it because of the influence of these Yugoslav neighbors? Yugoslavia has
common borders with three other satellite countries. Was it because
Hungary had a strongly rightist past? But East Germany's past
was more strongly rightist.

Naturally, all these factors had important implications, and, in
a way, they even complicated each other. But there was another
factor in addition to these—a peculiarly Hungarian factor which
became the decisive one. It was only in Hungary that in July, 1953
—four months after Stalin's death—a forthright denunciation of
the Stalinist policy had occurred: that the regime had made a
public—and shocking—self-criticism. And it was only in Hungary
that, in the following months and years, two contradictory and
visible currents had expressed themselves inside the Party. It was
Nagy's consequent fight against Rakosi—plus the fact that (because

of the possibilities inherent in the one-party system) the leading role in this struggle was played by Communist Party-members— which granted a moral standing for these men in the eyes of the nation. This moral standing could hardly be denied even in the future political fights of a multi-party system.

And from what milieu would the new Party be recruited? There were the old Party militants who had been ousted or purged by Rakosi. There were also the young Party members of the Petofi Circle, and there were the working class, the students, the peasants who were to the left of the Social Democrats, and the many convinced Marxists among the intellectuals. Recruiting would be the most difficult among the working classes. It was this group which, more than any other, had been duped by Rakosi and had received the most promises and the least advantages. And it was this group in whose name the dictator had ruled. In the beginning, the new Party would be a Party in which the intellectuals, more or less, would play a large part. Numerically, it would perhaps not be large, but it would represent a high-level group. Perhaps, its influence would be felt more in the intellectual life of the nation than in its political life.

And the writers? What would become of the writers who had been members of the old Party? Among these Nagy had many friends. Would the new Party be able to count on them? The answer to this question would not be easy. The writers would have to fight their own battle if they were to impose their own opinions. Many people were minimizing the role that had been played by the writers in the struggle against Rakosi. In addition, many people were accusing the writers of having supported Stalin and his Hungarian disciples. Already, a broad first attack had been launched against one of these, the poet Laszlo Benjamin, in the paper *Magyar Fuggetlenseg*: "We other friends of literature have not forgotten you. You have ecstatically welcomed each Stalinist move. You have furthered the Rakosi cult among the poets to the point where you have believed that those who never dedicated a poem to the dictator did not have the right to call themselves Hungarian poets. You have poured out crocodile tears, in rhyme, to the death of Stalin ('Great Stalin,' according to you). . . . We bid you goodbye, Benjamin, and recommend that you look for other outlets for your trashy verse than the pages of the Revolutionary press. If you would like to sing one last hymn to the 'Great Premier,' hurry to the corner of Acacia Street and Rakoczi Avenue, where the free people of Hungary have broken his statue to bits. Go quickly, and perhaps you can still find a little piece for a souvenir."

Yet Benjamin was one of the first to denounce his own mistakes, accusing himself pitilessly. For the past three years, he had fought unflinchingly against Hungarian Stalinism. The public was now aware of the position taken by the writers and, for months before the insurrection, issues of *Irodalmi Ujsag* (The Literary Gazette) had sold like hot cakes. But, at the same time, the struggle among the writers went on largely behind closed doors in the meetings of their association's Party cell. People knew that Tamas Aczel had won a Stalin Prize, but who knew about his part in drafting the memorandum of the writers which had been submitted to the Central Committee in November, 1955, protesting against the suppression and seizure of various newspapers? The poem of Zeltan Zelk, dedicated to Stalin, was better known than was his courageous stand at the general assembly of the Writers' Association Party cell in November, 1955.

At the start of the rebellion, the writers, most of whom were Party members, had joined in the cause of the Revolution. They had supported it even before they understood the real meaning of events, and they supported it when it was clear that it had gone much farther than they had expected. And this was neither out of cowardice nor out of opportunism. It was simply because, to employ an old Marxist formula, these writers had "gone beyond the bulk of their class." The regime had given many of them a privileged status. They were not paid on the basis of copies sold, but on the basis of copies printed. The Writers' Association had large resources at its disposal and frequently showed great generosity toward its members, advancing them funds so that they could concentrate on a large work or sending them to "creative centers" in the country, where they could work at peace in pleasant surroundings. But the system of privileges consisted not only of those which the regime gave, but also of those which the regime could take away. Many writers of great talent were condemned to silence or assigned to hack-writing jobs. The scale of official values didn't correspond to that of real values.

Nonetheless, most of those who had been so privileged in the past were now ready to pay the price for the favors won by their credulity or their conformism. These men could no longer live as before, and, even though their situations might become more difficult, the improvement of the general situation—that of the people —would prove some compensation for them. In exchange for their lost privileges, they would be gaining something more precious— their freedom. Those who were sure of their talent had no fear of future freedom. On the contrary, they were impatient for it, behaving a little like race-horses at the starting line.

Naturally, to continue the comparison, each horse would run more willingly without the bit and without the jockey. Even though the literary policies of the new Party should be infinitely more pliable than were those of the old Party, most of the writers would show little willingness to adhere to them. In spite of everything, a Communist Party without a certain unity and discipline is inconceivable, and the mood of the writers now was to think with their own minds. Some would join out of a sort of defiance, saying to themselves that, since they had been Party members in those days the Party was useful to them, they would continue to be Party members in those days, too, when, at best, the Party would not be harmful. Most, however, would follow the example of Gyula Hay, an old Party militant who told a French journalist: "I will always be ready to support a pure and clean Marxist movement, but I never again want to be a member of a Party."[18] Yes, to sum it up, Nagy could count on the support of the writers—though not without debate and disputes. But, in the end, they would not let him down.

The writers were not the only ones who had had enough of the Party; in fact, this was to some extent the case with most people. And this did not apply only to the Communist Party but to all parties. This statement is in conflict with the impression created by the fact that one of the most popular demands of the people was freedom of political party activity. The truth is that this demand for a multi-party government was less an expression of love for the parties than it was a demonstration of their hostility toward the Party of Rakosi, toward the dictatorship of a single Party.

The extraordinary pace at which the parties were reconstituting themselves was accompanied by a number of phenomena that were either new or that had, at least, been unknown for many years. Bitter rivalries sprang up among the parties over the allocation of office space, or of automobiles, or of representatives in the Government. Discord broke out within the parties themselves. The first issue of the Smallholders' daily paper, *Kis Ujsag,* which was once very popular and which was now, like a phoenix, being reborn from its ashes, railed against those who had formerly betrayed the Party in favor of Rakosi and who now were hurtling themselves into it in the hope of laying their hands on their share of the pie. The newspaper said: "We demand the immediate expulsion of the pseudo-Smallholders so that their political juggling may not prevent us from realizing our real objectives. We shall not allow the most faithful equerries of Rakosi to discover suddenly that they were once members of the Smallholders Party. No! We have had enough!"

There was obviously much truth in this statement, and certainly the passion of it could easily be explained. Still, the date was November 1, and quite a few people were asking: Is it really this point which is now most important? In the days of the fighting, the unity of the whole nation had been most impressive. Even if the people did not wish to see the faithful equerries of Rakosi returned to the Government, they nevertheless deplored angry Party struggles and loud quarrels. The strongest voices were demanding at one and the same time the end of the political monopoly of one party and the creation of a broad national union of parties. These two demands might appear paradoxical, but they existed side by side. The National Council of Northern and Eastern Hungary, by way of Miskolc Radio, drafted this recommendation: "We urge the parties not to begin their political struggle until after the withdrawal of the Soviet troops." The newspaper of the Csepel metal-workers voiced the wish that "many parties be legalized. But these parties must work for the same goal—the well-being of all. And, above all, they must not engage in partisan battles."

This feeling was particularly strong among the young students and the young workers and the soldiers. These young students and workers believed that the fruits of their efforts and their sacrifices would now go to those who were unworthy. They themselves would soon go back to their classrooms and their workshops, while the political professionals would divide the cake. And the same state of mind existed in the Army and among the men in the new National Guard. In the present political situation, the Army was an extremely important factor: it represented authority and force simultaneously. And the leadership of the Army was of strongly leftist background and conviction. Colonel Maleter, Colonel Marton, and General Kiraly were all Communists. These men, according to all probability, would not favor any slipping to the right or any exaggerated quarrel of the political parties. They had fought for a free, an independent, and a progressive Hungary, and not for an anachronistic blot in the center of Europe. They had fought for a clean and honest Government which would serve the people, and not for a hierarchy of new careerists to take the place of the former ones. It was the writer Laszlo Nemeth, one of the most important novelists of his generation, who strikingly summed up the disgust that these "pure in heart" felt for the sordid scramble of those who were now engaged in struggling for their own advantage: "I have seen only the events in my own province and, for the rest, I know only what I have heard over the radio. But already a double danger seems to be developing: an immediate danger that the nation, in its justified indignation and in answer to the call of vengeance might commit irreparable acts; and a more distant danger, but one that is beginning at this moment when attention is concentrated on the departure of the Soviet troops, that the political professionals will hurl themselves upon their new jobs, being concerned, above all, with recapturing their former splendor. There are some who seek to seize key positions in order to transform the Revolution into a counter-revolution, and thus to nullify the 1956 Hungarian struggle for liberty in order to set up something resembling the regime of 1919. Who are the ones to oppose these maneuvers, if it be not those others of us who know the stakes and the risks. Only death could keep us from raising our voices."

It was not necessary to be a great scholar in order to understand that the problem of uniting the forces of progress would become acute almost immediately. It would certainly not be "under the direction of the Communist Party," as the old cliché of propaganda leaflets would put it, but, instead, "with the active participation of Communists." If there was truth in Kadar's statement to the Italian journalist, it was still not at all certain that the Party would have to pass into the opposition, as Kadar seemed to believe. One could well imagine that the Party, to whatever extent it and its representatives could show an irreproachable past, would remain at the core of a national movement, and that it would even play an important role. The Twentieth Congress, which had developed many new and interesting elements, Nagy had thought, also recognized the possibility of achieving socialism by a parliamentary route. Why should not the new Hungarian Communist Party strive toward this goal through a new route—through a positive and an effective program?

Obviously, this raised the question of the future role which he himself would have to play. Nagy knew perfectly well that there were some who considered him a puppet and that others regarded him as a leaf carried along by the wind of events or as a "yes-man" who was incapable of forcefully opposing the demands presented to him. These men would have liked him to do their pick-and-shovel work, to take onto himself all of the unpopular tasks, and then, his tasks finished, they would have liked to remove him from power, or, at the very best, to pension him off in an honorary position.

One could not even say that he would not personally prefer a more peaceful way of life. The week he had just lived through had cost him more in nervous energy, in tension and in worry than had any ten years of his life. Still, as little as some knew Nagy, they would have known that he had too much sense of responsibility to be willing to cede his place as long as he had so many things to say and to do. He was too much of an individualist to play at puppetry, or to be a yes-man.

Neutrality

It was on Wednesday evening and during the early hours of Thursday morning that the first news arrived in the capital about the movement of Soviet troops across the frontier and toward the interior of the country. At first, Nagy thought that these were simply part of the maneuver of getting the Russian troops out of the country: in the past it had often happened that a military unit, leaving Hungary, had returned because of transport problems and left again by another route. The Russians were not particularly concerned with matters of border lines in the people's democracies.

But, from Thursday morning on, despairing warnings began reaching the Premier. Transport officials and railroad workers cried in anguish over the telephone: a veritable flood of Soviet troops was rolling back into Hungary in tanks and trucks, bringing with it artillery and ammunition. Nagy still believed that these reports were largely exaggerations reflecting the atmosphere of panic that still held the country in its grip.

Then, however, the details began to come in. Armored columns had just crossed the Tisza and had burst into the most important centers of northeast Hungary. Units of these were being sent in all directions and were taking up combat positions. Some of the troops that had withdrawn from Budapest had returned and were digging in outside the capital. The airfields were being encircled by Soviet armored vehicles. One would have had to be blind to ignore this evidence.

But could one give a definitive political meaning to all these troop movements? In troubled times, orders and counter-orders succeed one another, and one must wait before drawing definite conclusions. Might one not surmise that all of these measures had been put into operation before Mikoyan left for Moscow and that they no longer had any relation to the actual situation? It always takes a long time to make the immense machinery that is an army turn around. Mikoyan and Suslov had promised that, in the future, no new Soviet troops would be sent into Hungary.

Whatever the circumstances, Nagy ordered a blackout on all news of an alarming nature.* It would be useless to upset the people just when they were beginning to calm down. Incidents with the Soviet troops, even minor ones, could have disastrous results. Obviously, the blackout could not last forever; certainly not in such a situation. Then, too, for some reason which was not understandable, Mikoyan was playing dead. There should have been a telephone call, an explanation. But no word came from Moscow. The Russians had also imposed a blackout.

For days now, the entire country had been urging that a position of neutrality be taken. Delegations of workers, one after another, had called on the Premier, and each had made this demand. On Nagy's desk was spread out the November 1 issue of the newspaper *Magyar Szabadsag,* whose editorial proclaimed that Hungary, like Austria, must press resolutely for a policy of neutrality. "In the future," said the editorial, "we do not want to join any power bloc, nor to make any definite agreements in favor of one or the other, nor to cut ourselves off from each other. This position corresponds not only with our geographical situation and our historic traditions, but, above all, with the lessons that can be learned from those traditions." [19]

---

* Because of the blackout, the Budapest newspapers were unable to report the return of Soviet troops, in force, from November 2 on. The organ of the new Communist Party (that of Kadar), *Nep Szabadsag,* published information from correspondents from Debrecen, Szolnoket, and Cegled. "At the moment of going to press," the paper reported, "we have been informed that Russian troops are approaching Kecskemet."

Up to that time, Nagy had not been in favor of proclaiming a policy of neutrality, not because of the principle itself, but for practical considerations. He had presented his views on the principle of neutrality long before those who today were bombarding him with such demands had done so. In January, 1956, he had written: "The most practicable plan, seemingly, is the active coexistence of progressive democratic socialist or similar countries with those other countries having a different system, through a coordinated foreign policy, through cooperation against the policies of the power groups, and through neutrality or active coexistence. This path is made easier for Hungary by its geographical location, through its neighboring states, through neutral Austria and countries building socialism—among them the Soviet Union and neighboring Yugoslavia, which stands on the principle of active coexistence. It is the sovereign right of the Hungarian people to decide in which form they believe the most advantageous international status will be assured, and in which form they think that national independence, sovereignty, equality, and peaceful development will be attained."

"It is the sovereign right of the Hungarian people . . ." But the Hungarian people in the streets, in their Revolutionary Councils, and in the Workers' Councils, were demanding a declaration of neutrality. All the same, it was a delicate question. As long as Hungary remained a member of the Warsaw Pact, such a declaration would bring the country up against at least formal obstacles. And the Russians would not be pleased. Mikoyan and Suslov had already gone far enough in giving their assent to Hungary's withdrawal from the Warsaw Pact. It would do no good to try to stretch that inch into a mile. Hungary should do nothing that would provoke a breach for which she could be blamed.

For the moment it was much more important to know exactly what the return of the Soviet troops meant. With each passing hour, new information on troop movements reached Nagy. Finally, he summoned Soviet Ambassador Yuri V. Andropov to his offices.

He asked for explanation. What was the reason that the Soviet Government had not abided by its declaration of October 30? The ambassador replied that he did not have adequate information concerning the situation, but he was ready to request an explanation from his Government.

Meanwhile, a series of new delegations arrived at the Parliament Building to urge the renunciation of the Warsaw Pact. Peter Mod, minister-plenipotentiary and envoy-extraordinary, brought with him the declaration of the Revolutionary Committee of the Foreign Ministry, which demanded the renunciation of the Warsaw Pact and the proclamation of Hungary's neutrality. He added that the declaration had been approved by every leading official of his ministry, including Deputy Ministers Istvan Sebes and Karoly Szarka.

At 11 a.m., Ambassador Andropov returned to the Parliament Building. The new interview stunned Nagy. It was not that he had any illusions about Andropov, a narrow, sectarian man who had been partisan to Rakosi. In 1955 and 1956, when, out of courtesy, Nagy had sent him excerpts of his memoirs to be transmitted to the Party leaders in Moscow, the Soviet Ambassador had forwarded them to Rakosi and Gero. But, at this moment, Nagy was not concerned with his personal feelings or with the past. He asked for an explanation of what was happening.

If the Soviet Ambassador had given reason for the troop movements, explaining why they were necessary—if he had, in short, held to the language of reason—there would still have been time for them to seek a reasonable solution together. But that was not Andropov's attitude. That grey-haired man with the impenetrable countenance said without a smile that the troop movements were "completely normal." They were necessary, he said, to assure the departure of the units regularly stationed in Hungary, without incident. If armored vehicles were encircling the aerodromes, it was only to assure the safe evacuation of the sick and wounded, and of the families of officers and soldiers. They signified nothing more.

Nagy could only ask himself whether the ambassador took him for a moron. There was little chance that Nagy could be fooled. The situation was too grave. The ambassador was simply concealing the truth. Nagy, while he was living in Moscow, had learned to assess such attitudes. When the Soviets no longer even tried to be convincing, it was because they no longer cared about appearances. This was the beginning of the end. Something must have happened at Moscow. But what? He had no way of knowing. Mikoyan gave no sign of life. The troops were flowing back into Hungary. Yes, this was, he felt, the end.

It was the end of Moscow's confidence in him. That was certain. The confidence he had enjoyed no longer existed. No longer ago than yesterday he had been convinced that, at last, he had won the Russians over to his side. Only yesterday, he had allowed himself to believe that they had understood that he was a true friend. Only a year and a half ago, when the Russians had allowed him to be driven from the Premiership, he had sworn that he would never again walk at their side, never again believe in them. Yet he had walked with them once again.

It was the end, too, of everything that the Soviet declaration of October 30 had represented: "complete equality of rights . . . respect for the independence and the sovereignty of the states . . . respect for territorial integrity . . . non-interference in the internal affairs of other countries. . . ." Words, words, words, words. All of this had been published in *Pravda,* and only the day before yesterday. But, already, it was finished. . . . "The decisions of the Twentieth Congress, which had a historic importance. . . ." The Twentieth Congress was finished, too.

He tried to think things out calmly, to analyze the situation with his closest friends. What more could be done? He had asked Andropov to try to get some information from Moscow and to transmit his protests. Even if there were one chance in a hundred that there was some misunderstanding, he did not want to pass it by, though naturally he could not base a policy on such a possibility. He had to be prepared for the worst.

From the military point of view, the situation was desperate. Nagy had never thought, as had so many others intoxicated by the withdrawal of Soviet troops, that the people of Budapest had defeated the Soviet army. He knew very well that the Russian bear could, with a flick of one of its paws, have crushed their resistance. It was not possible to count on military aid from abroad. He would not ask for such aid, knowing that the mechanism that such a move could set in motion might result in the launching of a world conflict. He was also enough of a realist to know that, even if he asked for help, it probably would not be forthcoming.

So Nagy found himself at the crossroads. If he kept silent in the face of events and closed his eyes to the new invasion, he would lose the newly-reborn confidence of the people, who would then look upon him as a traitor. Under such circumstances, he would no longer be able to control the country without the support of the Soviet troops—assuming that they would give him such support—any more than could Rakosi, Gero, and Hegedus. But if, on the other hand, he were to resign as Premier, he would be letting the country fall into anarchy. The Russians would quickly replace him with a puppet. The only possibility open to him—which did not in any case offer any hope, though it would at least be honest—was to put himself at the head of his people and stand up against the Soviet perjurers. If the Hungarians could not bring military means into play, an attitude of moral courage might have a feeble chance for success. Perhaps—though who could say?—the moral weight of public opinion might protect a little nation that had so often spilled its blood in defense of noble ideals. He could do nothing else but raise his voice, as did Miklos Zrinyi in the seventeenth century, and say: "Here is the danger! Here is the devouring flame!"

At about noon, a new telephone call came from Andropov. Nagy summoned Gyorgy Heltai, Acting Deputy Minister of Foreign Affairs, and Peter Mod to his office. The Russian ambassador presented him with a five-point answer from Moscow. Nagy himself translated every point into Hungarian and dictated it to Mod, who diligently made notes. The essence of the answer was this:

The Soviet declaration of October 30 was still fully valid. The Hungarian Government should appoint a committee which should be authorized to begin negotiations regarding the political problems involved in the renunciation of the Warsaw Pact. And another committee should initiate negotiations regarding the military and technical details of the withdrawal of the Soviet troops.

Again Nagy asked Andropov: "What has become of the solemn promise that no further Soviet units would enter Hungary?" But to this all-important question the ambassador could give no new answer.

What could Nagy do? He summoned the executive committee of the Communist Party to a meeting. There were Kadar, Munnich, Lukacs, Szanto, Losonczy, Apro, and Kiss, and he informed them of the Soviet reply. The Party's leading body decided that the Soviet Union had *de facto* broken Hungary's obligations to the Warsaw Pact. Thus, the Communist Party proposed to the Government that Hungary should renounce the Warsaw Pact, and that, to avoid any provocations, the Premier should declare the neutrality of the country. Only Gyorgy Lukacs and Zoltan Szanto had objections to this decision. On the opposite side, Antal Apro proposed that the Deputy Minister of Foreign Affairs should immediately be charged with the preparation of the declaration of neutrality.

Following the Party's decisions, a meeting of the Cabinet was immediately held. Nagy presented the Cabinet with one proposition: It must, as a matter of principle, take a stand on the question of Hungarian neutrality. If the Soviet Government did not quickly furnish an explanation for this new invasion, the Hungarian Government would renounce the Warsaw Pact, declare Hungary's neutrality, and, through an appeal to the United Nations, demand that the four great powers (including the Soviet Union) help defend the neutrality of Hungary.

This would be only one aspect. The other would be to offer the Soviet Union definite guarantees. The Russians were afraid that Hungary, once it withdrew from the Warsaw Pact, would become a member of the Western bloc. Could they want a better guarantee than the recognition of her neutrality by the Big Four? There was, in the first place, an excellent precedent. Though it had occurred under other conditions, the declaration of Austria's neutrality had solved a problem that had appeared to be insoluble. Hungarian neutrality would mean that it could no longer be used as a base by the Soviets, nor could it allow Western troops to be stationed on its soil. For the Russians, this would be a solution less advantageous, perhaps, than to have bases in Hungary; but it would not threaten dangerous consequences.

Istvan Dobi, in his capacity of President of the State, was pleased with Nagy's proposals. The only objections raised by members of the Cabinet concerned questions of international law. In truth, the Warsaw Pact, as well as the agreement reached between Nagy and Mikoyan, was being trampled under the boots of the returning Soviet army. So far as the first Soviet intervention was concerned, it could always be claimed that it had come as a result of an appeal by the Hungarian Government. But now? Now the legal Hungarian Government was protesting against the arrival of new Soviet troops on its territory. Under the terms of the Warsaw Pact (not to mention the Soviet declaration of October 30) "the stationing of troops of one state that is a member of the Warsaw Pact on the territory of another state shall be by agreement of all the member states and only with the consent of the state on the territory of which, and on the demand of which, these troops are asked to be stationed."

Had there been previous agreement by all the member states of the Warsaw Pact to this wave of tanks rolling across Hungary? Had they given their consent? Had Hungary given its consent to these Soviet troops, or had it requested them? The Soviet Union was in the process of violating the Warsaw Pact, which it regarded as no more than a piece of paper.

Nevertheless, the Council of Ministers decided again to make one last attempt at a solution. Perhaps Andropov had already received some news from Moscow. It was better to wait, in order not to poison the situation further. The meeting was adjourned until the afternoon without taking any decision other than to give the Foreign Ministry portfolio to Nagy.

The Cabinet met again in the afternoon and, once again adjourned after deciding to ask the Soviet Ambassador to meet with it later.

That meeting took place in a tense, agonizing atmosphere. Andropov was as slippery as an eel. He minimized the military threat. It was an exaggeration, he said, to speak of a massive invasion of Soviet troops. They were only normal replacements. The whole question was of no importance.

Nagy himself spoke in a tone that was both nervous and solemn. More than ten years earlier he had launched an official protest to protect the fruit trees of Hungary from Soviet soldiers. Today, the stake was much larger: it was the whole orchard of Hungary.

Now, a decade later, the same Imre Nagy was speaking who had dared to be the only Communist to raise his voice to tell the truth to Marshal Voroshilov.

Now he told Ambassador Andropov that information from creditable sources, according to which new Soviet formations had crossed the Hungarian frontier, had reached the Government of the Hungarian People's Republic. He demanded the withdrawal of these troops. He said that Hungary had decided to renounce the Warsaw Pact without delay and to proclaim the country's neutrality. The Government would call on the United Nations and demand that the Big Four defend that neutrality.

Andropov listened to the protests and took note of the Government's demand. He promised to ask Moscow for an immediate reply.

One after another, the principal members of the Cabinet gave their support to Nagy. The most vehement of all was Janos Kadar, his future successor. "What happens to me is of little importance," Kadar said, "but I am ready, as a Hungarian, to fight if necessary. If your tanks enter Budapest, I will go into the streets and fight against you with my bare hands!"

As soon as Nagy's Government reached its decision, the heads of all the diplomatic missions in Budapest were informed of developments. Nagy addressed a cablegram to Dag Hammarskjold, Secretary-General of the United Nations, informing him of the situation and requesting that the Hungarian question be put on the agenda of the General Assembly's eleventh session, which was about to begin, for urgent action. Hastily, he directed Geza Losonczy to make a full report to members of the foreign press corps in the capital, and he himself went to Radio Budapest to report to the people.

"People of Hungary!" he said. "The Hungarian National Government, imbued with a profound sense of responsibility toward the Hungarian people and toward history, and giving expression to the unanimous will of Hungary's millions, declares the neutrality of the Hungarian People's Republic. The Hungarian people, on the basis of independence and equality, and in accordance with the spirit of the United Nations Charter, wish to live in sincere friendship with their neighbors, the Soviet Union, and all the peoples of the world.

"The Hungarian people wish to consolidate and to develop further the achievements of their National Revolution without joining any power blocs. The century-old dream of the Hungarian people is being fulfilled. The revolutionary struggle fought by Hungary's past and present heroes has at last carried the cause of freedom and independence to victory. This heroic struggle has made it possible for this country to reevaluate its relations with other countries from the viewpoint of its own fundamental interest: neutrality. We appeal to our neighbors, to countries near and far, to respect this unalterable decision of our people.

"Our people are truly more united in this decision than ever before in their history. Workers of Hungary, work and sacrifice with revolutionary zeal! Support law and order in our country! Defend and strengthen free, independent, democratic, and neutral Hungary!"

The die was cast. The decision had been made public.

Everything indicated that, now, the country understood Nagy and understood the gravity of the situation. All the things that Nagy had sought for eight long days—complete understanding of the responsibilities, a balance of public opinion, and unreserved rallying of public opinion behind the Government—all these were won suddenly, as though by the waving of a magician's wand.

At eleven o'clock that morning, important negotiations had been begun between the representatives of the Government, the unions, and the various revolutionary organizations. The question at issue was the halting of strikes and the resumption of work. The negotiators were unable to reach an agreement and were forced to adjourn until 8 p.m. Nagy had delegated Ferenc Erdei and Zoltan Vas to represent him.

The meeting began in an atmosphere of tension, but with an air of confidence. With total frankness, Erdei drew a picture of the complex situation. He said that the smallest incident could set fire to the powder train. It was now up to the nation to prove its maturity.

This was the same Erdei who, hardly a week earlier, had been driven from the balcony of the Parliament Building and who had been dismissed from leadership of the Peasants Party. Now he was heard with patience and even approval by the great majority of workers and intellectuals present. After hearing an analysis of the economic situation by Zoltan Vas, the meeting voted unanimously to support the Government. The Revolutionary Committees of the eighteen largest factories in Budapest, of the transport workers, and of the three largest workers' districts sent an appeal to all miners, to all gas and electricity workers, to transport and industrial workers, as well as to all intellectuals. This appeal proclaimed that their "unqualified confidence in the government [was] fully justified," and it urged all wage-earners to go back to work.

In spite of the dangers, Nagy was not discouraged. At last, work would be resumed and life would return to normal. It would have been better to have accomplished this earlier, but, perhaps, it was not too late. "Unqualified confidence in the Government is fully justified!" At last, it had come. If only Moscow would understand!

In any case, he must act as though everything were happening for the best. For the first time in eight days, he went home to Orso Street to sleep. He felt exhausted and filled with a dull anguish. But his conscience was tranquil. Come what may, he had done everything that he could.

Nagy's automobile slipped silently through the deserted streets. He was confronted by an imposing spectacle. The city was plunged in darkness. Street lights were almost non-existent. But in every window a candle burned. Tomorrow, November 2, was the Day of the Dead (All Souls' Day). Budapest's thoughts were on those who had fallen for liberty.

The spectacle was dramatic and sublime. The twinkling little lights seemed to be saying in a small whisper that perhaps, all the same, these cruel sacrifices will not have been in vain.

The next morning, on awakening, Imre Nagy learned that Janos Kadar had disappeared during the night.

Moscow's Decision

There is no reason to suppose that Mikoyan had not been sincere in negotiating an agreement with Nagy, Kadar, and Tildy for the withdrawal of Soviet troops from Hungary and the renunciation by Hungary of the Warsaw Pact. When he had consented to the proposals of the Hungarians—armed as he was with full power to do so—he had not as yet become aware that the attitude in Moscow had already changed. By the time he had returned to the Soviet capital, the decisions arrived at a few hours earlier in Budapest were already out of date, and he was confronted with a conflicting decision handed down by the Presidium. This supreme Communist body had decided that it would not tolerate Hungary's departure from the socialist camp and her reorientation toward the right through renunciation of the Warsaw Pact and renunciation of the "dictatorship of the proletariat." If necessary—and all the Soviet leaders were certain it would be—the Russians would oppose such moves by force of arms.

Such considerations certainly might have impelled the Soviet leaders to decide on a course of action diametrically opposed to the principles it had laid down hardly forty-eight hours earlier. But to assign this step to precipitancy or to morality would be as superficial as it would be to ignore these same two factors. If it is true that the real leaders of the Kremlin were lacking in well-defined and carefully thought-out political conceptions—or that these leaders were likely to be embarrassed by unforeseen events—it is no less true that they were not lacking in intelligence and that they had steady nerves. Thus, if the fact that they had given their word meant nothing to them, they would nonetheless not be too happy to have the entire world witness to the lightness with which they would break a newly-made promise.

Any real attempt to explain the Russian about-face as the result of only one factor would be false. The new decision was provoked by a variety of factors, all of which became simultaneously pressing. There are a few cases in history in which a great number of material factors have converged toward the same final result, while, simultaneously, a small number of moral considerations have been moving in the exact opposite direction. The tragedy of Hungary may be classed among such exceptional cases.

First of all, there were the interests of the Soviet empire. With the exceptions of Beria, who had already been executed, and of Malenkov, who supported him for a while, the Soviet leaders were in favor of maintaining the indivisibility of the empire built by Stalin. Convinced of the superiority, and, above all, of the strength of their regime, they would look upon the surrender of even a minute part of the Soviet sphere as an act of treason—even more so if there were any likelihood that the abandoned part might fall under the influence of the opposite camp. In spite of all differences in tactics and methods, and in spite of all personal animosities, the Soviet leaders were unanimous on that point.

Should Hungary leave the framework of the Warsaw Pact, the result would pose a threat to the Soviet empire such as it had not known since the beginning of World War II. The consequences, insofar as the other people's democracies were concerned, would be serious. Once Hungary was outside the Warsaw Pact, what arguments could be used to keep the Poles and Czechs in line if they should present the same demands? Acceding to Hungary's demands would undoubtedly arouse hopes of independence in such countries as Latvia, Lithuania, and Esthonia, which only recently had become autonomous republics within the Soviet Union. Then, too, nationalist sentiments would be strengthened in the Ukraine, in Georgia, and in Byelorussia. Once such a process of disintegration was allowed to begin, who could say where it would end?

On the other hand, there was no doubt that a new Hungary would benefit from the political sympathies of the West, even in terms of material support. Already, President Eisenhower had increased the U.S. offer to $20,000,000 for aid to Hungary, and the flow of gifts from all over the world, which had just begun, was likely to increase. The West would certainly seek to make of Hungary a "window on the West," just as it had of West Berlin. The rise in the Hungarian standard of living, thus displayed, would exercise such an attraction among the peoples of the other Communist countries that the Soviet Union and its "superior socialist system" would be seriously shaken.

The leaders of the Soviet Union were not the only ones who were worried by the course of events in Hungary. The heads of the "fraternal parties" in the other people's democracies were in the grip of an unprecedented panic. While Mikoyan was in Budapest— the period when *Pravda* began speaking more gently of the rebellion—*Scinteia* (in Bucharest) and *Neues Deutschland* (in East Germany) continued to proclaim with all their energy that Hungary was the scene of a savage counter-revolution and to launch threats in the direction of Budapest. Otto Grotewohl, East Germany's Premier, sent an anguished cry toward Budapest: "Do you wish to nullify all the victories we have won? Do you wish to abolish the socialist victories of the last ten years?" Walter Ulbricht, Secretary-General of the German Communist Party, warned: "The people must be vigilant. Those who make any concession to the forces of reaction, be they ever so slight, will end by paying with their lives." But it was Antonin Zapotocky, the Czech Premier, whose attitude was the most revealing of the state of nerves in the satellite countries. He said over the radio: "In neighboring Hungary, a counter-revolution has been raging for several days. It has unleashed a fascist white terror against the workers. Its hands are soiled with the blood of slain workers as well as with that of simple folk of all classes of society. The Hungarian reactionaries, hand in hand with the Western imperialists, are seeking to realize a plan which has long been in preparation and which is aimed not only against the people's power in Hungary but against all the socialist countries and against world peace."

All these leaders, seized by a nameless terror, launched desperate appeals not only toward their own people, but also toward their protectors in Moscow. Countless times during these days the telephone sounded in the offices of Khrushchev, Bulganin, Molotov, and Kaganovich, bringing the lamentations or supplications of Ulbricht, Siroky, Gheorghiu-Dej, Zhivkov, and their acolytes. And these men were not satisfied with pleading; they also threatened. If the Hungarian situation were not immediately put in order, there would be nothing left for them to do except hand in their credentials. The Soviet leaders certainly understood that the Stalinist edifice was beginning to crack at its foundations.

The opinions of the military leaders must also have carried great weight. In their eyes, nothing could justify the abandonment of the excellent strategic position that Hungary provided. Apart from the fact that it provided airbases and that, when the time arose, it would provide maneuverability to infantry and tanks, the territory of Hungary also provided Russia with a great advantage in the rocket era, being, as it was, near to many parts of Western Europe and, in particular, Italy. The marshals and the generals were indignant that they had not been given a free hand to crush the uprising in its first days and that they had been ordered to withdraw their troops from the capital at a time when, with even their limited means, victory seemed so close. The Soviet army had been forced to leave Budapest looking as if it had been defeated. If it were now to be obliged to leave all of Hungary under the same circumstances, who would be able to take responsibility for the defense of the other territories and for the army's morale? The flabby lack of resolution on the part of the political leaders could have catastrophic consequences. Thus, the military leaders were pressing for swift and energetic action.

The international situation, instead of interfering with a new Soviet move in Hungary, rather favored it. The attack on Suez had profoundly shaken, on the one hand, the Western world and, on the other, Asia; entirely apart from the question of the timeliness of the British-French-Israeli action, it seemed that Britain and her allies were at the moment taking advantage of the events in Hungary to pursue their own ends in the Middle East. The Soviet leaders felt themselves justified in reversing the situation; why should they not take advantage of the confusion created by the

Suez affair, which had distracted attention from Hungary in the General Assembly and forced that body to concentrate on the conflict in the Middle East? Then, too, the Suez affair had divided the West: the French and British favored pressing their intervention; the United States was for a peaceful settlement. Could a Soviet intervention in Hungary ever be carried out under better conditions or at a better moment?

Finally, the imminence of the presidential election in the United States, when added to all the other circumstances, seemed to the Russians like a veritable gift from the gods. The election campaign tied the hands of President Eisenhower even if he had wanted to act—which, in truth, he was not anxious to do. All the top leaders of international politics knew perfectly well that, by virtue of the Yalta and Potsdam agreements, Hungary lay within the Soviet sphere of interests—and that these agreements remained fundamental, inviolable laws for a world divided into two camps. (The trouble was that these fundamental laws were not known to the "heroic Hungarian insurgents," the citizens of Budapest "who attacked the tanks with their bare hands" and who, it seemed, "had opened a new chapter in the history of humanity.")

On the other hand, what were the considerations in the minds of the Soviet leaders that militated against intervening in Hungary? Almost all were questions of morality rather than of politics. They knew that the whole world would be deeply shocked. They knew that their action would bring "severe reproof" and that it would be bitterly denounced. But what weight would all that have if it were balanced against the benefits that would be derived from maintaining control over a country of ten million souls—a country which had become the westernmost part of its empire, with air and ground-force bases, with rocket-launching bases abuilding, and with deposits of uranium? If it left Hungary, the Soviet Union would suffer a loss of prestige. Rather than that, it would be better to stay. The Suez affair had made it easier from a moral point of view. Had anyone asked the Egyptians if they would welcome the return of foreign soldiers to their soil? But the foreign soldiers had gone back to Egypt. Miracles never last more than three days. The world is stunned. It acts and it talks; but after a few days everything returns to normal. It is not that the Soviet leaders were happy at the turn of events: they would have preferred it if the Revolution had never taken place. But, the situation being what it was, it would be best to act quickly during this most favorable conjuncture of circumstances, rather than to let matters drag on indefinitely.

Some leaders of the Kremlin, however, were delighted by the dilemma. These were the members of the Molotov-Kaganovich group, who were still at that time members of the Party leadership. The events in Poland and, above all, in Hungary, seemed to them to furnish proof of the correctness of their viewpoint. It was the Stalinists who were right, they felt, not Khrushchev. It was easy for them to demonstrate that the events for which Hungary was the stage were the direct consequences of the Twentieth Party Congress and thereby the results of the "heretical" theses of Khrushchev and of his "liberal" tactics. The "Hungarian counter-revolution" would never have taken place if Stalinist principles had been respected and if the iron hand of Rakosi had continued to hold the country in its grip. The proof was there: Khrushchev's policies were weakening the Soviet empire and providing grist for imperialist mills.

To which Khrushchev could respond, as he did, that the responsibility fell back on Stalin—on Stalin and his emulators and his agents. It was their crimes that had sapped the strength of the democratic people's regimes and that had propelled the people into a struggle against authority and against those who were supposed to represent it.

It would be difficult to say which of the groups that held these two viewpoints was right. In truth, both were right. Without Stalin and the crimes of Stalinism, things would not have been where they were. But, on the other hand, the toppling of Stalin's statue in Budapest had been only the aftermath of the symbolical toppling performed by Khrushchev at the Twentieth Congress. Only one conclusion could be drawn from this act: namely, that the contradictions of a Stalinist regime were, in the final analysis, too serious to be maintained when the choice was between the defensive measures recommended by Molotov and the reforms advocated by Khrushchev.

For the time being, what was important to Khrushchev was

not the moral or ideological lessons involved, but, rather, his own position in the Politburo. It was apparent to him that this position was somewhat precarious and that he would have to take the initiative. He had to outdo Molotov in proving the belief to be false that he was a "liberal" and in showing that he cherished the unity of the empire as much as anyone and that he was ready to crush any dissidence or "imperialist maneuver." In short, he had to prevent a coalition of Molotov supporters and generals from forming against him. He must, then, make himself the spokesman for the generals and he must insist, more loudly than anyone else, on intervening in Hungary. His own future, his own life depended on this, and he did not hesitate.

Obviously, the new decision contradicted the recent declaration of the government as well as certain fundamental principles of Marxism-Leninism. There was the frequently quoted statement of Marx: "A people that oppresses another people cannot be free." And Lenin had written: "Even if Finland, Poland, or the Ukraine separated from Russia, it would not be so bad. Those who hold to the contrary are chauvinists. It would be folly to follow the policies of Tsar Nicholas." But what good would it do to raise these questions? The situation had gone far beyond the point where preoccupations with quotations from Marx and Lenin could serve any purpose. Quotations could be found that would prove either side in the argument. The anniversary of the Russian Revolution, November 7, was approaching, and Suslov would have to make the official address. After his return from Budapest, he would not have great difficulty in finding an appropriate text. And, as for maintaining the empire, the policies of Tsar Nicholas were not so bad. . . .

These were the broad lines of the argument presented before the Politburo in Moscow on October 31, 1956. In summing everything up, the question might have been put thus: Should the Soviet Union behave like a great imperialist power or like a great socialist power? The members of the Politburo had no doubt that, in acting like imperialists, they were being socialists.

By the time Mikoyan had returned to Moscow, the decision had been taken. His quick intelligence enabled him to sense immediately what was afoot. The best that he could do, obviously, was to show that he was entirely in agreement with the decision and to support it by providing last-minute information on the counter-revolution and on the fascist assassins who had started it. Had he spoken in another tongue with Nagy in Budapest? Had he made certain promises? Yes, of course. But what importance could Imre Nagy possess when the major interests of international politics were at stake?

The Socialist Achievements

At the seat of the Government in the Parliament Building, the spotlight was on Kadar's disappearance. Where, and why, had he gone? There were many rumors about the circumstances of his disappearance, in all of which the name of Ferenc Munnich figured. One story was that he had asked for a car to take him home and had left in the company of Munnich, heading in the direction of the Soviet Embassy. Another was that he had left alone, but had been overtaken by Munnich in another car. The cars had halted. A brief, violent argument had ensued between the two, after which Munnich, almost forcibly, had pushed Kadar into his car and taken him to the Soviet Embassy. But these were, after all, only rumors.

A few minutes before he had left the Parliament Building, Kadar had made a radio speech in which he had announced the formation of the new Communist Party. "In these momentous hours," he had said, "the Communists who fought against the despotism of Rakosi have decided, in accordance with the wishes of many true patriots and socialists, to form a new Party." That Party's name would be the Hungarian Socialist Workers' Party— a name which, about twenty years ago, had been the official name of the only Communist organization having its roots among the Hungarian workers.[20] The members of the initial committee would be Ferenc Donath, Janos Kadar, Sandor Kopacsi, Geza Losonczy,

Gyorgy Lukacs, Imre Nagy, and Zoltan Szanto. Every one of these had been imprisoned for several years or had been openly opposed to the Rakosi regime; and, with the exception only of Kadar, none of these had had any role in the fake trials or in the executions of their fellow comrades. The first four had grown up in Hungary in the Hungarian Workers' Movement; the other three were "Muscovites," but there was no doubt that every one of them shared the views of Kadar, who had emphasized: "The new Party now defends and will continue to defend the cause of democracy and of socialism, the realization of which should be achieved not by servile imitation of foreign examples but in compliance with the economic and historical peculiarities of our own country, as supported by Marxism-Leninism (cleansed of Stalinism and of dogmatism) and by the teachings of scientific socialism and the revolutionary and progressive traditions of Hungarian history and culture."

These outspoken statements became even more heated and resolute when Kadar mentioned those Communists who had participated in the overthrow of the Rakosi regime. "In their glorious uprising," he had said, "our people have shaken off the Rakosi regime. They have achieved freedom for the people and independence for the country. Without these, there can be no socialism. We can safely say that the ideological and organizational leaders who prepared this uprising were recruited from among your ranks. Hungarian Communist writers, Hungarian journalists and university students, and the youth of the Petofi Circle, and thousands and thousands of workers and peasants, and veteran fighters who had been imprisoned on false charges—all fought in the front line against Rakosi despotism and political hooliganism. We are proud that you have honestly stood your ground in the armed uprising. . . . You were filled with true patriotism and with loyalty to socialism."

And he had been inflamed with hatred when he had spoken of the Party "which through the criminal policy of Stalinism's Hungarian representatives—Rakosi and his clique—degenerated into a purveyor of despotism and national slavery." Despotism and national slavery! Nobody had ever made a more annihilating judgment of the Hungarian Communist Party. "This adventurist policy," Kadar had continued, "unscrupulously frittered away the moral and ideological heritage which, in the old days, you acquired through honest struggle, through the sacrifice of blood in the fight for our national independence and our democratic progress. Rakosi and his gang gravely violated our national decency and pride. They disregarded the sovereignty and the freedom of our nation, and then lightheartedly wasted our national wealth."

This was Janos Kadar's best and most moving statement during the Revolution—and probably throughout his whole life. This was the statement of a man who had decided to take part with his whole being in the great task which faced his country. He asked people to join his new Party. He asked the other democratic parties—and first of all the Social Democrats—for cooperation, and he unalterably supported "the Government's decision concerning the withdrawal of all Soviet troops.

Why, then, had he left? Why had he deserted Nagy and the Party?

On Friday, he was sought everywhere. Some leaders of the new Party thought that he had been instrumental in planting the fears that were voiced for his safety. But his apartment was empty. There was no news of him.

Perhaps he had become frightened.

Kadar was known to have been upset by the death of Imre Mezo, an old friend, and by the attack on Party headquarters in Republic Square and the summary executions by the revolutionaries. Could he have been afraid that these manifestations of hatred of the Communist leaders would continue and intensify and even turn against him? Perhaps. In his last speech as a member of the Nagy leadership, he had emphasized the dangers of counter-revolution: "Hungary's youth, the soldiers, the workers and peasants, have not spilled their blood in order to see Rakosi's tyranny replaced by the tyranny of the counter-revolution," he had said. But he had been speaking of a danger against which it was necessary to fight, not of one before which one fled.

Perhaps he did not consider himself qualified for further political activity. His role in the past was replete with contradictions, muddled by confusions and waverings. Unlike Nagy, in whom there had been a clear consistency, whose every act fitted precisely into his character and followed a logical course, Kadar's career raised many questions as to where, precisely, he had stood in the Hungarian struggle.

It was Nagy, during his first term as Premier, who had brought about Kadar's release after several years in prison under the Rakosi regime. But, after Nagy's fall, Kadar had entered the Politburo headed by Gero, Rakosi's right hand. And worse, he had been Minister of the Interior at the time when Rajk was executed. Within the Party, the word was that he and Revai had voted against the execution. But it was also said that Kadar had stood beside the gibbet when Rajk died.

There was also this damaging fact: at the beginning of the year when Rakosi was under pressure, he, Rakosi, had, in order to remove from his own shoulders as much of the responsibility for Rajk's death as he could, played for the entire Central Committee a tape recording which had been made in Rajk's prison cell without the knowledge of the participants. On it were to be heard the voices of Kadar and Farkas seeking to persuade Rajk by every possible means to admit the charges against him in the interests of the Party, even though these charges were entirely fabricated. It was typical of Rakosi—and wholly in the Stalinist tradition—that, having dispatched Kadar and Farkas to Rajk's cell to wring from him a confession that could be used to support a death sentence, he dispatched on their heels another team to record the manner in which they carried out their mission. The tape would serve well to absolve Rakosi himself, should that be necessary, or for use against Kadar and Farkas. Kadar must have known all this, and he must have known that there would be Communists who would take little pleasure in his new rise to Party leadership. He may even have feared that their influence would be used against him.

Possibly these were among the reasons underlying his departure. While there were some in the Government who thought he had gone over to the Russians, others, Nagy among them, refused to believe it. After all, Kadar had openly embraced the cause of the Revolution and had publicly demanded the withdrawal of the Soviet troops. It was Nagy's belief that, under these circumstances, his defection to the Russians was unthinkable—in fact, impossible. And yet, Nagy felt that wherever Kadar had gone and for whatever reasons (whether it was out of fear or out of a desire to withdraw from political life), he should have told Nagy of his plans in advance, if only because he owed his liberty to Nagy.* It was not so long since Kadar had handed him for signature a document containing these lines: "These partisans of the Communist ideal have confidence in the future." Beneath these words were the signatures, side by side, of Janos Kadar and Imre Nagy.

And yet, it seemed, Kadar's confidence had been shaken.

The important thing for Nagy at this point was to make sure that there would not be the slightest provocation that could be used as a pretext for a new Soviet intervention in the country's affairs. Although the number of Soviet troops in the country continued to grow, Nagy strictly forbade any hostile gesture on the part of the Hungarians. When Soviet tanks began encircling all airfields, the Hungarian soldiers wanted to open fire. Nagy ordered them to offer no resistance. Under the circumstances, an armed struggle would have been suicidal.

Only calmness, coolness, and discipline would now, so Nagy felt, save the situation. He was informed that the radio network had authorized the broadcast of anti-Soviet statements. He sent Jeno Szell, an old militant in whom he had great confidence, to take charge, directing him to see to it that not only the old Stalinists were denied access to the microphones, but also that the revolutionaries were prevented from making inflammatory statements. He forbade the flourishing newspapers to print any provocative articles. He summoned to head the press service another of his old followers, Miklos Vasarhelyi, who imposed a requirement for governmental authorization before any new newspapers could be published.

Happily, Nagy was not alone. Kadar had left, but others—men who were the most responsible political leaders in the country and who commanded the most respect—ranged themselves at his side.

From Pecs came Bela Kovacs, the unchallenged leader of the Smallholders Party, with the intention of taking active part in the

---

* It was while Nagy was Premier in 1954 that Kadar was freed from the prison to which he had been sent by Rakosi in 1951.

Government. Seeing on the list of ministers the names of some who had been compromised under the Rakosi regime, Kovacs experienced a moment of hesitation, but then he saw where his duty lay. The Government's need, he told himself, was—if it were to face its grave situation before the rest of the world—for a strong national unity combined with an awareness of the times and a capability of exerting force for peace and order.*

The support brought to Nagy by the Protestant churches could be precious. Lajos Ordas, the Lutheran bishop who had spent two years in prison under Rakosi and who had not been able to resume his office until the Revolution, called on his flock to forget the past and to join in rebuilding the country. Another Protestant bishop, the Calvinist Laszlo Ravasz, took a similar position. Inviting his followers to beware of both anarchy and reaction, he exclaimed: "Let no one dare to think of reestablishing the system of the past."

It was obviously of the utmost importance that Cardinal Mindszenty make a similar declaration of faith in the new national union and that he recognize the efforts of the Government. Nagy asked Zoltan Tildy and Pal Maleter to negotiate with the Cardinal. They met with him once, but their negotiations did not bring the desired result.

The situation was equally delicate in regard to relations between the Government and the Social Democratic Party. Nagy had reserved a portfolio for this party at the top of his limited Cabinet, but he had been informed that the Socialists could not enter the Government until the newly reconstituted Party had had an opportunity to make a formal decision on the question. Meanwhile, the Party leader, Anna Kethly, had gone to Vienna to attend an inter-

---

* On February 20, 1959—twenty-seven months after the defeat of the Revolution and eight months after Imre Nagy's execution, and at the height of the new campaign to bring the Hungarian peasants into the cooperatives—an editorial was published in the Budapest daily *Magyar Nemzet* under the name of Bela Kovacs. The article supports the policy of the Kadar regime. It is impossible to determine the credibility of this editorial since the circumstances of its creation are not known. What is worthy of attention is the fact that Bela Kovacs *seven times* emphasizes in the comparatively short article that he is ill, that he is in bed, and that his faculties are gradually deteriorating.

national Socialist conference. Therefore, it would be necessary to await her return.

Then Nagy decided to see the Socialist leaders himself. He was well aware that it would be to their advantage at this time to remain outside the Government, and thereby, as its opposition, remain in a position to criticize it. It is always more advantageous to make demands than to negotiate with those who present them. Nagy understood that the situation of the Socialists was particularly delicate. They were afraid of being gobbled up by the Communists and would, in any case, prefer to remain in the background of any government headed by a Communist. All this was comprehensible, and yet to think in these days only of the interests of a party could be a grave mistake. When Nagy saw that his arguments were futile and that the Socialists would hold to their original decision, he rose slowly and headed for the coat rack. He took his overcoat and his wide-brimmed hat.

"Very well," he said. "Then I will leave. I will go back to my home. That would be the simplest thing to do. I am sixty years old and my health is not what it was. It is true that we still have the Russians on our backs and that there is danger of a counter-revolution of the right, but if you have taken your stand, what good would it do to insist? After us, the deluge. Suit yourselves."

His gesture carried the day. The Socialists quickly reconsidered and decided to enter the Cabinet. One factor influencing them was the fact that, from Vienna, Anna Kethly was reported as expressing full confidence in Nagy.

Across the country there was a rising tide of opinion in favor of a broad National Assembly. The fear that a dissident government might be formed now subsided. The National Council of Transdanubia voiced its confidence in the Premier after his radio address to the people. The National Councils in the north and the east voiced the opinion that it would be better if the struggle between the parties did not begin until after the withdrawal of the Soviet troops. The Writers' Association also convened in a spirit of unity. There were no attacks against writers who had worked for the Communists, except one by a writer who was no more than a dilettante. The non-Communist writers, most of whom had been condemned to silence for long years by the Rakosi regime, replied in protest. In the November 2 issue of *Irodalmi Ujsag,* Tibor Dery wrote prophetically: "The Revolution has been won, but, if we do not give it time to restore its strength, it can still be crushed. There are those to whose interests it would be to see it vanish. We must unite. We have only one country and one life. I repeat: Unite, and we will not be torn apart."

So it was that the Hungarian Revolution tried to define its program. Until then, it had been a spontaneous and disorganized movement. The rebels knew exactly what they were fighting against, but only in large generalities what they were fighting for. Now, it was necessary to define the Revolution's goals. Among the polyphony of themes, the insistence on the continuation of "socialist gains" became more and more dominant. Delegation after delegation voiced firm opposition to any attempt to restore the old bourgeois system. The peasants proclaimed that they would never surrender their land to the old landowners; the industrial workers insisted on keeping control of the factories. The Workers' Council of Borsod, composed of twenty-eight members, met with Nagy and protested strongly against a restoration "of feudalism." Afterwards, its spokesman, Sandor Burgics, a miner from Ormosbanya, said: "Imre Nagy is firmly on the side of the miners. The entire nation can range itself behind him."

The opposition to any capitalist revival stiffened. Strangely enough, it was a writer who never before had shown any socialist tendencies and who for long years had been condemned to silence, who now showed the most courageous and most touching attitude toward the "socialist gains." This was the novelist Laszlo Nemeth, who outlined in a publication of the Peasants Party a program which the most orthodox Socialists could not have amended. He saw very clearly the interests of the country and he believed more firmly in the future of socialism than did, for example, a man like Kadar. He wrote:

"Hungary has gone quite far along the road to socialism in these last ten years. It has, in truth, become a Socialist country. To ignore this fact simply out of a desire to destroy the old regime would be an error as gross as those committed by the Communists. Refusing to consider the true and progressive situation in our agriculture, the Communists reduced agriculture to its level in Russia after the October Revolution—and this for the sole purpose of instituting a reorganization along Leninist lines."

Emphasizing the fact that the Hungarian people favored socialism, Nemeth affirmed that such peoples as the Poles, the Yugoslavs, or the Indians, who are living under or tending toward a socialist system, would draw away from Hungary if it were to fall back, even though only on the surface, into what these peoples would call a bourgeois democracy. He wrote: "This vigilant attitude is commended to us by the respect which, I hope, we have won among the peoples of the Soviet Union by our attitude, and also by the attention we have created among the best sons of the West. . . . All, after this astounding Revolution, expect exemplary political institutions from us."

All of this, of course, did not mean that the program of the Workers' Councils, or that of a Nemeth, was certain to triumph in the new Hungary without a fight. The fact was simply that, after November 1, the Socialist forces in Hungarian society—or, at least that part of those forces that wished to safeguard the gains under socialism—had regained their confidence and their voice.

Nagy saw all of this clearly, and it tended to reassure him as far as he could be reassured under the circumstances. In any case, one thing seemed evident to him: if it were true that, from the start of the rebellion until the present, events had outdistanced him, it might now, in this second phase, be said that events were justifying his ideas. More and more, the people were coming around to him. Not all of these spoke his language, but the socialist concepts, which had their roots in Hungarian realities, were more and more frequently voiced.

History alone is capable of producing a situation as cruel and as false: at the moment when the Revolution was being consolidated and when the desire to protect the socialist bases of Hungarian life was increasing, Soviet troops were spreading out across the country preparatory to strangling the Revolution in the very name of those socialist ideals. As in the case of Yugoslavia ten years ago, it seemed that Moscow could not believe that anybody else could build a socialist state without Russian help. Or was it that

Moscow, believing it now was possible, had consequently become frightened? The telephone in Nagy's office rang ceaselessly. From Zahony, on the Soviet frontier, came word that the Russians were widening the railroad tracks to accommodate their trains, which use a wider gauge than do those in the West. From Debrecen came news that five hundred armored vehicles had crossed the frontier and were approaching the city. The airfield at Debrecen, like those at Szolnok and Budapest, was encircled by Soviet tanks.

Nagy's only recourse was to protest. One after the other, he sent three verbal notes of protest to the Soviet Embassy. In the first, he proposed that, in conformity with Soviet promises, negotiations begin without delay between Soviet and Hungarian representatives regarding the withdrawal of Soviet troops and the repudiation by Hungary of the Warsaw Pact. Nagy informed the Russians that the Hungarian delegation would be headed by Geza Losonczy. The second note raised the same question from a military point of view, requesting the formation of a mixed commission to set in motion on November 2 plans for the evacuation. The Hungarian delegation, the note said, would consist of Ferenc Erdei, Minister of State, and Pal Maleter, who had been promoted to general. The third note protested against the arrival of additional Soviet troops in Hungary and their movement toward the interior of the country.

Nagy also sent a new message to Dag Hammarskjold, informing him of the state of affairs and calling on him: 1.) to invite the great powers to recognize Hungary's neutrality, and 2.) to ask the Security Council to call upon the Soviet Union to enter into immediate negotiations with Hungary.

Obviously, these messages were simply gestures, not effective measures. The Soviet veto would block any decision by the Security Council. The great powers showed no eagerness to guarantee Hungary's neutrality. The risks involved would be too great. Yalta and Potsdam tied the hands of the powers. London announced that "the Foreign Office was studying the Hungarian note with care." Washington announced that "a State Department spokesman refused comment for the time being on the message of the Hungarian Government relayed by the U.S. Embassy in Budapest."

Early in the afternoon, a verbal note arrived from Yuri Andropov. The Soviet Ambassador informed the Hungarian Government that demonstrators were threatening the Soviet Embassy and that, if the Government was unable to maintain order, he would be obliged to call for the help of Soviet troops.

Nagy reached for the telephone and called Bela Kiraly, who was in charge of the defense of Budapest. He directed the general to leave whatever he was doing and to go immediately to the Soviet Embassy. The Russians could not be permitted to use such a feeble pretext for a new Soviet intervention.

Less than an hour later, there came another verbal note from the Soviet Embassy. The Russians agreed to create a mixed commission with a view to planning the withdrawal of their troops. A Soviet delegation headed by General Malinin would present itself at the Parliament Building the following morning.

What did this mean? Nagy could hardly believe his ears. Was there, then, still hope? His telephone rang again. It was General Kiraly, calling from the Soviet Embassy. When he had arrived there with motorized infantry and armor, there was not a single demonstrator in sight. He had spoken with the ambassador and the incident was closed.

So, then, all was not lost. In spite of the massive invasion of Soviet troops, perhaps there was still a way out and, perhaps, the treacherous path along the edge of the precipice would not end in a fall. Who could say?

During the course of that night—a night filled with uncertainty and mysteriously silent—two Hungarian journalists made their way through the suburbs east of Budapest toward the airfield at Matyasfold. Their observations were published in *Nepakarat,* the newspaper of the National Federation of Hungarian Trade Unions, on November 3:

" 'Where are the Russian tanks?' we asked the sentinel, a member of the newly-formed Hungarian militia.

"The young militiaman wiped his brow. His clothes were dripping from the rain; he had been on guard for several hours in the open. He returned our press cards; then, with a wide gesture, he indicated the surrounding countryside. Toward the airfield were numerous spots of grey and brown, blurred by the rain. One would have said they were bushes, but the long rifles of their artillery betrayed them as tanks encircling the field. Tanks and armored cars were stationed along the edge of the forest; what there might have been back among the trees, we naturally could not tell."

Accompanied by members of the militia, the two journalists approached the Soviet encampment under a driving rain. Some Russian soldiers were bringing water to a white house, in front of which stood an armored car. The soldiers seemed tired and apathetic. The account continued:

"They saluted the Hungarian militiamen, who wore tricolor brassards, and we began to question them. It was a strange interview on the edge of a capital surrounded by foreign troops. What did they know of the reasons for their being here, we wondered?

" 'Where did you come from?' we asked [one of the Russian soldiers].

" 'From Temesvar [a Rumanian city near the Hungarian frontier],' he replied, after a moment's reflection.

" 'And what are you doing here?'

" 'We were told that German fascists had attacked Hungary and that we would have to help defend the country.'*

"We exchanged a look. We had just come through Ulloi Avenue, where, in the pock-marked walls, we could see the kind of aid they would bring. But what could this soldier, who had come from so far away, know of all that? He had never been to Budapest and he asked now what the situation really was. Night had fallen. Bright reflectors illuminated the sodden runway of the airfield. Along the roads there were tanks, and more tanks, and still more tanks. All around them, Soviet soldiers were trying to warm themselves at small fires. These were the army of occupation. It was not the people of Hungary who had called them. Those who had summoned them were long since across the frontier, where they were trying to picture the uprising as a counter-revolution.

"We returned toward the city. The two young men who accompanied us pointed out electric cables that had fallen to the street and the shell holes in the walls of the buildings.

" 'There will be work to be done here,' one said.

---

* The soldiers of other units thought they were being taken to the Suez to "fight against the imperialists." Seeing the Danube, they thought it was the canal.

"The other, a younger boy—seventeen—a fitter in a Budapest factory, said in a low voice:

" 'It's time we got back to our jobs. . . .' "

That same night a reception was held in Moscow in honor of President Kuwatly of Syria. Among those conspicuous by their absence was Khrushchev. It was also noted that Marshal Zhukov and Foreign Minister Shepilov made only brief appearances.

"Black Soup"

It is said that when a man is fatally sick, he frequently experiences a day of euphoria a little before his death, when the functioning of his organs seems almost normal, giving him the illusion that recovery is possible.

In the history of the Hungarian Revolution, that day was November 3.

In the morning, tens of thousands of people hastened toward their places of work. Not all of them had to go by foot, because the streetcars had started to run along those lines where the rails had not been torn up and where the wires were intact. To many, it was a pleasure to be able to climb once again the steps of one of those yellow cars, and they paid their fares almost cheerfully. Many factories had sent out trucks to fetch their workers. The strike was almost over. If there were many who did not go back to work, it was not because they were still on strike, but because it was Saturday, and it hardly seemed worthwhile. By Monday, all the factories and offices would be running full-blast.

There was a bustle around the stations. The first commuter trains bringing workers from the suburbs were running. The first train bringing medicines arrived at the East Station, coming from the west. The big railroad yards at Miskolc announced that traffic had been completely reestablished in its sector. Similar news came in from all corners of the country.

The stores also reopened their doors, the food stores among the first. Queues of shoppers lengthened along the streets, waiting to buy bread and potatoes, and the housewives could be sure that they would not have to return home empty-handed. There was no threat of famine in the capital. In the *espresso* shops, there was already black coffee to be had, and some were even able to serve *patisserie*. On the street corners, chestnut-sellers offered those paper cones of warm nuts which were so welcome in the crisp chill.

Since merchandise was in short supply, some speculation appeared. In one market, a country woman offered eggs at three *forints* each, instead of the customary two *forints*. Members of the militia took her basket of eggs from her and sold them for her quickly at two *forints*, returning her empty basket and the money.

Professors and teachers went back to the schools. Classes would begin again on Monday. The post office resumed deliveries of mail. Glaziers were kept busy; before anything else, they had to replace the broken windows at the hospitals. Locksmiths, barbers, cleaners, and shoemakers were kept so busy that they hardly knew which way to turn. The bakers, who had not stopped working through the rebellion (thus earning the esteem of the entire country), were exhausted and looked forward to a day of rest on Sunday.

In the theaters, where Revolutionary Committees had been elected and where the programs were more or less modified to remove the Rakosi taint, rehearsals were resumed. Motion-picture cameramen, directed by a group of young producers, began filming in the streets a documentary about the uprising.

Newspapers appeared on a normal schedule. Their content was less emotional in tone—and more careful—than during the preceding days, as though their editors had suddenly become more conscious of their responsibilities. Plans for new newspapers were discussed at the press center on Lenin Boulevard. The Szechenyi Library, the country's largest, which was seriously damaged in the fighting, published an appeal that was a touching sign of the rebirth of confidence in the future. It asked the people to contribute documents on the Revolution. It said: "The library will consider as confidential any material received before the victory of the Revolution is definitive."

On the initiative of young university students, the Writers'

Association started to collect money for the families of the martyrs of the Revolution. They placed big green boxes on the most frequented spots in the capital. There was no guard at the side of the boxes. And the *forints* accumulated there in higher and higher heaps.

In apartments and offices the telephones jangled ceaselessly. In these days the radio was the pulse of the public life and the telephone the pulse of private life. Relatives who were separated, friends whose flats were far from each other, and lovers on both sides of the Danube kept contact by these telephone calls. "How are you?" "Is there still any fighting in your quarter?" "Have you enough to eat?" "Do you still love me?" Thousands of questions and answers were exchanged. During the days of the heaviest fighting, most of the lines became silent; but on Saturday they came alive again, burning and gay.

Automobiles from abroad, driven by journalists or members of the Red Cross, were quickly surrounded wherever they stopped. Sometimes the foreigners offered the Hungarians cigarettes from their country, or tins of sardines, or chocolate bars—items rare in the diet of Budapest. Some people fought for these gifts; others drew away, insulted and humiliated by such scenes.

What was it that filled the people with so much confidence and optimism, when they knew that, never since 1945, had the Soviet threat to their country been so serious? It was a hope which had been born in the days of combat and which now—surely after a victory—was being reinforced. Hungary was not alone. The West, the United Nations, would not allow her liberty, won at the cost of so much sacrifice, to be endangered. Every new radio announcement heralding the shipments of medicines and food and funds from abroad served to fortify this hope. So did every tin of meat or stick of chewing gum handed out in the street. And so did every word of praise from the West. Rumors spread like wild-fire: an airplane carrying sixteen officials of the United Nations to Budapest had landed at Prague. The daily *Valosag* published an exclusive story: A young revolutionary, driving a car, had arrived at the Austro-Hungarian frontier during Thursday night. He had spoken with United Nations troops stationed all along the frontier. The soldiers had told him that their units, composed of British and

American troops, had been put on an alert status, though they would not cross the frontier until formally invited to do so by Imre Nagy.

Neither story was true. But both were nonetheless characteristic of the state of mind of the people. What was true was that the Security Council had placed the Hungarian question on its agenda on Friday night. The people might have asked themselves why it was not an emergency session of the General Assembly which was considering the question (as was so with the Suez question), instead of the Security Council, in which the Russians had the veto power. But the average Hungarian was ignorant of such subtleties. And if he were indignant to learn that the Soviet delegate Sobolev had characterized the reports of the arrival of new Soviet troops in Hungary as "unfounded," he was considerably reassured to hear the radio announce in its broadcast on Saturday, at 5:30 a.m., that Henry Cabot Lodge, the United States delegate, had said firmly: "The United Nations cannot remain a passive spectator to the events in Hungary." There were few who would suspect that this was only a pious hope and not a statement of fact. And no reader of the Budapest papers was aware of this statement which appeared in the *New York Times* that same day: "The big Western powers appear to have decided to keep the Hungarian question to one side for the moment, until such time as it becomes clear that the anti-Soviet rebellion has either attained its objectives or has been checked."

Just as on the preceding days, the people were reassured by the knowledge that the United Nations continued to interest itself in the Hungarian situation. If the debate was adjourned until Saturday night, they reasoned, it was undoubtedly a sign of the West's concern for the matter, and there were few who suspected it was a sign of weakness.

"The eyes of the entire world are upon us," was a phrase repeated at every Budapest street corner. The implication was that they could not be robbed in broad daylight of a cause that was under such close scrutiny.

But the principal reason for reassurance lay in the change that the people believed they saw in the attitude of the Russians. They saw that the hopes inspired by Andropov the evening before were being confirmed. At midday, a full Soviet military delegation presented itself before the Parliament Building to begin negotiations with the Hungarian delegation. They were given full military honors. The brilliantly bedecked officers, headed by General Malinin who wore a green uniform, his breast covered with decorations, climbed the steps on a thick red carpet.

These negotiations began in a strained atmosphere. The precise question as to whether or not the Soviet soldiers would leave Hungary was never put forth. The discussion covered only the conditions and circumstances of their withdrawal.

The Soviet delegation had arrived armed with its demands. The Hungarian Government would have to repair those monuments, in honor of the Soviet soldiers who had fallen during the war, which had been damaged during the rebellion. It must guarantee that these monuments, as well as the tombs of Soviet soldiers who had fallen in Hungary, would be respected in the future. The last Soviet units to be evacuated from the country would leave after a ceremony that would demonstrate that these troops were not members of an army of occupation. In general, the Soviet demands were concerned with such questions of the honor of the army as were aimed at restoring army morale as well as at improving Hungarian-Soviet relations. The Hungarian delegation had no reason to refuse these demands.

However, no date was fixed for the withdrawal of the Soviet troops, the Soviet officers emphasizing that this would require, understandably, some time. There was also no agreement reached on the technical details of the evacuation.

After this promising beginning, the two delegations adjourned their sessions until 10 p.m. This time, in following the usual diplomatic courtesies, the Hungarian officers would go to the Soviet headquarters at Tokol, near Budapest. Until that time, the Soviet delegation promised, no additional Soviet convoys would cross the frontier into Hungary.

For a moment, Nagy asked himself whether the bride was not too beautiful. Not only did the Soviet demands seem entirely natural to him, but he had been ready to make similar proposals himself. As much by temperament as by conviction, he, too, had deplored the mutilation of the monuments to the Soviet dead. Those honored dead had, after all, fallen in the war against Hitler; and in the tombs that had been profaned rested the remains of soldiers who had died driving the German and Hungarian fascists from the country. Much had happened in Hungary since then, it was true, but whatever role the Russians had later played, whatever their attitude toward him had been, Nagy had never for a moment forgotten the heroic role played by the Red Army in the war against the Nazis. There was nothing wrong in having overthrown the statue of Stalin—indeed, the act had served a purpose—but Stalingrad was still Stalingrad, in spite of everything, and Nagy had never thought of letting the Russians leave Hungary like a defeated army. He was delighted that the Russians had proposed a solemn ceremony with martial hymns, speeches, and waving flags; handkerchiefs would be waved as a sign of farewell.

It was true that the conciliatory attitude exhibited by the Soviet military delegation conformed in no way with the news that new Soviet units were continuing to roll across the frontier throughout Friday night. There were reports that, along with the Soviet tanks and armored cars, there were to be found railroad workers who had taken command of some rail stations. And at Eger, for example, thousands of Soviet soldiers were digging themselves in on the edges of the city. But these developments could, of course, be explained by the Russians' insistence on negotiating their departure from a position of strength. The Russians wanted to leave no impression that they were leaving Hungarian soil either because of pressure from the Hungarian people or because of the pressure of world opinion. They would want to show that they were leaving by their own will, in full awareness of their strength—and only in accordance with the spirit of the Five Principles enunciated at Bandung.

His experiences in Moscow as well as in Budapest had taught Nagy that top-level decisions were often made at the last moment and that, sometimes within the space of a few hours, the most contradictory resolutions could be given birth. There was good reason to believe that—even though the Kremlin may have been in favor of crushing the rebellion at the time that Mikoyan and Suslov had returned to Moscow—the liberals and the moderates had, on Friday, been able to tip the balance toward a peaceful solution. This hypothesis did not seem unreasonable in the light of Andropov's changing attitudes and in the light of the conciliatory views expressed by the Soviet military delegation. Moreover, if one admitted that one of these two tendencies could suddenly take precedence—and this had been shown to be possible during the last two days in the case of those Russians who favored a tough policy— one would also have to admit that the other tendency had succeeded no less suddenly in reversing the situation.

And there were other factors that might also have intervened. After eleven hours of debate, the emergency session of the General Assembly had accepted a United States proposal to bring about a cease-fire and to stop the movement of troops into the Suez. If the Russians had seized upon the Suez affair as a reason for behaving more harshly to Hungary, this U.N. resolution may well have cautioned them to behave a little more prudently, impelling them to try to avoid finding themselves in the painful situation in which Britain and France now found themselves. The moments of hope which Nagy was experiencing were not resulting simply from his own changing moods; they were based to a certain degree on facts, or, at least, on well-founded reasoning. Though this reasoning might, in the end, prove to be false, it was essential that Nagy act as if everything were going well. Though he was powerless to influence the Kremlin, he could still make a great effort to consolidate the situation inside Hungary and to take new measures for the restoration of order.

That Saturday morning, the new Government had taken definite form. The Communists, the Smallholders, and the Social Democrats were each represented by three ministers; the Petofi Peasants Party was represented by two. The revolutionary armed forces also had their representative. The composition of the Government was as follows. Premier and Foreign Minister: Imre Nagy (Communist). Ministers of State (but without portfolios): Zoltan Tildy, Bela Kovacs, and Istvan B. Szabo (all Smallholders); Anna Kethly, Gyula Kelemen, and Jozsef Fischer (Social Democrats); Istvan Bibo and Ferenc Farkas (Petofi Peasants); Geza Losonczy (Communist); and, though he had disappeared, Janos Kadar (Communist). Minister of Defense: Pal Maleter.

Never in the past ten years had a Hungarian Government enjoyed such a measure of confidence among the people. Of this fact, there could be no doubt. Even though the Government had not been formed as the result of free elections, it expressed the will of the people far better than had its predecessors. Certain commentators, even in the Western press, spoke of the Government's "drift to the right." Actually, if such Stalinist personalities as Apro, Tausz, and Nyers—not to speak of Rakosi and Gero—could be regarded as of the "left," then, now that these were all gone, it was true that the Government had drifted to the right. But the new Government really represented a combination of various leanings, some more to the left, others more to the right—although, regardless of this fact, neither the Government as a whole nor any of its members had voiced the slightest criticism of the "socialist gains" or had sought to make an issue of them. On the contrary, all those ministers who were regarded as rightist had come out flatly in favor of those gains. As Anna Kethly had said at Vienna:

"The Hungary of tomorrow will be a socialist state. . . . We must be watchful so that the results of the Revolution do not disappear, as was the case in 1919." It was widely known that Istvan Bibo, a member of the Cabinet, shared the views of Laszlo Nemeth, who had proposed: "The parties in the coalition Government should publish a joint declaration guaranteeing that they will respect certain broad principles of socialism. Industry should continue to be directed by the State, and no property of an area greater than twenty-five to forty holds [one hold = 1.38 acres] should be restored to its old owners. In addition, worker participation in the management of factories and of small cooperatives should be encouraged."

Such were the views of the political leaders of the "right" during the early days of November.[21] In reality, one would have to go back to October, 1918, and to the Government of Mihaly Karolyi in order to find a Cabinet oriented so far to the left.

Order and public security had improved steadily as the National Guard became better organized. The Revolutionary Committee for Maintenance of Order had decided to name General Bela Kiraly as the commander of this militia, with Sandor Kopacsi, until then a colonel in the police, as his adjutant. Mixed patrols circulated through the city. These consisted of militia members and police-men. They answered the most insignificant calls and examined the papers of motorists and pedestrians at night, disarming those who were unable to show membership in either the National Guard or the police force. It could be said that order and security had been almost entirely reestablished.

The last noteworthy demonstration occurred during Friday night at the offices of the Ministry of Foreign Affairs. A group of armed young men had surrounded the building and, on the pretext that members of the AVH were hiding inside, begun searching the offices. They found two locked rooms which could not be opened. The invaders tried to force the locks by firing at them. Outside, their companions assumed that they were in danger and opened fire on the building. Within, the others thought they were being attacked from without, and so they returned the fire. Almost imme-diately leaders of the Revolutionary Forces for Maintenance of Order arrived. These lined the rebels up in order to examine their papers. The leader of the demonstrators wore the insignia of a lieutenant colonel, but his papers showed he was only an army corporal. His "promotion" to the rank of lieutenant colonel was signed by one Jozsef Dudas.

Dudas, commander of an insurgent unit of considerable strength, was one of the most enigmatic and troubling figures of the Revolution. Some foreign correspondents who encountered him considered him one of the heroes of the rebellion; others saw him as a fascist adventurer. He had begun his career in the workers' movement in Transylvania and had been a member of the Com-munist Party, from which he had later been expelled. In 1944, he was a member of a delegation which had been sent to Moscow by the Horthy Government to sound out the possibilities of an armis-tice. After the war he had been elected to the municipal council in Budapest as a representative of the Smallholders Party. At the end of 1946, he had been arrested by Rakosi's men under suspicion of participating in a counter-revolutionary plot. He had been turned over to the Rumanian authorities (Transylvania being, by that time, under Rumanian control). The Rumanians had kept him in prison for seven years. Freed in 1954, he had returned to Budapest and earned his living as a factory worker.

In the course of the uprising, Dudas had succeeded in group-
ing about himself several hundred armed insurgents. They occupied
the offices of *Szabad Nep,* published a daily, the *Magyar Fuggetlenseg,* and founded a "National Hungarian Revolutionary Committee," with himself at its head. During the rebellion, in company
with other leaders of insurgent groups, he had been received once
by Imre Nagy. At first, he had refused to recognize the Government and had kept presenting ever-changing lists of demands.
Later, in the name of national unity, he had set himself up in
opposition to all party rivalry and had declared that he would
oppose all attempts to restore "Stalinism, capitalism, or monarch-
ism." It is difficult to assess his program clearly. One day he would
demand United Nations intervention in Hungary and the next he
would not only reject such a proposal but voice indignant opposition to it. On October 31, for instance, his newspaper had said:
"We want no one from the outside world to come here in place
of the Russians. We no longer welcome foreigners to our country,
because, once they are here, it is too difficult to get them to leave."

Dudas had told a Polish journalist that his program was
"national, revolutionary, democratic, and socialist." He said that
he had entered into direct contact with Moscow in order to "resolve
the situation." In reality, his sole contact with Moscow was by way
of *Szabad Nep's* correspondent in the Soviet capital—a correspondent who, unaware that his newspaper had been seized, had telephoned for information on the situation and had been put through
to Dudas. The rebel leader had immediately told this correspondent, in a firm voice, to go to Khrushchev and Bulganin and to
present them with his demands.

Those who had contact with Dudas were of the opinion that
he was not a man of ill will. In him was combined a sincere desire
for freedom with a strong personal ambition, plus a kind of political
liberalism with an individual aggressiveness. He was willing to
listen to the opinions of others, but, at the same time, he nursed
some abortive Napoleonic tendencies. The chances are that, in
giving the order to attack the Foreign Ministry, Dudas had not
been looking for members of the AVH but that, instead, he had
wanted to install his headquarters there and thus to gain for himself
a hand in the supreme direction of the country's affairs.

But, by this time, Nagy felt strong enough to deal with such adventurers. Irresponsible gunfire, attacks on public buildings, and individual action were no longer to be tolerated. Nagy issued an order for Dudas' arrest, and the order was executed promptly, providing a convincing demonstration of the Government's strength.*

There was another development which was indicative of the Government's consolidation of power. The Government had called on former members of the AVH to make their identity known, promising that those who were guilty of no brutality would be freed as soon as their cases were examined. The registering of AVH men got under way in perfect order. Men who, two days earlier, had fled for their lives and were hunted through the streets were now unmolested. Confident that the authorities would protect them, they arrived in such numbers on Saturday that most of them were asked to return home and to come back the following Monday.

The organization of the new Communist Party also progressed without incident. The new Party organ, *Nepszabadsag,* was sold freely in the same streets where copies of *Szabad Nep* had been burned a few days earlier. On Saturday, the paper's editorial included these lines: "We will no longer be a Party of a million members. We will operate in a more modest framework, with limited resources. Those who wish to join the Party must understand that their membership will bring them neither an important post nor an elevated position. In short, it will bring them no advantage that would distinguish them from other people. Daily tasks, arduous and devoid of any gratitude, will be their lot. We face a harsh and laborious future, inconspicuous, without honor, without any false supremacy guaranteed by bayonets. We have lost much, but we have regained the honor of socialism."

Party organizations were being formed in the large provincial cities, such as Szeged and Debrecen. On Saturday afternoon, at the corners of the main boulevards and Wesselenyi Street, young Communists distributed the new Party's first leaflet from a balcony. It contained passages from Kadar's radio speech: "The

---

* Though Dudas was soon released, he was again arrested by Kadar's militia and executed in January, 1957.

heroic uprising of our people has delivered us from the Rakosi regime." Neither those who distributed the leaflets, nor those who read them, were aware that the leader of the new Party had disappeared.

At the same time, the responsible political leaders were making new efforts to make the Soviet Union understand that the new Hungary would not be its enemy—that, on the contrary, its friendship would be stronger than had been that of a satellite Hungary under Rakosi. Imre Nagy received the Austrian minister and thanked him for the note by which he, Nagy, had been informed that the Austrian Government was clearing a zone along the frontier to prevent the return of previous Hungarian political emigres, with or without arms. Ferenc Farkas, the Minister of State, announced on the radio: "We desire, once our neutrality has been recognized, to enter into the most friendly and sincere relations with all other socialist countries, in economic as well as cultural affairs."

Toward the end of the afternoon, the Hungarian Government called a press conference for foreign correspondents in the Gobelin Room of the Parliament Building. Here, Tildy and Losonczy answered questions in the name of the Government. The journalists were interested principally in the progress of negotiations between Hungary and the Soviet Union regarding the withdrawal of Soviet troops. Losonczy said: "The negotiations have already yielded some results. We hope that others will follow. There has been a certain relaxation of tension." Tildy, however, made it clear that "the reply of the Soviet Union has thus far been satisfactory" to Premier Nagy.

Later, in answer to a question as to whether the Soviet Union had imposed conditions for its evacuation of the country, Tildy replied: "The restoration of national independence cannot be bound by conditions. Only after we have achieved the evacuation can friendly relations be reestablished."

There was an atmosphere of drama about the conference. The Government representatives did their utmost to answer the questions frankly, but they did not want to risk injury to Soviet sensibilities. Tildy noted that the Hungarian troops had been ordered to refrain from any hostile act. "I believe," he said, "that such a tragic conflict cannot be allowed to take place. It would be terrible for the Hungarian people, for the Soviet Union, and for the entire world. I do not think that it will come to that."

At the end of the conference, Losonczy made a short statement setting forth the broad lines of the new Government's policies: "The Government has announced that it will make no concession as far as the positive accomplishments of the past twelve years are concerned: for example, the agrarian reform, the nationalization of industry, and the social legislation. It demands also that the gains of the present Revolution remain intact: notably our national independence, our equality of rights, and our freedom to build socialism, not on the basis of dictatorship but on the basis of democracy. The Government is determined not to tolerate the restoration of capitalism in Hungary.

"I wish to emphasize in this grave situation that the Hungarian Government wishes to settle all questions now in dispute between the Soviet Union and the Hungarian People's Republic by negotiation, and that it wishes to avoid any friction between the two countries. This is our wish, not only because we are a much smaller country than the Soviet Union, but also because we wish to maintain and even strengthen our good relations with the Soviet Union, as with all countries that are building socialism. I emphasize this because, even in the socialist countries, there are signs that the character and the policy of the present Hungarian Government are misunderstood and misinterpreted."

Shortly after the press conference, Cardinal Mindszenty went on the air with an address that was to become the subject of a violent controversy which has not yet subsided. On questions of foreign policy, it must be said, the address tended to be reassuring and to reflect a realistic understanding of the situation.

"Even in our difficult situation," the head of the Hungarian Catholic Church said, "we hope that we do not have enemies, because we are hostile to no one. We desire to live in friendship with all peoples of all countries. . . .

"Our entire situation depends on what the Soviet empire, that vast empire of 200,000,000 inhabitants, will do with its troops stationed within our borders. The radio announces that the number of Soviet troops in Hungary has increased. We are neutral. We give the Russian empire no cause for bloodshed. Do not the leaders of the Russian empire realize that we will respect the Russian people even more if they do not oppress us? It is only an enemy people which is attacked by another country. We have not attacked Russia, and we hope that the Soviet military forces will soon leave our country."

This attitude reflected the country's interests, and it promulgated nothing which was likely to be injurious to Soviet sensibilities. But the Cardinal's opinions on internal matters contained many more shadings. On the one hand, he urged the people to resume their work, but on the other, he asserted: "The world must know that the struggle in this country was not a revolution but a battle for freedom." He demanded free elections under international control and open to all parties, and, at the same time, he spoke out against an internal struggle: "The country now needs many things, but it needs as few parties and party leaders as possible."

He emphasized insistently that he placed himself above the parties, but the scornful—and even a little menacing—tones with which he spoke of the coalition Government clashed with his words. He called the Government leaders "heirs to the deposed regime," and added: "Since 1945, after a lost war which for us was purposeless, there was set up here a regime whose heirs now enthusiastically stamp each fragment with the seal of loathing, disgust, and condemnation. That regime has been swept aside by all the Hungarian people. Its heirs should seek no further proof of that fact."

As far as social measures and the demands of the Church were concerned, the Cardinal equivocated to some degree: "I will define the general lines of the practical measures that we must take, since we want to live in a constitutional state and in a classless society and to increase democratic progress. We are in favor of private property within just and equitable limits of our society's best interests. We want to be a country and a nation with a pure cultural and national tradition. This is the desire of all the Hungarian people.

"And as the head of the Hungarian Roman Catholic Church, I declare (as was said by the Council of Bishops in a collective letter in 1945) that we do not oppose the direction of former progress and that we further desire a healthy progress in every field. The Hungarian people understand that we have to care for our institutions, which have a great value and a great past. I say, briefly, to the six and a half million Catholics in this country that within the framework of the Church we will wipe out all traces of the violence and the legal processes that characterized the fallen regime. That is a natural consequence of our ancestral faith and our moral precepts, and of laws which are as old as the Church. . . ."

Even though the Cardinal had said that he did not at that time want to go into detail, his listeners were a little perplexed by his statement in favor of "private property within the just and equitable limits of our society's best interests," and above all, that "within the framework of the Church we will wipe out all traces of the violence and the legal processes that characterized the fallen regime." Was he alluding to the eventual reestablishment of the Church's broad domains, which had been broken up and distributed to the peasants without indemnity to the Church in 1945? Did he regard indemnity as a right?

In general, the import of the speech was largely discounted, even by the faithful.[22] It diminished, rather than augmented, the popularity of the prelate, though obviously, it was in a free country only one freely expressed opinion among many others. It is fitting to emphasize that the speech, since it was broadcasted at 8 p.m. on November 3, could no longer have influenced the course of events. These were already implacably determined. The outcome had already been set in motion, and all attempts to blame this speech for having provoked the Soviet decision are attempts to justify that decision through hindsight.

It was characteristic of the atmosphere of these dramatic hours that whatever the leaders of the Government were trying to accomplish at the summit, the people, the simple inhabitants of Hungary, were trying to accomplish at the base. It was touching to watch the efforts of the people in the countryside and in the cities to explain to members of the Soviet units that continued to advance across the country that the Hungarians were not enemies of the Russians and that they were not counter-revolutionaries.

The Pecs radio broadcasted the following message to the Soviet troops stationed in the city:

"The enemies of the Hungarian people have spread the rumor that a counter-revolution is in progress in Hungary, that power is in the hands of those fascist and reactionary elements which seek to restore the detestable old regime, and that it is for this reason that you have been brought here.

"This is false! The Hungarian people have only taken the power into their own hands. We want to be a country free and independent and democratic. We do not want bankers and large landowners on our backs, but neither do we want Rakosi's Stalinist clique—a clique which has plunged our country into suffering and misery . . . You are Russians. Live the way you want to live. We are Hungarians and we demand that you let us organize our lives in our country in our own fashion. Twelve years ago you brought us our liberty, and we are grateful to you. Why do you wish to take it away today? We want to live in friendship with you, as with all other nations. Russians, our people have suffered greatly. Go back to your own country so that we can begin to live calm and peaceful lives."

This kind of popular diplomacy was being carried on throughout the country. At Dunapentele (formerly Stalinvaros), representatives of the population and of the Russian soldiers reached an agreement to resume their discussion the following morning, November 4, in order to dissipate any remaining misunderstandings. At Bekescsaba, a lieutenant colonel who was a member of the department's Revolutionary Council told a representative of the Hungarian News Agency: "In the course of a conversation, the Soviet commander of a motorized unit stationed in the region told us he had arrived here believing that he was going to fight the fascists and the partisans of a fascist restoration. Our people told him that there was no such thing, that the Hungarian people simply wanted a free and independent existence. They explained to the Soviet commander the painful situation into which the Rakosi regime had plunged the Hungarian people. After that, the Soviet soldiers declared they would never fire on the Hungarian people."

Crowning all these efforts at the "base" by the people themselves, the Hungarian military delegation composed of Ferenc Erdei, of Generals Pal Maleter and Istvan Kovacs, and of Colonel Miklos Szucs, left for its evening meeting at Tokol, a little hamlet on the island of Csepel. They were received at Soviet headquarters by Generals Malinin, Stepanov, and Cherbanin. The time was nearly ten o'clock that Saturday night.

At the same time, with the news of the resumption of Hungarian-Soviet negotiations, the U. N. Security Council, which, on Saturday night, had resumed its debate on the Hungarian situation, now decided unanimously to adjourn until Monday morning. Several delegates voiced doubts as to the sincerity of the Russians, and France's delegate made a blunt allusion to Prague, demanding: "Is this not what Soviet forces are about to repeat in Hungary?" But Sobolev, the Soviet delegate, assured the Council that the negotiations were even then under way, and, with the Hungarian and Yugoslav representatives confirming this fact, the adjournment was voted.

The negotiations were, in fact, in progress. The atmosphere was cordial, even friendly. At eleven o'clock, General Maleter telephoned to General Kiraly in Budapest in order to tell him that all was going well. Until midnight, the Hungarian delegation remained in touch with members of the Government in the Parliament Building, keeping Nagy informed of the progress of the talks.

At midnight, the telephone connection was broken. A man in civilian clothes, who was completely unknown to the Hungarian delegation, burst into the room followed by several armed men. It was General Ivan Serov, head of the Soviet security forces. He announced he was arresting the members of the delegation. The Soviet General Malinin protested forcefully, even exploding into oaths, but, after General Serov had taken him aside and whispered several words in his ears, General Malinin gave the others in the Soviet delegation the order to leave the room and followed them, visibly upset.

Hungary's history contains a precedent for such an incident. In 1544, the Turkish Sultan Suleiman invited to supper a Hungarian lord named Balint Torok. In the course of the banquet, the Hungarian's suspicions were aroused and he expressed a desire to leave. The Sultan, however, insisted he stay, saying, "There is still the black soup," meaning the coffee. At the moment the coffee was served, the Sultan's janissaries hurled themselves on the Hungarian and placed him in irons. Since then, the term "black soup" has been a Hungarian synonym for treason.

Sunday, November 4, 1956

It was toward midnight of that Saturday when Nagy went to bed in the Parliament Building. A few minutes before four o'clock, he was awakened to the news that the Soviet troops had attacked Budapest. His first thought was for the safety of Maleter and the other members of the military delegation. There was no word of their fate. The Soviet military headquarters was not answering its telephone.

Of all the members of the Government, Tildy was the only one in the Parliament Building at that hour. Of Nagy's old friends, the only ones present were Donath and Szilagyi. Calls were sent out for the other ministers. When Bibo arrived, he was still able to reach the building. Bela Kovacs was able to approach only within a few blocks. In the building were also Istvan Dobi, head of the Presidential Council of the Hungarian People's Republic; Istvan Kristof, Secretary of the Council; and Sandor Ronai, President of the National Assembly.

Nagy gathered them all into session. Tildy raised the question of how the news was to be announced to the country. Nagy took that mission upon himself. Donath scribbled the broad outlines of the situation on a piece of paper. Nagy tossed his coat over his shoulders and left his office, making his way through the chilly corridors to the far wing of the building, where there was a radio studio. His ministers followed him. The technicians on duty set up a microphone.

Toward 5 : 20 a.m., Nagy spoke:

"This is Imre Nagy, President of the Council of Ministers of the Hungarian People's Republic, speaking. Today at dawn, Soviet forces launched an attack against the capital with the obvious purpose of overthrowing the legal Hungarian democratic Government.

"Our troops are fighting.

"The Government is at its post.

"I notify the people of our country and the entire world of these facts."

At this moment, the boom of artillery and the crackle of small-arms fire could be heard in the distance.

A few minutes later, the radio broadcasted an appeal to Pal Maleter, the Minister of Defense, and to Istvan Kovacs, head of the General Staff, calling on them to return immediately and resume their duties. Then, after a few more minutes, another communique was read:

"The Hungarian Government calls on the Soviet officers and soldiers to hold their fire. Avoid bloodshed. The Russians are our friends and will remain our friends in the future."

But no one was under any illusion that either of these appeals would be answered.

Gyula Hay, the dramatist, and his wife, arrived then at the radio studio. The writer scribbled a few words on a sheet torn from a notebook, then read the text over the air:

"This is the Hungarian Writers' Association speaking to all writers, scientists, writers' associations, academies, and scientific organizations of the world. We appeal for help to all intellectuals in all countries. Our time is limited. You all know the facts. There is no need to review them. Help Hungary! Help the writers, scientists, workers, peasants, and all Hungarian intellectuals. Help! Help! Help!"

This was also a hopeless plea. There was no hope anywhere.

It was toward six o'clock that Nagy learned of the formation of an opposition government presided over by Janos Kadar. This news was perhaps a harsher blow to Nagy than the Soviet attack had been. As recently as the previous night he had still insisted that Kadar's name be included in the list of Government members. He would have been willing to admit that Kadar had fled out of fear, but he would not have considered it possible that Kadar was a traitor to his country and to Nagy himself. "The supporters of the Communist ideal must have confidence in the future. . . ," Kadar had written. In the future or in the Soviet tanks? What must they have said to make him go their way? Something like this, no doubt: "Comrade Kadar, the future of socialism in Hungary is in your hands. That of the camp of peace, that of world peace. . . . In any case, there is little ahead for you in another Hungary because of your part in the Rajk affair. . . . Well, then . . .?" The stakes had been too big, the character too small.

Cardinal Mindszenty arrived at the Parliament Building. He asked to see Tildy.

"I don't feel very secure in my palace in Buda and so I have come to you to seek your protection . . ."

"Whatever we can offer in the way of protection is at your disposal," he was told.

There was a short pause. Then Mindszenty broke the silence.

"Actually, I also came here to find out what was going on. But I see that you have nothing good to tell me. So I would rather leave. . . ."

By that time, Dobi, Kristof, and Ronai had left. All three were creatures of the old regime. They had nothing to say against the Soviet intervention.

Nagy's telephone rang. Soviet tanks were approaching the Parliament Building. What good would it do to wait longer? The play was over. And all was lost. He had tried to do the impossible. Was it strange that he had failed? He had wanted to be a man among monsters, a Hungarian in a hostile world. It was impossible. He had wanted to be a good Communist and a good patriot at the same time. That, too, was impossible.

A good Hungarian and a sincere friend of the Soviets. Those who had impeded him had been those for whom he had endangered himself—the Kremlin leaders—those in whom he had had confidence, whom he had—why not say it?—served for a while, whom he had not betrayed when they had abandoned him. Now he found himself crushed by these very men—men whose real interests he had respected more than his own and in whom he had believed, even after having once been duped by them. Now they had drawn him into a last ambush.

This was how he was being repaid for a whole life, for so much effort, so much humiliation. This was how he was being repaid for his career of nearly forty years as a militant Communist, for his undermined health, for his faithfulness to the cause, for his sacrifice of personal honor. Soviet tanks, rumbling through the streets of Pest, were coming now to crush him.

In these most difficult hours he had thrown his body as a footbridge across the gulf that separated the Party from the people, Soviet power from little Hungary. Now the gulf gaped wide. Under the weight of the tanks, the fragile footbridge had collapsed and fallen into the emptiness.

And with him, into the vacuum, had gone Hungary's liberty—for, after all, he and it were one. True, he had made mistakes, had shown weakness, had waited too long to act. But even as he was—with all his errors, his faults, his weaknesses, and his delays—his name will be forever linked with Hungary's liberty. Whatever else the judgment of history will be, this would not be contested. Whatever could be saved of his person, there also would be the liberty of Hungary. True enough, he had no desire to give his life as so much fodder. Yet, still and above all, it was of the cause and of the future of that cause that he was, as always, thinking at the moment he stepped into the street in the grey light of that November morning.

The possibilities open to him were severely restricted. The tanks were approaching. There was no question of leaving Hungary. With his closest friends, with all those who, because of their Communist past, were in greatest danger of arrest and of Soviet revenge, he took his place in an automobile, and they started for the Yugoslav Embassy.

They were going to seek asylum.

BOOK III

**The
Finale**

I

Nagy remained twenty-two days in the Yugoslav Embassy. Shortly after he and his friends reached their asylum, a Soviet tank, firing at a window, killed an embassy functionary. It could be that this was an accident and that the incident had nothing to do with the presence in the embassy of Nagy.

During those twenty-two days of Nagy's asylum, the Soviet army, thanks to its enormous material superiority, succeeded in crushing the Hungarian Revolution, except for scattered kernels of resistance that were to hold out in the mountainous regions of Mecsek, Matra, and Bukk until the middle of December. Though the Hungarian youths fought on like heroes, the battle had been lost in advance. When a shot was fired from a window, Soviet tanks would bring the entire building under fire from their artillery. When scattered resistance would start up in a street, the entire population of that street would be dragged from the buildings by force. The destruction was much greater than during the first Soviet intervention. Part of Rakoczi Avenue, the main boulevards, and part of Ulloi Avenue were in ruins. Trains laden with deportees headed for the frontiers; the nation's entire youth was in danger of being taken into captivity.

All of these acts were carried out under the pretext that a

"Revolutionary Workers' and Peasants' Government" had been formed and that this "Government" had called again on the Soviet army to help "defend the supporters of socialism and the socialist conquests." Ferenc Munnich made the first announcement of the constitution of this new Government, broadcasting over a previously unknown transmitter. He said that Antal Apro, Janos Kadar, Istvan Kossa, and himself, all former members of the Nagy Government, had broken with Nagy and resigned to form a new Cabinet. In reality, with the exception of Kadar, the other three ministers had been dismissed from office by Nagy on November 2, along with the bulk of the former members of the Government.

The announcement that it was these men who had formed a "Revolutionary Workers' and Peasants' Government" contained not a grain of truth. Although the circumstances under which it was formed remain confused, it seems much more reasonable to state that it was formed by the Russians. What is certain is that some of its members had fled the country during the rebellion and had crossed into Czechoslovakia, whence they were taken to Moscow. Just as the ancient kings reigned by the grace of God, this Government had been installed by the grace of the Kremlin.

To say that Hungary's history had never known a leadership more thoroughly detested than this "Revolutionary Workers' and Peasants' Government" would in no way be an exaggeration. The people recognized that this government, imposed by Soviet tanks, was neither Hungarian nor revolutionary, since it owed its existence to the fact that the revolutionary movement had been crushed; nor was it a "workers' government," since the workers fought it with all their strength; nor, moreover, did it represent the peasants, since the peasants had nothing in common with it. Conceived in treason, it had been born amid a massacre and baptized by a lie.

In its first declarations, this Kadar Government promised the world on a silver platter. It would protect the nation's independence and maintain the country's sovereignty. It would not tolerate persecution under any pretext. It denounced the criminal reign of the "Rakosi-Gero clique." Once order was restored, it would negotiate with the Soviet Government and with the other members of the Warsaw Pact for the withdrawal of Soviet troops.

None of these promises was kept. The newborn independence

and sovereignty of the country, which had lasted only a few days, were tossed into the discard. Those who had taken part in the revolutionary struggle were subjected to pitiless persecution. Internment camps, prisons, and even the gibbet awaited those who had fought against foreign oppression and against the terror of the old regime. Little by little, the reign of the "Rakosi-Gero clique" was restored. This was done with less show in some areas, but it was also done with much more perfidy because the Revolution had effectively exposed the lie on which the entire regime was based. One of its first moves was to sign an accord with Moscow, continuing the Soviet occupation.

The activities of the Kadar Government soon gave the lie to the glowing promises with which it assumed power. Yet, even if it had kept its promises, the people would never have forgiven the treason that had presided at its birth. They compared its leaders with those traitors of 1849 who were called "Muscovite Guides" because they had conducted the armies of the Tsar to a point from which they were able to surprise and attack Kossuth's army from the rear. Hungarian history has never pardoned those earlier traitors.

Now, once armed resistance had been crushed, the struggle against the Russians took on a new form, too. The working classes took over the leadership in this phase, thus justifying in an unexpected fashion the Marxist-Leninist dogma regarding the leading role of the proletariat. In the factories, the Workers' Councils formed at the start of the rebellion ordered a general strike in protest against the brutality of the occupying forces and the activities of their agents. The strikers demanded guarantees of national independence, the withdrawal of Soviet troops, and the recognition of the authority of workers' organizations. Most of the Workers' Councils also declared that they would not recognize the legality of the Kadar regime. For them, the legitimate Government remained that of Imre Nagy. They demanded the resignation or removal of Kadar and the return to power of Nagy.

For several weeks Hungary lived under the auspices of a double power: that of the Kadar government, supported by Soviet tanks, and that of the Workers' Councils, which represented the popular will. Under these conditions Kadar, or more precisely his Soviet advisors, did not feel that the time was ripe to oppose the workers' demands openly. They reefed sail and temporized. Realizing its political weakness and isolation, this Government pretended, despite its military power, that it regarded its role as purely provisional, and it even indicated a willingness to negotiate with Nagy with a view to finding a place for him in the new Government.

One of the first official declarations of the Kadar regime spoke only of the "weakness" of the Nagy Government. In his first big radio address on November 11, Kadar characterized Nagy as "the only Communist in [Nagy's] Government" and reproached Nagy's Cabinet with a "total impotence" that had "opened the door to counter-revolutionary forces." He added: "I must say in all frankness, having been a member of Imre Nagy's Cabinet, that neither Nagy himself nor the political group of which he was a part, would knowingly have helped the counter-revolutionary forces." Kadar denounced his predecessor simply for having given way under counter-revolutionary pressure and for not having made known to the people the true situation.

On November 13, several workers' delegations went to see Kadar at the Parliament Building. They asked news of Nagy. Kadar repeated that he did not "feel that Nagy had knowingly aided the counter-revolution, but that he had been overwhelmed by events." He said: "Imre Nagy is not being held. He left the Parliament Building of his own free will. Neither the Government nor the Soviet troops had any desire to restrict his freedom of movement. It is up to Nagy alone as to whether he will participate in political life."

On the following day, Kadar received a delegation from the Central Workers' Council of Budapest. He told its members: "The recent events in Hungary cannot be looked upon as a counter-revolution. But the fact cannot be ignored that, quite apart from the deep indignation of the workers—an indignation which was provoked by the grave errors of the past and by the small heed given their demands—there were also counter-revolutionary manifestations in the rebellion." Kadar at that time confirmed "definitely" that no one would be punished for having taken part in the "great popular movement of these last weeks."

He said that the demand for Hungarian neutrality was completely understandable but that, in order to realize it, the relative strength of the great powers would have to be taken into consideration. It would depend on the international situation, he said.

Kadar also voiced his opinions regarding the subject of free elections and regarding a multi-party government. "We want a multi-party system and really free elections," he said. "We know that this will not be easy, because, if the power of the workers can be crushed by bullets, it can also be crushed by ballots. We must envisage the possibility of total defeat in the elections, but, if we take part in an electoral campaign, the Communist Party can again find the strength necessary to win the confidence of the working masses."

During the conference, the workers expressed their desire to see Nagy resume direction of the Government. To this, Kadar replied: "Imre Nagy is still in Budapest. He is in a foreign embassy, from which he has asked asylum." Under those conditions, he, Kadar, could not negotiate with Nagy, and thereby it must be understood Nagy could not resume the Premiership. Said Kadar: "As soon as Nagy abandons his extraterritorial refuge and returns to Hungarian soil, it will be possible to consult with him and to arrive at an agreement."

It is important to recall these statements because they are indicative of the atmosphere in which negotiations began between the Kadar regime and the People's Republic of Yugoslavia regarding the question of Nagy's leaving the Yugoslav Embassy. In the embassy with Nagy were his wife, his daughter, his son-in-law Ferenc Janosi, Nagy's two grandchildren, and a number of his supporters who had accompanied him from the Parliament Building or who had joined him there later. Among these supporters were Zoltan Szanto, former Hungarian Ambassador to Paris and Warsaw and an old adversary of Rakosi; Zoltan Vas, who was in charge of food and supplies during the rebellion; Gyorgy Lukacs, the philosopher who held the post of Minister of Culture in the Nagy Cabinet; Geza Losonczy, Minister of State; Ferenc Donath, the agrarian who had been imprisoned by Rakosi; Gabor Tanczos, Secretary-General of the Petofi Circle; Julia Rajk, widow of the executed Minister of Foreign Affairs (she had returned from a trip to East Germany on November 2); Sandor Haraszti, President of the Association of Journalists; Jozsef Szilagyi, Nagy's secretary; Miklos Vasarhelyi, head of Press Information Services; Szilard Ujhelyi, President of the Film Bureau; Gyorgy Fazekas, a journalist who had taken part in the organization of the militia; Peter Erdos, a journalist; and Ferenc Nadas. Many of them had their wives and children with them, the group including fifteen women and seventeen children.

All had been members of the Communist Party. Many— Losonczy, Donath, Julia Rajk, Haraszti, Erdos, and Ujhelyi—had spent years in prison as a result of the Rajk or the Kadar cases. Another striking fact was that five of the seven members of the Provisional Central Committee of the Hungarian Socialist Workers' Party recently formed by Kadar were among those who had sought asylum. A sixth, Sandor Kopacsy, had been arrested by General Serov in person. In short, of the entire leadership, Kadar was the only one at liberty.

During the negotiations with the Yugoslavs, Kadar's representatives suggested that Nagy and several of his friends ask Rumania for the right of asylum in that country, where they could remain until the situation returned to normal in Hungary. The Yugoslavs replied that they had nothing against this solution, but that its acceptance would be up to the refugees.

The political refugees themselves voiced a desire to remain in Hungary if possible, as much for the general interest as for the privilege of taking part in the country's normal life. In such a case, they would demand guarantees of their safety. And if such a solution should prove impossible, they would prefer to go to Yugoslavia, a Communist country that was not under Soviet domination. It was for this reason that they had in the first place chosen the Yugoslav Embassy.

On the sixteenth of November, Kadar let it be known that he was ready to give Nagy written guarantees which would allow him to leave the Yugoslav Embassy the following day. When the Yugoslav Ambassador Dalibor Soldatic went to Kadar to obtain his signature on these guarantees, Kadar presented some new requirements. Nagy and Losonczy would have to renounce their ministerial titles; they would have to recognize the justice of the positions taken by the new "Revolutionary Workers' and Peasants' Government"; they would have to make a public confession of error and to agree to abstain from any action against the new regime. Then Kadar said that, on second thought, it might still be preferable for Nagy and his friends to seek asylum in one of the socialist countries of Eastern Europe.

Nagy and his colleagues rejected these demands immediately. They were indignant at being confronted with humiliating and dishonest conditions by the very man who had betrayed them into their situation.

The Yugoslav Government then sent Doubrivoje Vidic, its Deputy Foreign Minister, to Budapest. Vidic sent Kadar a personal letter and subsequently had several conversations with him.

Finally, on November 21, Kadar, in a letter addressed to the Yugoslav Government, confirmed in writing the position he had made known in several conversations: namely, that he had "no intention of dealing severely with Nagy and the members of his group because of their past activities," and adding: "We think that this declaration henceforth makes pointless the right of asylum accorded those in question. Those persons can leave the Yugoslav Embassy and return freely to their own homes." In other respects, the Hungarian Government accepted all the conditions of the Yugoslav Government.

Having obtained typewritten guarantees, Nagy and his friends decided to go home. Four members of the group, Lukacs, Szanto, Vas, and Erdos, had already left the embassy, the first three undoubtedly for political reasons, since they had not taken so firm a position in favor of the Revolution's objectives as had the others. As for Erdos, he was acting largely out of bravado. He was impatient to learn what was going on in the city and he did not feel that he was important enough to be in danger of serious consequences. However, he left his wife and little daughter in the embassy.

What could have persuaded Nagy and his friends to renounce their asylum and to put faith in the promises of Kadar?

The Revolution had been crushed. Further armed resistance was impossible. True, the United Nations, to which Nagy had twice appealed for support, had, in a series of resolutions, called on the Russians to be sensible, to respect Hungarian independence and the people's will, and to withdraw their troops from Hungary. They had gone so far as to denounce Soviet armed intervention vigorously, but without obtaining the slightest result. Only the resolution against deportations of Hungarian youth had succeeded in making an impression, the deportations having thereby been stopped. In general, however, the Soviet Union scorned the resolutions adopted by the United Nations, accusing it of intolerable interference in Hungary's internal affairs. Britain and France had been forced to bow before the U.N. decisions on Suez; but the Soviet Union had no intention of following suit. On the Hungarian case, the U.N. had failed miserably.

In the United States, the elections were over. President Eisenhower, in his first statement after his reelection, voiced his admiration for the Hungarian people and condemned the Soviet Union, adding, "We have never encouraged the captive peoples to rise up in armed revolt." Those in Hungary who still hoped for help from the West were now forced to admit to themselves that such hopes were in vain. The conviction that the West could not let them down had now, after all the words of praise that had poured out over the radios, to be abandoned. There was nothing left for the Hungarian people to do but to continue their resistance, either actively or passively, or to flee the country. In the course of these weeks, nearly a quarter million men, women, and children crossed the frontier, which was still lightly guarded, heading west or south.

In Kadar's attitude, which was clearly inspired and directed by the Russians, Nagy saw two tendencies. On the one hand, Kadar wanted to rid himself of Nagy as a disturbing element. On the other hand, Kadar was somewhat persuaded to leave Nagy in peace, with a view to arriving at a compromise with him.[23] The fact was that the people were demanding more and more insistently the return of Nagy as the one person in whom they saw the possibility of a solution, and Kadar and his associates were so completely isolated that they found it necessary to make a gesture toward Nagy in order to pierce the wall of hatred that the people had raised against them. It might be possible, Nagy thought, that it was such considerations that had brought an end to Soviet hesitations and dictated the written guarantees given the Yugoslav Government.

Whether or not Nagy believed Kadar's new promises, one reason for his decision to leave the Yugoslav Embassy lay in the fact that he and his friends did not feel comfortable there. On November 11, seven days after their asylum was granted, it so happened that Marshal Tito visited the Dalmatian port of Pula and that in the House of the Peoples' Army there he made a long speech to the Istrian activists of the Communist League. In addition to analyzing the general world political situation, plus the internal situation in the Soviet Union (during the course of which he strongly attacked Stalinism and its representatives in the Kremlin), he also dealt in detail with the events in Hungary. With the assurance of a man who had long ago prophesied many of these events, he mercilessly condemned the policies of Rakosi and of Gero. Then, in examining the events of the Revolution, he said: "If Imre Nagy's Government had been more energetic, if it had not always vacillated instead of taking a strong stand against the chaos and against the fact that Communists were killed by reactionaries, and if it had energetically opposed reaction, then perhaps things could have been straightened out and perhaps the intervention of the Soviet Army could have been avoided. But what did Imre Nagy do? He asked the people to take weapons against the Soviet Army and he asked the Western countries for help. This intervention was exploited enormously by the West. It was exploited by the imperialists in attacking Egypt. The imperialists chose exactly this moment of the Hungarian tragedy to begin their attack—hoping as they did that the Soviet Union would be too busy to oppose the aggression. Then new fighting began in Hungary. The Soviet troops were strengthened. Nagy fled, and a new Government was established."

Another part of Tito's speech dealt with the events preceding the Soviet intervention. He condemned the intervention itself, though he also at the same time considered it necessary,[24] and, in speaking of the pursuit of Communists and of the deeds of the fascist mob, he added: "Imre Nagy's Government did nothing to counteract this situation. Instead of fighting against it and instead of showing in some way his desire to block the murder of Communists and of progressives, he simply lamented on the radio continuously, begging for help."

At the same time Marshal Tito spoke of the Kadar Government in this manner: "In examining the present Hungarian events from this perspective—that it stands either for socialism or for counter-revolution—we have to protect the Kadar Government and give it our help. . . . I can tell you, comrades, that I know the men who are now members of this new Government, and, according to my opinion, they represent the most honest forces of Hungary. . . ."

Quite apart from the question of whether or not Marshal Tito's analysis of the events was correct, or of whether it was objective, or of whether he "had an axe to grind"—quite apart from these possibilities, it was not hard to imagine the effect of this speech on Imre Nagy. After all, this was the statement of the head of the state which had granted him asylum, and it was a statement which attacked him who hoped for protection while it protected Kadar from whom he had asked to be protected. Nagy had too much pride and too much dignity to stay in the Yugoslav Embassy now—even if there were only one chance in a hundred that he would be allowed to live in his native Hungary.

The fact that Kadar guaranteed his safety with his own signature gave Nagy some confidence. Not that he any longer had confidence in Kadar. But he considered the position of the Kadar Government to be too weak for it to take the chance of openly breaking such a promise. Even more important, the guarantee was not addressed to Nagy but to the Yugoslav Government. Thus, the entire affair was on an international level, and he and his friends were protected by international law. And, above all, Yugoslavia was at this time the only country outside the Soviet bloc which not only recognized the Kadar regime but even promised to help it. So it did not seem at all probable that Kadar, isolated as he was, would like to provoke Tito's anger.

Nagy and his friends left the Yugoslav Embassy on November 23, at 6:30 p.m. Before doing so, they addressed a letter to the Yugoslav Government expressing their gratitude for the help and asylum granted them. Many of them telephoned their relatives or their families to tell them they would be home for dinner.

The Deputy Premier of the Kadar Government, Ferenc Munnich had sent a bus for them. They thought that the first to be taken home should be old Sandor Haraszti and his wife, for the Harasztis lived in Damjanich Street, a few minutes from the Embassy.

Near the Embassy there were Soviet armored vehicles. This fact was not at all extraordinary, since the building had been under constant surveillance since November 4. A few people who wanted to visit Nagy in the Embassy had simply been arrested.

But the unexpected—the surprising—fact was that there were Soviet MVD officers in the bus.

When Imre Nagy started to climb into the bus, somebody— allegedly the driver—leaned over to him and whispered: "Attention, Comrade Nagy! You will not be taken to the place they have promised."

Nagy immediately turned and climbed out of the bus, and those who had already boarded the bus followed him.

On the street, Nagy said he would not board the bus again as long as the Soviet officers remained in it.

The MVD officers then climbed out.

The Yugoslav ambassador, who accompanied Nagy to the bus, protested strongly and requested Milan Georgijevich and Military Attache Milan Drobac to board the bus and to accompany Nagy and the others to their homes.

Then Nagy, followed by the other Hungarians, climbed into the bus again.

The bus began moving, and at that moment a Soviet MVD officer jumped into it.

The bus went in the direction of the Gorki Allee. This seemed to be all right, for it was the direction leading to Haraszti's house.

But the bus did not stop in front of the house. Instead, it stopped in front of the building occupied by the Soviet Military Command.

A Soviet lieutenant colonel emerged from the building. He told the passengers to leave the bus and enter the building.

The two Yugoslav diplomats protested, but they were dragged out forcibly.

Milan Georgijevich stated that these measures were contradictory to the agreement signed by the Hungarian and Yugoslav Governments.

The Soviet lieutenant colonel replied that he had nothing to do with that agreement and that he was carrying out the orders of his superiors.

Imre Nagy and the others refused to leave the bus, but they were then forced to disembark.

The women and children were crying while the small group was swallowed up by the building.

II

Friends of Nagy and his companions spent most of the following day trying to reach them by telephone. There were no answers at any of their homes. The Yugoslav Embassy telephoned Ferenc Munnich, Number Two man in the Kadar Government. Munnich promised to look into the question of their whereabouts. At eight o'clock that night, Radio Budapest read the following communique:

"It is well known that Imre Nagy, former Premier, and several of his followers asked the Yugoslav Embassy on November 4 to extend to them the right of asylum. This was granted them. The right of asylum expired on November 22. For more than two weeks Imre Nagy and his comrades had been asking the Hungarian Government for permission to leave the territory of the Hungarian People's Republic and to go to another socialist country. Permission to go there having been granted by the Government of the Rumanian People's Republic,[25] Imre Nagy and his comrades left November 23 for that country."

There were none who believed the communique, including those for whom it was intended and those who themselves had drafted it. Yugoslavia protested immediately. Belgrade's note made official what everyone already knew—that Nagy had had no intention of leaving the country and that, on the contrary, he and his companions had "during their stay at the Yugoslav Embassy . . . rejected the proposal that they go to Rumania." The Kadar Government's reply to this note did not come until December 1. It bluntly informed Belgrade that the Nagy case was an internal matter and demanded that the Yugoslav Government consider the matter closed.

The news that Nagy had been carried off, plus the cynicism of the Government's communique, fell on the country like a thunderbolt. Together they confirmed what many already knew: that nothing could be expected of the Kadar Government, that it was ready to violate within one day the promises of the morning, and that not even its signature was to be trusted. The kidnapping was unsettling to those who still nursed illusions about the Kadar regime—even to those who were attached to it by self-interest. An editorial in the Kadarist paper *Kisalfold,* published at Gyor, said:

"The news is spreading everywhere that Imre Nagy, who is held in the highest esteem by the people of this country, all of whom follow his fate with interest, has been seized by Soviet troops and taken to Rumania. Obviously this story is an invention inspired by foes of the regime, but, nonetheless, the Government keeps quiet and does not release sufficient information on the question. The Government must understand that its silence only makes the situation worse. It serves only to confuse those who would still have confidence in it."

To reassure those who would still believe in him and to quiet those who had never trusted him, Kadar set about providing the necessary "information." Three days after the abduction of Imre Nagy, he told a delegation of workers which questioned him about the incident: "These people . . . were not taken to their own homes for their own protection. The Government had reason to believe that the counter-revolutionary elements still at large in the country might resort to provocation, killing Nagy or one of his collaborators so that responsibility for the murder might fall on the Hungarian Government."

To dissipate any fear for Nagy's safety, Kadar made it known the following day over the Hungarian radio that there was no longer any cause for such a fear: "We have already said that we have no intention of bringing Nagy and his friends to trial for the charges to which they have laid themselves open in the past. . . . We will keep that promise. We do not regard their departure as permanent, but, in the present situation, we think that it is preferable for Nagy and his followers to leave Hungarian territory for a while."*

In view of the fact that the General Assembly was in session at the United Nations and that several delegates had violently protested against the events surrounding Nagy, the representatives of the "socialist camp" considered it wise to make some concession to world opinion. On December 3, the Rumanian People's Republic's Foreign Minister, Grigore Preoteosa, made the following statement: "I wish to make it clear that the steps which were taken to grant political asylum in Rumania to Imre Nagy, former President of the Hungarian Council of Ministers, and his friends, were necessary, as much to guarantee the personal security of those concerned as to facilitate the reestablishment of order in Hungary. Taking into consideration the desire expressed by the group to go to a socialist country and the interests of assuring the safety of the group, the Hungarian Government asked the Rumanian Government to grant its members the right of asylum.

"At that time, the Rumanian Government gave assurances that Rumanian asylum for the group would be in conformity with all the rules of hospitality and that all measures would be taken to guarantee the safety of the former President of the Council of Ministers and his friends. At the same time, the Rumanian Government gave assurances that it would take into consideration the international rules of political asylum. The stay of Imre Nagy in Rumania is a temporary measure. These are the conditions under which former Premier Imre Nagy and his group have been in Rumania since November 23, 1956. They will have the benefits of all the rights of political asylum. I can affirm that the persons concerned are grateful to the Rumanian Government for the hospitality it has offered them. I can also state to the [U.N.] Assembly that the attitude of Imre Nagy and his group is characterized by good humor and understanding. . . ."

Thus, everything was for the best, in this best of all people's democracies! Everyone was in good humor: Imre Nagy and his friends, and Kadar and his cohorts, and the Rumanians who were

---

* After the execution of Nagy, Kadar declared on June 30, 1958: "Some have said that in the Nagy affair we violated our commitments. That is slander." (*Nepszabadsag,* July 1, 1958.)

guaranteeing their respect for the right of political asylum. During this period of euphoria, the official Hungarian press reproached Nagy at most for a certain "weakness" or "slackness." The first statement of the reorganized Communist Party, on December 8, was even disposed to recognize in him and his friends a certain merit, though it did not in any way pass over their mistakes in silence: "The activities of this opposition group in the core of the Party could be considered as a positive one only so long as they were together with other opposition groups, directed against the policies of the Rakosi-Gero clique."

It was only four weeks later, in early January, 1957, that the epithet of "traitor" was hurled at Nagy and his friends. Between January 1 and January 4, the leaders of the Hungarian, Rumanian, Czechoslovakian, and Bulgarian Parties, met in Budapest with Krushchev and Malenkov, the leaders of the Soviet Party. Two days later, on January 6, the charge of treason was made for the first time by the Kadar Government. The statement read: "Imre Nagy and his Government, by their treason, opened the way to the fascist counter-revolution."

In mid-January, Premier Chou En-lai of Communist China visited Budapest. He went a step farther than had the Kadar Government, declaring that the "Imre Nagy clique was up to its neck in the swamps of treason." The joint communique, issued at the close of his visit, spoke several times of Nagy and his companions as "traitors and renegades."

From that day on, the Party press in Hungary and abroad continued to speak of Nagy and his followers in this manner. The Central Committee, which, as recently as December, 1956, had, while condemning his role during the Revolution, still considered his function in the period that preceded the uprising a positive one, declared on February 26, 1957, that Nagy and his companions "before October 23 played the role of the advance guard for the counter-revolution and, after November 4, the role of rear guard in the same counter-revolution." The Soviet Government handed down an identical judgment. At the end of March, Kadar went to Moscow at the head of a Hungarian delegation, and Bulganin, who was then the Premier (before being himself accused of anti-Party activity), declared: "Under the mask of Communism,

Imre Nagy served the enemies of the Hungarian people long before the events of October."

By the beginning of 1957, such statements had begun to make it possible, or even necessary, to bring Nagy to trial. Karoly Kiss, one of the Kadarist leaders whom Nagy had once protected from Rakosi's vengeance and who later had helped to expel Nagy from the Party, was the first to say publicly: "The general public is more and more of the opinion that, as a result of his grave faults, Imre Nagy must be brought before the bar of justice." In Communist jargon the term "general public" has a special meaning, and those who know the jargon understand immediately what is about to happen when it is used. It was the "general public" that demanded the execution of Rajk and the reduction of the standard of living. Within the Party, certain leaders to whom Kadar's policies seemed too liberal and even timorous, made themselves the spokesmen for the "general public."

On March 7, 1957, Jozsef Revai, one of the famous Rakosi quartet, violently criticized the "patience" which the Party leadership was showing to Imre Nagy, who, he said, was no more than a "traitor." "The Party," he said, "must condemn Nagy without reserve and without appeal." But it seemed that neither the Buda-pest Government nor the Soviet authorities were ready to take such a step. On the contrary, in response both to the demands for Nagy's trial within the Party and to the speculation that was appearing in the Western press to the effect that he would be tried, the Government issued denial upon denial of such intention. On February 27, 1957, the spokesman for the Hungarian Foreign Ministry said: "The Government has no intention of bringing Imre Nagy to trial." On April 4, 1957, Kadar, in speaking to a group of foreign journalists, declared that, in view of the delicacy of the situation, there would be no trial of Nagy.

It became more and more clear that the fate of Nagy and his friends depended on the evolution of international politics and, particularly, on Soviet-Yugoslav relations. No one could say for sure what had become of the Hungarian exiles, and there were a variety of rumors, often contradictory, in circulation. According to some reports, they were being held in the former summer palace of the Rumanian kings, at Sinaia. According to other reports, they were imprisoned in the dungeons of Doftana. From Budapest came word that Nagy had been seen in the corridors of the prison on Fo Street while he was being taken to an interrogation session. The only thing that one could know with any certainty was that he was in the hands of his jailors, and that he was at the mercy of a great and pitiless power which, if its diplomacy would thus be advanced, would save him from a violent death, but which would not hesitate to sacrifice him if the contrary were the case.

In November, 1957, several leaders of the intellectuals' movement that preceded the Revolution were brought to trial and severely punished. Tibor Dery, sixty-three, an old Communist militant and one of the masters of Hungarian prose, was sentenced to nine years in prison. Gyula Hay, an excellent dramatist who had been in Moscow as a political exile, was given six years. The property of these two men was confiscated. There were articles and statements in the press which inferred that the Government intended to bring to an end the series of trials stemming from the "counter-revolution" and that those who had not yet been judged would soon have to appear in court. Radio Budapest announced that procedures against Pal Maleter had been initiated. The Kadar Government published the fourth volume of its *White Book,* devoting a whole chapter in it to "the counter-revolutionary activity of Imre Nagy." One did not have to be a great scholar to divine that its juridical language and circumstantial charges were drawn up from an act of indictment which had already been written or which was at least in the process of being prepared. It looked as though Kadar and his henchmen were readying their charges for the moment when the Russians would be ready to move.

In the fall of 1957, the celebration of the October Revolution brought together in Moscow the representatives of the entire world's Communist parties. Khrushchev was then at the height of his power. The fact that he had taken under his wing the Soviet intervention in Hungary had demonstrably paid off; all his rivals— Malenkov, Molotov, Kaganovitch, and Zhukov—had been eliminated. Then, too, the Yugoslavs were there to take part in the celebration, attesting to another Khrushchev political success.

Yet, when Khrushchev presented a joint statement of Communist principles for the delegates' signatures, it was the Yugoslavs alone who refused to sign it. This unforeseen development brought a sudden halt to Khrushchev's march toward the stars. At a stroke, Yugoslav-Soviet relations deteriorated, and the outlook for Nagy and his friends darkened.

A short time later, the Budapest Government received the necessary instructions to begin the trial. On January 28, 1958, the public prosecutor presented formal charges against Nagy and "his accomplices," and, on the basis of these accusations, the first session of the trial was held on February 6, 1958.

At this point, it can be surmised that an unforeseen development occurred in Moscow, for the court suddenly interrupted the proceedings and ordered further investigation of the case. It is possible that new overtures were being made in Tito's direction and that the Russians did not want to prejudice the Yugoslavs by condemning Nagy. In March, during a session of the Hungarian Party's Central Committee, Kadar was asked whether or not Nagy would be brought to trial. He replied: "At the moment when such a trial would have been timely, we were not strong enough to bring it off; now we are strong enough, but it is no longer timely."

A sudden visit by Kadar to Tito at the end of March proved—if that is necessary—that an attempt at a rapprochement with Tito was under way. The fact that the Yugoslav leader was willing to receive the man who had broken his word to Tito in the Nagy affair indicates that Tito was not insensible to these advances. Most certainly, Kadar made many promises as to Nagy's impunity, but he showed himself refractory toward Tito's advice that Hungary follow a little more independent policy toward the Russians and that the country should from time to time show such firmness as the Poles had shown.

It was only a few days later, during the celebration of the anniversary of Hungary's "liberation," that Khrushchev visited Budapest. He was the victor visiting the vanquished, the conqueror in the humiliated province. Affecting a wide smile, Khrushchev toured several provincial cities, making speeches to workers and scientists, to Party functionaries and to peasants. He broke through police lines to mingle with the people, picking up babies to pose for photographers. All of this was to show the world that order reigned in Hungary and that a people in revolt had submitted and had even begun to have a certain affection for their conquerors. But the countryside, its wounds still open, welcomed the visitor with an obstinate silence. Radio broadcasts of the mass meetings at which Khrushchev spoke were enlivened by the "canned" sound effects of "frantic applause." These effects had been "canned" during the days of Stalin, but they now proved themselves useful for Khrushchev's celebration, too.

In the course of his meetings with Khrushchev, Kadar gave a detailed account of his conversation with Tito. The Yugoslav leader's "attempt to debauch" the Hungarians roused Khrushchev's anger. On his return to Moscow, he sang the praises of the Hungarians, saying in substance that they were not like Tito: they did not try to ride two mounts at once or to be on good terms at one and the same time with the "Western imperialists" and the Soviet Union.[26]

This was the episode that seems to have sealed the fate of Imre Nagy and his friends. It appears that the Kremlin finally arrived at the conviction that the Yugoslav revisionists would cause less difficulty if they were outside the "great house" of the Soviet Union. Already, the Hungarian and Polish uprisings had served as a warning.

The situation became worse when the Yugoslav Communists published a new program which, while critical of Western policy, also voiced some reservation regarding Soviet policy. The diatribe that this program evoked recalled the worst period of the Stalinist era. It seemed to be forgotten that, not so long before, Khrushchev had gone to Tito, hat in hand, to apologize for unjust accusations against the Yugoslav leader. Now he was saying that the Yugoslavs were not Communists. They were "supporters of imperialism" and its "central representatives in the workers' movement."

In this chorus that sang now in full voice an anthem composed ten years earlier, it seemed that the dominant theme was carried by the Chinese. Peking had undergone a harrowing experience in its attempts to liberalize its regime. The theory of "let a hundred flowers bloom" had resulted in an unexpectedly strong wave of criticism against the leaders and the mistakes of the system, and the regime had quickly had to weed Mao Tse-tung's flower garden. As a result, the Chinese leaders had again become uncompromising. In the press and at their meetings, they attacked the Yugoslavs with a vigor that far exceeded that of the Russians, and they carried the Kremlin leaders along in their wake. It must be remembered that Khrushchev's principal support in the struggle against the Malenkov-Molotov "anti-Party clique" had been the Chinese. And, as a result, the influence of Mao Tse-tung and his friends had increased, their words carrying more and more weight. Though it is true that the Chinese were always careful to underline and to emphasize the Soviet Union's leading role, it is also true that the ideological leadership had slipped more and more into the Chinese hands and that, as a result, the Kremlin gave increasing consideration to that country's interests. If it was not yet precise to say that China was leading the Soviet Union, it was possible to point out that, in any case, the Soviet Union was not leading China and that whatever Peking wanted had begun to be more important than what Moscow wanted. Khrushchev's anger over Tito's infidelity, plus the regard he had for the loyalty of Mao Tse-tung, gave rise to trumpets which were sounding ever more strongly and which were intended to shake the walls of Jericho-Belgrade. Old arguments were dug up from the grave of the Comintern; and old muskets were reloaded and old sabres rattled. In reality, of course, there was only one new argument against Tito: it was the Hungarian "counter-revolution" and the asylum granted Nagy and his friends in the Yugoslav Embassy in Budapest.

At the beginning of June, 1958, Khrushchev went to Sofia. He made a number of speeches and he used each of them to make some point against Bulgaria's Yugoslav neighbors. As proof of Tito's felonious behavior, Khrushchev said: "At the moment of the counter-revolutionary putsch of Budapest, the Yugoslav Embassy became the headquarters of those who had launched a fight against the Hungarian People's Democracy. In the end, the embassy became the asylum of the Imre Nagy-Geza Losonczy group, all traitors and cowards."

This speech can be taken as the signal for the condemnation of Imre Nagy to death.

III

Fifteen days later, during the night of June 16-17, Radio Budapest and Radio Moscow announced the news of Nagy's execution. The published communique left unanswered a series of important questions. For example, it neglected to name the public prosecutor, the counsel for the accused, or the witnesses; and it also neglected to describe the testimony of the accused. There was no indication of the place or of the date of the trial. A short time later, Geza Szenasi, public prosecutor for the Hungarian People's Republic, in replying to questions from foreign journalists, consented to reveal —"smilingly," the news services reported—that "hearings" had been held before the verdict and that the trial had lasted twelve days in all. A month later, the Kadar Government, in answer to a Yugoslav protest, said that the trial had taken place from the ninth to the fifteenth of June and that the verdict had been handed down on June 15. The contradictions between these two statements raise questions about the extent to which the Hungarian Government, or at least its representatives, were informed about the details of the trial.

According to the official communique, Nagy was brought before the tribunal along with eight of his codefendants. These others were: Ferenc Donath, Miklos Gimes, Zoltan Tildy, Pal Maleter, Sandor Kopacsi, Ferenc Janosi, Jozsef Szilagyi, and Miklos Vasarhelyi. Of them, Donath, Szilagyi, Vasarhelyi, and Janosi, had, like Nagy, been granted asylum by the Yugoslav Embassy—after which, having been taken to Rumania by Soviet troops, they had been given the right of asylum there. Never did any communique announce that they had given up the right of asylum; nor did any reveal the manner in which they had been returned to the Hungarian authorities—a process that could have been accomplished only by the most flagrant violation of international procedure. On the other hand, Pal Maleter had been arrested by General Serov at the moment when he was negotiating with the high command of the Soviet forces in Hungary. His arrest—he was then Minister of Defense and charged with the negotiations on behalf of his Government—constituted another violation of human rights, not to speak of Hungary's rights; and the act of placing him on trial also was highly irregular. Of the other three defendants, Kopacsi had been arrested in November, 1956, also by Soviet forces. Gimes had been arrested in December by a mixed group of Soviet and Kadar troops. The arrest of Zoltan Tildy had never been previously announced. It was announced only in the communique giving the verdict.

It was this communique, too, which announced that Geza Losonczy, who was the Minister of State in the Nagy Government and who had passed long years in prison under Rakosi and who had also taken refuge in the Yugoslav Embassy, had "meanwhile died of an illness." Since he had contracted a grave pulmonary ailment in Rakosi's prisons as well as a serious nervous ailment, it is possible that his new imprisonment had finished him off. But the communique did not specify the nature of his illness or the place or date of his death. The communique also made no mention of the fate of the fifteen women and seventeen children in the group. It was not until December, 1958, that it was announced in Budapest that the members of the families of the deported, along with Zoltan Vas and Zoltan Szanto, had been authorized to return home from Rumania.

By contrast to these omissions, the actual record of the accusations which were presented at the trial was so wordy as to be tiresome regarding the "crimes" of the group concerned. In general, the "criminals" were accused of having formed an illegal organization and of fomenting a plot to overthrow the legal government of the Hungarian People's Republic. In addition, Nagy was accused of high treason; and Kopacsi and Maleter were charged with mutiny. This document also accused Nagy and those closest to him of having organized, in December, 1955, a plot directed against the State "for the purpose of seizing power by force and of overthrowing the Hungarian People's Republic." Nagy was accused of the crime of having drafted his dissertation— the same one of which he had sent copies to the Central Committee and one to the Soviet Ambasador. For the purposes of the trial, this thesis was nonetheless described as a "*secret* document" in which the author had "set down the political platform of the plotters against the Hungarian People's Republic and [had] defined the immediate tasks and the ultimate goals of that plot." Nagy was held responsible for the activities of the Petofi Circle. (It should be recalled that Kadar, then First Secretary of the Party, had said that the Party would always be proud of the youth who had grouped themselves in the Circle.) The former Premier was held responsible for the "armed revolt launched with the active collaboration of imperialists on October 23, 1956"—a revolt which Kadar, ten months earlier, had called the "glorious uprising of our people." Nagy was also held responsible for the renunciation of the Warsaw Pact, though the communique made no mention of the visits of Mikoyan and Suslov to Hungary during the Revolution, nor of the policy that the Soviet Government had officially set forth in its note of October 30 defining the rights of the people's republics regarding that pact. Finally, Nagy was held responsible for the execution of 234 defenseless members of the army and the AVH, though no mention was made of the really defenseless citizens—2,700 of them —who had been killed by Soviet troops in the course of crushing the Revolution.

There were countless other inconsistencies in the charges. Nagy was accused of being responsible for Cardinal Mindszenty's rehabilitation (he was said to have reached an agreement with the Cardinal), and he was accused of abetting Mindszenty's opposition to the Hungarian People's Republic (when, in fact, the Cardinal, in his only public statement, had criticized Nagy as the "heir to the deposed regime"). In connection with the charge that he had collaborated with "imperial circles and, in particular, with the American imperialists," Nagy was accused of having instigated the Hungarian broadcasts of Radio Free Europe (which, in fact, attacked Nagy). He was accused of having demanded in his speech of November 4 "the open and armed intervention of the Western imperialists" (when actually not a word of that speech could be interpreted as soliciting armed aid from the West).

But facts were no hindrance to the authors of the charges. According to their version, a "secret meeting," presided over by Nagy, was held on the morning of October 23 "in the apartment of Geza Losonczy . . . at which Nagy, Miklos Gimes, Miklos Vasarhelyi, Ferenc Janosi, and Sandor Haraszti" had drafted a list of members of the Government which they wished to form "after the forceful overthrow of the legal Hungarian Government." The fact that Nagy had not even been in Budapest at that moment was of no importance.

On the basis of all these "incontestable facts" the communique concluded: "The documents in the case have established and proved that Imre Nagy and his companions, conforming to their revisionist and nationalist tendencies, have been led to betray the workers' power, the democratic people's regime, and the socialist fatherland, in an alliance with the most reactionary forces. . . . The Council of the People's Supreme Tribunal, having considered the gravity of these crimes and the circumstances that provoked them, as well as the extenuating circumstances, and having deliberated, has declared that the accused are guilty of the crimes listed in the charges. In consequence, Imre Nagy, Miklos Gimes, Jozsef Szilagyi, and Pal Maleter have been condemned to death; Sandor Kopacsi, to prison for life; Ferenc Donath, to twelve years in prison; Zoltan Tildy, to six years in prison; Ferenc Janosi, to eight years in prison; Miklos Vasarhelyi, to five years in prison. . . ."

By the time that the official communique was being read over the radios, Imre Nagy was no longer alive. The official text ended with these phrases: "The sentences are final, with no right of appeal. The death sentences have been executed. . . ."

Such was the nonchalance with which these men were killed! The judgment was pronounced in the name of those for whom the victims had fought all their lives. They were called traitors by those who had betrayed them. The press of the "socialist camp" welcomed the verdicts with unanimous satisfaction. "The list of their crimes could be enumerated at great length," said the journal *Esti Budapest*. It added: "But could one name greater crimes than those in the communique? Is any further proof necessary" . . .? The Soviet press, expressing itself in a dignified manner, found that the verdicts were "severe but just." The Bulgarian press, more emotional, reported with satisfaction that "the dogs have been destroyed." The Poles were the most discreet: according to some reports, the Polish Communists paid homage to Nagy at their cell meetings by rising when his name was mentioned. In any case, more than ten days passed before the Polish Party press and Gomulka himself officially took a position of finding the trial emphatically fair.[27] The Chinese press was the most loquacious: "Good news has just come from Budapest," was the way *Jen-Min-Ji-Bao,* organ of the Party's Central Committee, opened its report.

The Yugoslav Government sent a note protesting against the violation of the written guarantees it had been given and also against those passages in the communique which said that the Yugoslav Embassy in Budapest had aided Nagy and his friends in the alleged illegal activity. In those countries of the East and West where men retain the right to express their true sentiments—to smile when they are happy, to weep when they are sad—the news of the executions was received with a wave of indignation. Individuals and organizations, newspapers and governments made known their disapproval. It can be said that the indignation was even more unanimous than that which had followed the crushing of the rebellion on November 4, 1956. There were some who had been able to explain that action in terms of political considerations, but men of good faith and healthy minds were unable to find an excuse for this assassination. "Ten months after the Hungarian Revolution, we were expecting an amnesty," said Pietro Nenni, head of the Italian Socialist Party, which was then linked to the Communists by a policy of united action. "It was this course that I had urged, and I was officially informed that such an amnesty was not only possible but that it would be announced in a short time. Instead, it was the executions that were announced. They have reopened old wounds and poured into them the salt of hate."

In France, the leaders of the labor unions, the representatives of the League for the Rights of Man, and a whole galaxy of writers protested; while both the Conservative and the Labor Party leaders in Britain—and both Republicans and Democrats in the United States—joined in the unanimous protests. There was no divergence here, either from the right or from the left. The indignation even swept through Communist ranks. Henri Lefebvre, one of the theoreticians of the French Party, spoke of the "cancer that had attacked the socialist revolution, the cynicism, and the baseness." He wrote, in substance: "A great man has just been killed, coldly and at a moment calculated in advance to serve as a warning to the world. The methods of political communication used [by the Russians] are life and death." Arthur Lewis Horner, General Secretary of the British Miners' Union and one of the leaders of the British Communist Party, said: "I can keep silent no longer. I must say what I think. . . . The fact that Imre Nagy and his companions have been assassinated is horrible and absurd." The cultural editor of *Unita,* the Italian Communist Party organ, resigned in protest against the executions.

In Copenhagen, the windows of the Soviet Embassy were broken. In Buenos Aires, several hundred demonstrators penetrated the offices of the Soviet Trade Delegation and burned effigies of Khrushchev, Serov, and Kadar in its main hall. Students at Zurich raised a cross twenty-five feet high on a raft anchored in the waters of the Limmat River. On its base were engraved the names of Nagy and Maleter, and a memorial light burned at its foot.

Since there was no doubt that the executions were only a means to a political end and not an end in themselves, the question on every lip was what would be the final end of a system of government employing such means. "The news of the execution of Nagy," said Prime Minister Nehru, "is sad and tragic in itself as well as in its consequences."

But neither the anger nor the indignation, neither the protests nor the anguish, could do anything more for Imre Nagy. He was dead. He had to die, not because the accusations against him were true, nor even for the same reasons as Laszlo Rajk had been executed before him. Nagy's death was not the outcome of a fabricated trial. It was the price—terribly high but fully sublime—of a Revolution that was victorious in itself. If a comparison between the assassination of Nagy and Rajk is possible, the assassination of Nagy must be the happier one because Nagy, at least, had acted, had accomplished great things, had performed heroic deeds. He had to die because, in a system that would not tolerate them, he wanted to give his people liberty and independence. He wanted to give to the workers of Hungary more bread and to help them live like human beings.

IV

The communique announcing Nagy's execution published nothing of what Nagy had said during either his imprisonment or his trial. Months passed before some light was shed on these events. The Budapest Government published a book of documents entitled *The Counter-Revolutionary Plot of Imre Nagy and His Accomplices.* The aim of this so-called *White Book* was not to seek the truth but to advance propaganda, to blacken the accused, to rouse against them the hatred of the people. Unlike other documents published after the trials of Mindszenty, Rajk, and others, this one did not contain a stenographic record of the proceedings, but only such fragments as sought to present the Kadarist leaders in the most favorable light and to make Nagy and "his accomplices" appear to be sinister conspirators and traitors. Such as they were, however, these fragments told considerably more than those who chose them suspected. It is evident that, failing some historic upheaval, we will have to be content for a long time with material furnished by such Hungarian authorities. There remains only one task—to try to reconstruct the attitude of the accused before their accusers.

The central target of the charges was Imre Nagy. The president of the court and the prosecutor did everything they could to persuade the witnesses and the "accomplices" to shift all responsibility onto Nagy. He was charged with being responsible for everything—ranging from the fact that his sixtieth birthday had been celebrated by his friends to the fact that President Eisenhower had offered $20,000,000 in aid to Hungary.

After nearly two years under detention, Nagy still continued the battle. Weak and humiliated before the tribunal that was to judge him, he fought, parried, explained, refuted, proved. He fought for his honor and for the truth. This is what stands out, above all, in the *White Book* published by his foes.

The charges sought to prove that, in October, 1956, Nagy designated himself as Premier, an accusation which was particularly poorly founded since it was well known that the entire country resounded with the name of Imre Nagy and that even the official

Party newspaper (in its issue of October 23, 1956) recognized the necessity of giving him the reins of power. Rejecting this charge, Nagy said to his judges:

"The charge that I expressed the desire to be Premier is false."

At another time, when the president of the tribunal tried to make him admit another false charge, Nagy burst out:

"On this point, the indictment is contradictory to the fact. I regret to say it, but this is a question of established fact, and it is I who know the fact."

He categorically denied every lie; but on the other hand, he did not hesitate to recognize whatever was true and to accept the responsibility. Such was the case, for example, when he was accused of not having enforced the state of siege—that is, of not having executed the young insurgents who had been captured with weapons in their hands. Without hesitation, Nagy accepted this responsibility. This was the exchange:

> PROSECUTOR: Do you contend that you were not responsible for proclaiming the state of siege?
>
> NAGY: I have not said that. In my statements on the radio, I did invoke the state of siege and put it into force.
>
> PROSECUTOR: Did you do your utmost to enforce the state of siege?
>
> NAGY: That was not within my power to do. Whatever was my task, I carried out. In my mind, the state of siege should not have been enforced except against common criminals.
>
> PROSECUTOR: You did not want the state of siege enforced against persons who were found to be in possession of arms illegally and who had fought against the Hungarian People's Republic with those arms?
>
> NAGY: Not in that way. I did not want to enforce the state of siege against them.

His tranquil acceptance of responsibility on a question as grave as this gave added weight to his denial of such fabrications as those which accused him of being in league with "imperialist circles." For example, the indictment dwelt at great length on the period the accused spent at the Yugoslav Embassy. It sought to exploit the fact that the accused wanted to let their friends and relatives know where they were, and it went on to charge that Nagy and his friends had "entered into contact with Radio Free Europe through the connivance of Yugoslav journalists." This is how Nagy replied to that charge:

"There were, certainly, attempts on our part to make known our whereabouts and the names of those in our party—to let it be known that we were still alive. But these communications were not destined for Radio Free Europe. Such a version corresponds in no way to the facts. Apart from the list of names, we did not announce anything at all. At the time, we asked the Yugoslavs to announce that we were under their roof, that they had accorded us the right of asylum, that they had invited us, and that we had not fled to them, because it was being said at that time that we had been killed or that we had sought refuge at the United States Embassy."

Nagy's statement that the Yugoslavs had invited the Hungarians to seek asylum at their Embassy was a revelation supported by other witnesses. Miklos Vasarhelyi, the journalist who was sentenced to five years in prison, testified: "I went on foot to . . . the home of the assistant military attache, Voukmirovitch. He had with him Ferenc Nador, Commander of the Air Force, and his family, as well as Peter Erdos. Voukmirovitch informed me that the Yugoslav Embassy was offering us the right of asylum." Gabor Tanczos, a leader of the Petofi Circle, gave this deposition: "On November 4, 1956, toward 7:30 in the morning, I received a telephone call. M. Milovanov, in the name of the Yugoslav Ambassador, invited me to go to the Embassy, where several Hungarian leaders were already assembled. He said he was advising me to go immediately, in my own interest, taking along my wife. That was how I went to the Embassy, with my wife, toward nine o'clock."

To prove the crimes of the accused, the indictment presented a long list of witnesses. While the communique announcing the verdict mentioned only twenty-nine witnesses for the prosecution, the *White Book* mentioned the testimony of forty-seven. It is difficult to say whether their testimony was made during the trial, or in the course of the investigation by the police. Ten of the witnesses had never had any contact with Nagy or with others of the accused. A pensioner from Hajduboszormeny, for example, declared that in mid-October, 1956, during a public meeting at which Geza Losonczy took part, a landowner rose and spoke against the Government. Nothing more. A Budapest woman testified simply that the National Guard leader of the Eighth Ward had taken part in robberies and pilferings. Another group of witnesses, among them Generals Janza, Toth, and Berecz, and Police Colonel Vegh, and Mme. Agnes Sagvari, a high Party functionary, were representatives of the old Rakosi faction whose impartiality toward Nagy was highly suspect. The individuals who might have been able to furnish the most interesting testimony concerning the rebellion—Mikoyan, Suslov, Kadar, and Munnich—did not appear at the trial.

It is clear from the *White Book* that these testimonies could not undermine Nagy's determination. More than once, he engaged in cross-examination with the witnesses. He denied their depositions and stuck to his own testimony. His conduct became him during that terrible fight: it was one of honorable obstinacy. Even if he did not recall every detail exactly, he never gave in and he did not change his testimony. He seems to have been both proud and persistent. He would concede nothing to these people.

For Nagy, the painful moments could not have been those which saw such witnesses as these parade past the tribunal. It must have been far more tragic for him to have to turn against some of his most faithful friends, who had been his companions-in-arms during the most difficult periods of his life.

The fragments of testimony published in the *White Book* gave the impression that several of Nagy's followers and that several political figures who were not Communists had been broken by imprisonment or arrest and had made "confessions" that were described as complete and as even containing accusations against Nagy. It must be stated that most of these had already spent long years in prison under Rakosi. Did they feel that further resistance was hopeless? One cannot be surprised if this was so. From one point of view, they were in a worse situation than were the witnesses in the Rajk case, for their wives, their children, sometimes even their little babies, had been arrested with them and were in the hands of the police. It was these broken and desperate men who were brought before Nagy to convince him of his crimes.

Poor old Sandor Haraszti! He was a militant in the Communist underground for nearly forty years who, after having been imprisoned under the Horthy regime, was returned to jail for four years in the Rajk case without having done anything. As Secretary-General of the Hungarian-Yugoslav Association, he was condemned to death. True, his sentence was commuted shortly thereafter, but his jailors did not tell him so until two years later, so that for two years he lived in daily expectation of the executioner. Arrested at the same time as Nagy—and after having lost his son-in-law, Geza Losonczy, in prison, he was brought before the tribunal at a time when his wife, already old, and his daughter with her baby were still under arrest. Is it surprising that he "confessed"?

What torture it must have been for Nagy to have this life-long friend, this charming old man, confront him. Haraszti was used by the prosecution to prove that Nagy's famous 1955–1956 thesis, which, according to the indictment, established "premeditation," had been given wide circulation. The *White Book* said:

"During the session of June 10, Sandor Haraszti, questioned as a witness, and Imre Nagy were confronted with each other. Sandor Haraszti declared:

"The work by Imre Nagy was well known to his group. For my own part, I told Imre Nagy that I disapproved of his intention to spread his ideas in such a way."

Nagy, however, persisted in his denials:

"I deny that this work was to be found in every hand. Some of my studies were circulated among a limited group. I deny that Haraszti ever told me that he thought my writings were to be found in too many hands."

To anyone who knew these two men—Haraszti, full of a fire and ardor which at times made him imprudent, and Nagy, always reserved and scrupulously concerned for the Party's spirit—it is not hard to divine which told the truth in this confrontation.

Equally painful for Nagy must have been his confrontation before the tribunal and the members of the prosecution with Zoltan Tildy, who had been at his side, resolute and courageous, during the troubled days of the rebellion; with Sandor Kopacsi, former Budapest chief of police who had succeeded in preventing worse bloodshed during the rebellion; or with Ferenc Donath, that friend of long standing who had spent four years in prison under Rakosi and who was now going back for another twelve years.

Donath, as has been stated earlier, had been at Nagy's side in the first hours of the Revolution, after which he had withdrawn because he felt his friend was too tolerant of the Stalinists. He had not returned to the Nagy leadership until Gero and Hegedus had been eliminated. He had then become a member of the Provisional Committee of the reorganized Communist Party, and had been at Nagy's side at the moment when the Russians were launching their attack against the seat of the Hungarian Government.

It was this moment which became the subject of critical examination during the confrontation of the two men. The question at issue was this: Who drafted the now historic declaration read over the radio by Nagy at dawn on November 4, 1956? The *White Book* said:

"At the June 9 session, Nagy unexpectedly presented a version according to which he did not draft the text of the statement he read over the radio at dawn on November 4. While he could not deny the fact that he had read the statement at the microphone, he tried to shift all or at least part of the responsibility for this criminal act on to his codefendants, Ferenc Donath and Zoltan Tildy.

"There were several confrontations during the session. We herewith print one of the statements:

FERENC DONATH: At dawn on November 4, I was awakened by the news that the Soviet troops had reentered Budapest. I was told to summon together the members of the Party's administrative committee. I telephoned Zoltan Szanto, and, while I was calling him, Zoltan Tildy and his wife arrived, after which we went to the Parliament Building. Tildy turned to Nagy and said that, as long as the possibility of broadcasting over the radio remained, the Government should issue a statement making the facts known. This statement was dictated by Imre Nagy. I began to put it down in pencil and, when I had finished, he said, if I remember correctly, that a text scrawled like that could not be deciphered. So I began to recopy it on a typewriter. I made some remark as to the style, but, as far as the sense was concerned, I did not intervene in the writing of the statement. Apart from Imre Nagy, Zoltan Tildy was present during this dictation. This was how the text was drafted.

IMRE NAGY: I did not dictate the text. Donath wrote it in

pencil while I occupied myself with fifteen or twenty telephone calls.

Who told the truth, Imre Nagy or Ferenc Donath? Who drafted that historic document? Happily, we have this time a witness whom the prosecutors overlooked. Thirteen months before the trial, the central organ of the Kadar Party, *Nepszabadsag,* in its issues of May 31, June 1, 1957, had published under the title of "Their Last Day" the memories of an eye-witness who had spent the night of November 3 to November 4 in the Parliament Building (and who had later become a confirmed Kadarist). This was how he described the incident:

". . . Zoltan Tildy asked Imre Nagy how he planned to announce the news [of the Russians' entry] over the radio. Imre Nagy replied that he would take this upon himself in his capacity as Premier. Ferenc Donath had already drafted the text of the statement. Imre Nagy made a few modifications and, without having discussed the text with the ministers present, put on his overcoat and left the office of the Premier, heading toward the studio situated on the mezzanine in the other wing of the building."

But why did Nagy argue such minor points as these? Did he thereby hope to diminish his responsibility or to see his penalty reduced? This seems unlikely. By having read the statement over the radio he was just as responsible as if he had drafted it. On the other hand, he could not have been ignorant of the fact that sentence had been passed even before the trial had begun. There is, therefore, only one possible explanation: he wished passionately to see the trial record set forth the truth, less so as far as his own role was concerned than as far as the reporting of the Revolution was concerned. Whatever might happen to him, there was a chance that the trial record would be preserved. Perhaps the day would come when it would be opened to the world. This was a reasonable hope. The *White Book* itself bore him out, even though it published only a slender portion of the testimony. Without wishing to do so, Kadar and his people had rendered a service to Nagy's memory.

After the confrontations, the prosecution introduced another method of attempting to break the spirit of the accused. According to the *White Book:*

"During the session of June 13, the prosecutor announced that the chief prosecutor had acquired reels of films made during the Revolution by journalists of East and West, as well as photographs depicting acts of terrorism that appeared in the Western press. At the request of the prosecution, the president of the tribunal ordered the film projected. After this showing, several of the accused gave their opinions of what they had seen:

ZOLTAN TILDY: I have been terribly upset by this film. I regret that my name has been linked to such acts.*

FERENC DONATH: Reports of this white terror reached us in the Parliament Building. The fact that we still continued to support the point of view of the Government can be explained but cannot be embellished. . . . I consider it my moral duty to make honorable amends before the memory of those Communists, those Hungarians, and those Soviet soldiers who lost their lives during the counter-revolution.

SANDOR KOPACSI: I am aware of my guilt and I am ashamed that my name should appear before my friends under such infamous colors. There has just been shown a documentary film that illustrates how these people were assassinated. I feel myself indirectly responsible for these murders. I have seen before my own eyes Soviet soldiers being brought out of the tanks in which they were found dead. Their commander, weeping, said that these men were to have been discharged from active service the following day, and now they were dead. I regret having committed acts for which I must now reproach myself."

And what did Imre Nagy say? According to the authors of the *White Book*:

"Imre Nagy had nothing to say."

After the presentation of this picture painted by Governmental propaganda, several of Nagy's codefendants must have made their *mea culpas*. But the same incident also made it clear that three of the eight accused with Nagy fought before the tribunal with the same courage and the same intransigence as their leader. These were: General Maleter, Jozsef Szilagyi, and Miklos Gimes. The *White Book* published only a few phrases from their testimony, but these contained not a word directed against Nagy or against any

---

* In the form of a partial amnesty, Zoltan Tildy's imprisonment was suspended in April, 1959, "considering his repentance and his age." (*Nepszabadsag,* April 3, 1959.)

of the other accused. In this connection, the *White Book* described a scene which must have been pathetic to behold. Szilagyi's defense counsel tried to lead his client into shifting onto Nagy the responsibility for one of his own speeches. The speech was given on the eve of the Revolution, October 22, at the Polytechnical University, where Szilagyi was taking a night course. After classes, the students decided to participate in the demonstration scheduled for the following day. At the trial, this was the exchange:

> SZILAGYI'S COUNSEL: In your statement at the Polytechnical University on October 22, did you make it plain that you were speaking as an intimate of Imre Nagy?
>
> SZILAGYI: In my opinion, the problem is not quite that. In reality, I spoke twice. The first time, I said that Imre Nagy must be brought to the Premiership. The solution was at hand: Imre Nagy to power. . . . During the course of the discussion, the question arose as to whether or not the demonstration of the next day should be carried out. The rector, Cholnoky, took a position against the demonstration. This impelled me to take the floor again. I spoke only one or two minutes. I was of the opinion that the demonstration should be carried out. There had also been the question as to whether or not the students should present their demands to Nagy. In my second statement, I said that there would be no point in this, since Nagy was not yet in power. I said the students should not present their demands to him, but should take part in the demonstration. So far as I myself was concerned, I knew Imre Nagy personally. Those were approximately the words I used.

Just as Szilagyi refused to testify that the demonstration of October 23 had been ordered by Nagy, so also Miklos Gimes could not be persuaded to accuse Pal Maleter of complicity with thieves and other common criminals. On October 31, the Revolutionary Defense Committee of the Hungarian Republic had been formed at a meeting in Kilian Barracks. In connection with this meeting, Pal Maleter's counsel posed several questions to Gimes, who had been present. According to the *White Book,* this was Gimes' testimony:

> GIMES: On October 31, I was present at a meeting in Kilian Barracks without taking an active role. It is a fact that one of the

speeches was directed against Maleter. The meeting had been opened by Maleter. Then Bela Kiraly spoke. After that, there were several speakers, among whom was a man who was wearing a leather jacket and who spoke in a raucous voice, but whose name I did not know. He attacked Maleter violently, accusing him of having struck a man in the Corvin Passage and having taken from him his machine gun—"his guitar" in the man's own words. Maleter replied that he had found a gold pin in the man's pockets and that the man was fortunate not to be shot, and for good reason. After that, he asked if this explanation satisfied the speaker, and the two men shook hands.

PROSECUTOR: Then there was between them no political disagreement?

GIMES: No, there was not.

It was not accidental that those fighting on Nagy's side up to the last minute of the trial were the same ones who, during the days of the Revolution (when the men of the Rakosi and Kadar regimes were lurking cowardly in the background), had had the courage to protest against the lynchings and all the other excesses of the Hungarian Revolution.[28] In the cases of at least Szilagyi and Gimes, who had filled far less important positions during the Revolution than had most of the other accused, the death sentences meted out to them must be explained by their intransigence in the course of the trial, by their categorical refusal to disavow the ideals of the Revolution, and by their fidelity to their cause to the last gasp. It is to be noted that, in any comparison of the Nagy trial with such other fabricated trials as that of Rajk, one particular difference stands out: the accused were this time given the right to make denials. This time, in effect, instead of being required to confess to their crimes, the accused were allowed to bring upon themselves the death penalty.

In announcing the executions, the communique of the Ministry of Justice made it clear that Nagy had not pleaded guilty. It stated that Szilagyi and Maleter had also refused to plead guilty, but that Gimes had recognized and regretted his errors. However, the fragments of testimony in the *White Book* and the penalty of death pronounced in Gimes' case, cast doubt on this assertion. In any case, there were frequent instances where the *White Book* and the communique were in disagreement.

To refuse to plead guilty when one's sick and fragile body was at the mercy of physical and psychological terror, and when one's wife and daughter and grandchildren were being held as hostages, and when the only hope for life and freedom lay in fully admitting everything—was not this the best proof of human courage and of human greatness? What was it that gave him the strength not to break? What did he think in these most difficult days? Nobody knows. He may have recalled the words he learned as a young worker in the MAVAG factory: "Iron-worker, do not give in!" He may have recalled his walks in the Vaci Avenue, or the bus drivers who stopped to allow him to climb aboard, or the men and women who spoke to him on the street and assured him of their confidence. He may also have recalled his life-long hero, the leader of the Revolution of 1848-1849, Lajos Kossuth.

In 1949, as a speaker in the cathedral at Debrecen during the centenary of the Hungarian Declaration of Independence, Imre Nagy had quoted the following words of Kossuth: "God can dispose of me in whatever way He wants. He can make me suffer. He can offer me the cup of hemlock or the fate of exile. But there is one thing He can not order to me to do. He cannot order me to become the subject of the House of Austria."

And Imre Nagy stuck to Kossuth's oath. He preferred death to becoming the subject of the newest oppressor of his fatherland, the "House of Moscow."

The "House of Moscow"? Such a "House" seems to be no exaggeration. Neither is it intended only as a symbol.

There are certain clues that make the reader of the official documents ask himself whether, in reality, the Nagy trial was conducted by Hungarian authorities or by a tribunal composed of, at least in part, Russians. One of these clues is the fact that, while numerous public pronouncements were made by the Hungarian Communist Party Central Committee during the time when the trial was said to have taken place, there was no mention of Nagy or of the trial, although, in other such cases, steps would have been taken to prepare the public for the outcome. Then, too, there is the fact that both the communique of the Ministry of Justice and the extracts of the trial record in the *White Book* were couched with phrases written in questionable Hungarian. Might they not be translations which still bear the traces of the original foreign tongue? Admittedly, there were errors that might be simply faults in grammar. But why would a Hungarian jurist or judge find it necessary to state that the counter-revolution in question was the one that had taken place *in Hungary*? There were many other suspect phrases which would have meaning only to the Hungarian reader of the original text, but the inference that can be drawn from this useless reference to Hungary is apparent to all.

The most troubling detail, however, lies in the assertion that sentence was pronounced on June 15, 1958. The fifteenth of June fell on a Sunday. Never, even in the period of the great purge trials, when the courts worked on an assembly-line basis, did a Hungarian court sit on a Sunday, much less meet to pass sentence on that day. Sessions of the trials of Mindszenty and Rajk were always adjourned on Saturday to be resumed on Monday. This verdict, assertedly handed down on Sunday, seems to indicate on the one hand a strange haste, the final execution of a task for which a deadline had been set, and, on the other hand, the action, at least in part, of a non-Hungarian court.

It is said that history never repeats itself. But sometimes, it seems, it offers startling parallels. The Hungarian Revolution of 1956 began as a student demonstration, like that which had taken place one hundred and eight years earlier; it was followed by an armed uprising against a foreign power possessed of crushing military superiority, and it ended with the execution of its leaders.

In 1849, at least, the House of Austria allowed the condemned Premier and the condemned generals of that Revolution to write their last letters; and it announced the date and manner of their execution. But the House of Moscow did not grant even so little to Imre Nagy and his comrades. Long months afterward, we are still in total ignorance about the details. In Hungary, capital punishment is carried out by hanging, but an East German publication has reported that Nagy was shot. True, there is no guarantee of the accuracy of this information. No one knows whether it was day or night when they died, and there was no one to report their last words.

According to unofficial reports circulating in Hungary, Imre Nagy passed his last night writing. If it is true that judgment was passed on June 15, this must have been the night of June 15-16. At midnight on June 16, the radio announced the executions. In the absence of more precise information, June 16 must be set down as the date of Imre Nagy's death.

Apart from the contents of the *White Book*, the last official information that seems worthy of belief dates from January, 1957. At that time, the leaders of the Rumanian Communist Party arrived in Hungary. They complained to their Hungarian colleagues of the attitude of Imre Nagy, who, it will be remembered, was then in Rumania where, so it was said, he was enjoying the benefits of asylum. It was impossible, the Rumanians said, to make him "listen to reason" or to persuade him "to admit his crimes" or to "obtain from him any reasonable statement." To everything that was said to him, he made one reply:

"Monday (he was speaking of Monday, November 5, the day after the final Soviet intervention) . . . Monday, work would have been resumed. Monday, everything would have been settled. . . ."

Notes

1. Speech at Kaposvar on May 1, 1946.

2. Zoltan Szabo, the distinguished writer who at this time was editor-in-chief of the Provisional Government's official journal, has set forth in an article in *Irodalmi Ujsag* (now published in London) this memory of Nagy, whom he knew well at the time: "When he had accomplished the decree [for agricultural reform], he gave no sign of pride in having carried through a social reform which was the most important since the emancipation of the serfs. It must, however, be understood that this piece of legislation gave meaning to his life. In fact, he went so far as to take the final text, revised after laborious negotiations, in person to the editor-in-chief of the official journal, which post I held. It was with a certain solemnity that he handed me the typewritten text bearing his signature. 'I have brought you something that you will no doubt take pleasure in printing,' he said, smothering a smile in his moustache and extending his hand to me."

3. Within the period of a few weeks an immense task was completed: 34 per cent of the total territory of the country (7,752,000 acres, in round numbers) was distributed among 642,342 peasants. There is no question that the reform, having been carried out in such haste, bore the marks of that haste. But there is also no doubt that it marked a historic turning point, not only for the peasants but also for the entire nation.

4. "In September, 1948, the idea prevailed in the domain of the agricultural cooperatives that Hungarian agriculture would have to

be collectivized within a few years. I do not agree. I consider such plans . . . unrealistic, erroneous, and excessive. Their execution would inevitably mean that we would leap over an entire transitional phase of our evolution. This would isolate us from the most important representatives of the peasantry and would deal a blow to the foundation of the worker-peasant alliance—which is the only solid basis for socialism in the countryside as well as in the cities." (Imre Nagy, "Relations with the Middle Peasantry," *Discussion,* 1948–1949.)

5. François Fejto, a specialist in Hungarian questions, believes that Beria and Rakosi hesitated for some time in choosing between Rajk and Nagy as the principal victim of the proceedings against Titoism. Their choice did not fall immediately on Rajk. (François Fejto, *Portrait d' Imre Nagy* [Paris: Plon, 1957.])

6. From what can be learned by what followed, Rakosi was not entirely wrong, although the situation was far more complex than he imagined. In a way that can only be called paradoxical, it was, of all the Kremlin leaders, Beria, who had the most reason to be anti-Stalinist. The details of the so-called "doctor's plot" persuaded some of those next to Beria to believe that their next victim was to be the chief of the secret police. After the death of Stalin, Beria took a position in favor of a more liberal foreign and domestic policy.

7. In the same resolution, Rakosi disposed of Mihaly Farkas, dismissing him from the Politburo. By this time the entire country was aware of the crimes committed by the two Farkases, father and son. It is quite characteristic of the Party's Secretary-General that he should have tried to associate Nagy with the disgrace of these two criminals. If Nagy's former accomplices were now banished, it was not for their crimes in the past but for "deviationism of the right," which is to say, for the support which the father had given Nagy.

8. "We must snatch the weapons of chauvinism, of anti-Sovietism, and of anti-Semitism from the hands of the enemies of the people and of Socialism." (*Imre Nagy on Communism* [New York: Frederick A. Praeger, 1957.])

9. Before the militants of the federation of Budapest at the Sports Palace on May 18, 1956, Rakosi said: "Until now we have spoken to this great audience only in general terms about the cult of personality that reigned here. That is not enough. The truth is that I myself tolerated this cult of personality and more than once encouraged it. But we must go even further. It must be said, openly and frankly, that if these illegal acts were possible here among us, I am at fault myself, since I hold the most important post in the Party. But the other leaders of the Party are also in some measure at fault. And

you can be sure, comrades, that we deplore and profoundly regret—and that I, above all, deplore it—that such grave violations of socialist legality have been possible."

10. According to the reports and communiques published by the Kadar Government, the "counter-revolutionaries" first opened fire. On the other hand, Peter Fryer, then correspondent for the *London Daily Worker,* gave this account of a talk he had with his colleague Charles Coutts, also a Communist: "Entering Parliament Square they [the demonstrators] met another Soviet tank which had been sent to fire on them, and this tank, too, turned and joined the demonstration. In the Square were three more Soviet tanks and two armored cars. The crowd went right up to them and began to talk to the soldiers. The Soviet commander was saying: 'I have a wife and children waiting for me in the Soviet Union. I don't want to stay in Hungary at all,' when suddenly from the roof-tops there were three salvos of gunfire. Some of the people ran to the sides of the Square for shelter. Others were told by the Russians to take shelter behind the tanks. Some thirty people were left lying either dead or wounded on the Square, including a Soviet officer. Tanks and cars opened fire on the roof-tops.

"It is still not clear to me who it was that began the shooting. It is more than likely they were security police." (Peter Fryer, *Hungarian Tragedy* [London: Dobson Books, Ltd., 1956], pp. 46–47.)

11. Attila Szigeti was arrested some time after the final Soviet intervention for having supported the Nagy Government. According to information that seems worthy of belief, he committed suicide in prison.

12. For the first time in the history of the Hungarian Communist press, *Szabad Nep* dared to take a position contrary to that of the Soviet Party organ. "In the latest issue of *Pravda*," wrote Miklos Molnar, the journalist, "one can read an article by the Budapest correspondent on the Hungarian events. The article has as its title: 'The Failure of the Adventure Against the People.' That is one error. What has happened in Budapest is not an adventure, is not against the people, and it will not fail. . . . The revolutionists of Buda and Pest wanted liberty—liberty for the people, without equivocation, without fear, without terror. More bread and national independence. Could this be called an adventure? What has failed? The thing that can really be said to be against the people is the reign of the Rakosi-Gero clique."

13. Edjaz Hussein, the Pakistani journalist who reported from Hungary during the Revolution, wrote: "Before [the] Parliament

[Building], where the Revolution began, we saw two tanks. They were guarding the building. As we were parking our cars, a Hungarian soldier came out of one tank and approached us. Seeing the U.N. press symbol on our windshield, he asked us excitedly: 'Are the United Nations here already?' We replied regretfully that we were not representing the U.N. and that we were only members of the press accredited to the U.N. 'That is not enough,' he said, turning to leave us with an air of having been deceived." (*Dawn* [Karachi], November 15, 1956.)

14. The Treaty of Trianon of 1920 gave to Czechoslovakia, Rumania, and Yugoslavia territories populated by Hungarians. This had given rise to a violent propaganda campaign between the two wars and had been the source of unrelenting hatred between the Hungarians and their neighbors. Hitler had frequently taken advantage of the national problems of the states that succeeded the Austro-Hungarian monarchy in order to win them to his side or to blackmail them.

15. It is not without interest to cite in this connection the official communique that followed the condemnation of Imre Nagy: "Imre Nagy and his group of conspirators dissolved the regular administrative organizations, including the economic councils and supervisory committees, in order to replace them with so-called Revolutionary Committees composed chiefly of bourgeois and fascist elements." Of those who took part in the founding of the Revolutionary Committee of the Ninth District referred to in this document, Ferenc Munnich was at the time of Nagy's execution the Premier, and Janos Kadar was First Secretary of the new Communist Party.

16. On Free Radio Kossuth on October 31, a student of the Technical University, Istvan Szanto told the story of his and his colleagues' trip to Vienna for medical aid from the Austrian Red Cross for St. Rokus Hospital. In his talk, he said: "On the way back something interesting happened on the border. Unexpectedly, a young man in an open leather coat stood in front of us; he told that he was an S.S. soldier, and he wanted to cross the frontier to scout the terrain. My friends and I looked at each other wondering what he meant."

17. At the time of the arrest of the Jewish doctors in Moscow, in the beginning of 1953, Rakosi started to prepare the anti-Zionist campaign in Hungary. Dr. Benedek, the director of the Jewish hospital, and several other doctors were arrested. Further purges were stopped only by Stalin's death.

18. Conversation with François Bondy, editor-in-chief of the Paris monthly, *Preuves.* (*Preuves* [Paris], December, 1956.)

19. During the Revolution, *Magyar Szabadsag* was the organ of former Communist journalists. Most of these journalists had worked for the central organ, *Szabad Nep,* and had been dismissed for the support they had given Nagy's policies. They had gone far beyond Nagy in their ideas before the Revolution, but this fact did not prevent them from retaining great esteem for him and from lending him their support. One of the directors of the paper, Miklos Gimes, who from a one-time sectarian Communist had become an uncompromising supporter of freedom of thought, was condemned and executed with Nagy. The author of this article, Peter Kende, is a former foreign editor of *Szabad Nep*. In December, 1954, he was excluded from the Party for "rightist deviationism."

20. The Hungarian Socialist Workers' Party knew a brief existence between 1928 and 1929. It was headed by a Communist, Ferenc Vagi. Since the Communist Party was suppressed by the Horthy regime, this organization was in reality the "legal front" for the Communist movement. In its turn, it was not long in being dissolved.

21. It was of these political men and their ideas that the communique announcing Nagy's execution said: "On November 2, he [Nagy] reorganized this Cabinet and brought into it the determined representatives of extreme reaction and the leaders of the counter-revolutionary insurrection." The communique was speaking of Anna Kethly of the Social Democrat Party, of Istvan Bibo of the Peasants Party, of Istvan B. Szabo of the Smallholders Party, and of Pal Maleter.

22. The communique announcing Nagy's execution tried to attribute this speech to the Premier: "In order to assure their seizure of power, the group of conspirators around Imre Nagy even contracted alliances with groups representing the extremes of reaction, going so far as rehabilitating ex-Cardinal Mindszenty and pitting him against the Hungarian People's Republic. After having reached agreement with this group through the intermediation of Zoltan Tildy, Mindszenty proclaimed over the radio on November 3 the program for the capitalist restoration." If it is true that Nagy freed the Cardinal, who had been imprisoned eight years earlier and condemned by a fabricated trial, it is nevertheless absurd that he would "contract an alliance" with him. On the Cardinal's part, it would have been, at the very least, curious of him to describe these "allies" several times as "heirs of an overthrown regime" and to give their testimony so little sympathy.

23. The fifth volume of the *White Book* issued by the Kadar Government gave sufficient indication that Nagy and his friends were

counting on a peaceful settlement and were preparing themselves for
it. This volume, which took into account the Nagy trial, said on pages
127–128:

"At the Yugoslav Embassy, Imre Nagy and his followers declared
themselves the administrative committee of the Party. [N.B.: They
had a clear right to do so, since of seven members of the committee,
five were in the Embassy.] This so-called administrative committee
had an interview on November 4 with Ambassador Soldatitch. Here
is what Szilard Ujhelyi had to say about this interview in a deposition:

> This meeting took place after Geza Losonczy came back from seeing
> Soldatitch. He invited the members of the administrative committee
> who were present—namely, Zoltan Szanto, Gyorgy Lukacs, Ferenc
> Donath, and Sandor Haraszti—to meet in Soldatitch's office. So far
> as Haraszti was concerned, Losonczy made the remark that that
> one, though he was not a member of the committee, could partici-
> pate in his role as director of the Party's central organ. . . . Imre
> Nagy was already in the ambassador's office. I know from Losonczy
> that no minutes were kept of the meeting, but that the debate was
> later summarized and recorded by Losonczy. It was also he who
> declared that the administrative committee had drafted a plan for
> a solution after the events of November 4."

"The notes on the debates of the so-called administrative committee," continued the *White Book,* "were later confiscated from Geza
Losonczy and Ferenc Donath. The outcome was that Imre Nagy and
his group, in the name of the self-styled administrative committee,
drafted a counter-revolutionary platform. They demanded the withdrawal of Soviet troops, a multi-party regime, and the denunciation
of the Warsaw Pact; and they took a position in favor of a declaration of neutrality by Hungary. In addition, they demanded that the
central power of the Hungarian People's Republic repose, above all,
in the Workers' Councils and in the organizations created over the
past weeks by the peasants, the intelligentsia, and other social groups.

"In the plan for a program, Imre Nagy insisted on the liberation
of all political prisoners."

24. The fifth volume of the *White Book* published by the Kadar
regime seems to confirm a theory gaining more and more support in
the West, according to which the Tito Government is believed to
have been informed in advance of the Soviet intervention of November
4, 1956. *See* Richard Lowenthal, "How Imre Nagy and his Followers
Found Themselves in the Yugoslav Embassy," (*Encounter,* [London],
October, 1958), p. 126: "In his deposition made before the tribunal
on June 13, Zoltan Szanto said:

On November 4, 1956, toward one o'clock in the morning, I was informed by the Premier's office that Ambassador Soldatitch of Yugoslavia wanted to speak with me on a matter of urgency and that I should telephone him without delay. I did so. Milovanov, of the Yugoslav Embassy, told me to come immediately to the Embassy, where Soldatitch wanted to speak with me in person.

The ambassador told me that he had reported to Belgrade on the conversation he had had with Losonczy and me, and, in the course of his report, he had asked if, because of the state of insecurity in the city, it would not be advisable to bring to the Embassy some of our wives and children. He had, a few hours earlier, received a reply to this question. The ambassador gave me the essential details of that reply: The situation was very grave. Events were evolving very rapidly. A new attack by Soviet troops against Budapest could begin any moment. Also, the Yugoslav Government had decided to accord the right of asylum to Imre Nagy, to the members of his leadership, and to all those whom his leaders thought worthy of it."

25. At this time a delegation of the Rumanian Party and of the Bucharest Government was in Hungary. (See *Nepszabadsag*, November 25, 1956.) It is to be presumed that it was during the course of this visit that they approved, as a matter of form and after the event, the action of the Soviet forces.

26. There is every reason to believe that, when Khrushchev visited Budapest in April, 1958, the final decision to bring Nagy to trial had not yet been made. In the flow of words Khrushchev poured out while he was in Hungary, he mentioned Nagy only once. On the other hand, during a reception in Khrushchev's honor, Kadar told a group of foreign journalists: "Nagy is living in a rest home that he himself chose." It was apparently after Khrushchev's return to Moscow that it was decided to try to execute Nagy.

27. When Gomulka finally took a position in the Nagy affair, he went so far that he could not have had the approval of the Polish people. In speaking of Nagy, he seemed to have forgotten that the crushing of the Hungarian revolt must have contributed in a certain measure to the stabilization—however temporary—of the conquests of Poland's October uprising, and he must also have forgotten that the sacrifice of Nagy had perhaps saved himself. "However, when the counter-revolution began to hang Communists," Gomulka declared, "Imre Nagy, Hungarian Premier, said over the radio: 'We will not punish anyone for participation in armed resistance.'" And Gomulka added: "Imre Nagy, who was a revisionist, retreated step by step before the counter-revolution, hostile to the power of the people over

whom the wave was rising; he accomplished his task [*sic*]. He has ruined the socialist order in Hungary." (Speech at Gdansk, June 28, 1958.)

28. "The fighters, the heroes of the armed struggle, are calm. I ask the people of the capital to remain calm in order that nobody may create any confusion among us and that no propagator of rumors should have any success. I tell you that the troops of the Army, the Hungarian Honveds, together with the armed youth, will assure the peace and order of Budapest." (Statement by Pal Maleter, in the Hungarian press, October 31, 1956.)

"All honest people should resolutely oppose the troublemakers. . . . Unfortunately, there are also still weapons in the hands of those who misuse the situation created by the Revolution. . . . The lynchings should cease immediately. There is no mercy for the criminals, but they should be responsible for their crimes in the orthodox way, before the courts of the nation. . . . Those who are menaced—even in their homes—by the troublemakers should ask the help of the commander of the National Guard in their sector, who will take the necessary steps." (Statement by Jozsef Szilagyi, in the Budapest newspaper *Valosag*, November 3, 1956.)

"We should not allow the purity of our Revolution to be violated. . . . We are speaking of the so-called popular judgments, of the lynchings, of the declarations whose spirit is foreign to our Revolution. We openly declare that all of these are harmful for the purity and honor of the Revolution. . . . There should be judgments, but not on the streets, not in the passion of the moment. These should be stopped so that the just severity of the law may find the forms worthy of the law." (Editorial in the revolutionary newspaper published by Miklos Gimes and his friends, *Magyar Szabadsag* [November 1, 1956.])